Celtic Blessings,

Jeanne Crane

CELTIC SPIRIT

A Wee Journey to the Heart of It All

Jeanne Crane

DEDICATION

To my parents,
Howard and Emily Bunting Crane.

Their unconditional love for me, their hard work to provide opportunities for me to pursue my dreams, and their faith in the goodness of everyday people gave me a great start on my life's journey. I am forever grateful.

And to my grandparents,
James and Eliza Jane Finlay Bunting

At the age of sixteen, they separately journeyed from Northern Ireland to America to seek a new life. Their quiet courage, optimism, and simple faith are at the heart of my passion for Celtic spirituality. I still hear their Irish brogue encouraging me to follow my heart.

TABLE of CONTENTS

Céad Míle Fáilte
One Hundred Thousand Welcomes

The power of place is never more palpable for me than among the sacred sites of ancient Ireland.

Celtic spirituality has a simplicity that can be found in the green, blue and purple hills, the deep blue of the waters, and the wondrous roar of the sea. Yet, there is so much more. I am ever so grateful to Tanis Helliwell, founder of the International Institute of Transformation, for leading the tour that introduced me to the Celtic Mysteries and offered an experience that both deepened and widened my understanding of Celtic spirituality. This book is inspired by that tour.

This is a fictional story of a group of Americans embarking on a journey to sacred places often overlooked by most tourists. I have never met a traveler to Ireland that did not rave about their experience. Yet, I have met many who have never seen many of the places I have chosen for this wee visit. All of the places in the story, with the exception of the lodgings and pubs, are real. Only the characters are fictional. Each is a traveler and seeker. Each provides a different lens to illustrate the universal nature of the trip.

Whether you are a potential traveler looking for ideas, a past visitor wanting to savor your memories or a reader who may never get to step foot on the Emerald Isle, I hope you will climb aboard and enjoy this very special ride.

MAP OF IRELAND

Marking the Sites We Will Visit on Our Journey

We gather at the Park Inn across from Shannon Airport. After lunch in a lovely tea room near Doolin, we travel to the spectacular Cliffs of Moher. The day ends at Salmon Lodge, our County Clare home for three nights. From this base, we will visit Brigid's Well, Poulnabrone Dolmen, Alliwee Caves, Craggaunowen. Day Three will offer options: hike of the Burren, shop in the village or relax creek side at the lodge.

On Day Four, we cross Ireland to the Boyne Valley, where we will stay four nights at the Bend of the River Conference Center. Clonmacnoise, the early Christian monastery and scriptorium, will be our main stop. On Day Five, we visit Dublin, seeing the Book of Kells and a play at the famous Abbey Theatre. Day Six we travel down to Glendalough, another early Christian monastery, nestled in the magnificent Wicklow Mountains. The following day we stay right in the Boyne Valley, going to both Newgrange and Tara.

Traveling back to the West of Ireland on Day Eight, we stop for lunch in Sligo Town before visiting Carrowmore, Carrowkeel and Queen Maeve's Tomb. The Sea Side Inn on the County Sligo coast offers a relaxing base for the remainder of our journey. Visits around Yeats Country and an optional pilgrimage to Croagh Patrick are scheduled. Our final stop will be the Turoe Stone as we journey back to Shannon Airport on Day Twelve.

DAY ONE

Doolin   *Cliffs of Moher*   *Salmon Run Lodge*

Our tour begins with an in-gathering and orientation at the Park Inn,
across from the Shannon Airport at 11 a.m.
Luggage (remember, one bag only) may be loaded on
our bus anytime after 9 a.m.
From Shannon, we will travel to Doolin, a picturesque sea village known
for its Celtic Music festival. After tea, we will continue on to the spectacular
Cliffs of Moher. Our final destination for the day is the Salmon Run Lodge,
a restored hunting and fishing inn, our home for three wonderful
days in County Clare.

TIMOTHY

"'Tis a grand beginning to the day, meeting up with you, Timothy Mulhearn."

"Dylan Boland, is it now? Let me get the full look of you. What brings you over to Shannon and away from the bank?"

1

"Meeting with the EU men. They come over checking up on us every fortnight now. At the start, I waited for them at the airline gate, hat in hand, polite and professional and all. Now, I say I am reserving a table here at the Inn. I have a cuppa and review files whilst I wait for them. Makes listening to their huff and puff about solvency and how grand they are being to us poor Irish a wee bit more tolerable."

"Aye, Dylan, seems I took the early retirement scheme just in the nick of time, did I not?"

"So now it looks as if you are planning to see around Ireland by coach?"

"You mean these bags at me feet? Did you not know I am now in the coach-for-hire business? Shortly after Sally passed on, Frankie rang me up to tell me of a great repo chance and encouraged me to give it a go."

"Jaysus, Timothy, you are a brave man to take on such a new enterprise at this point in the economy. But all the best to you, man. If anyone can make a success of it, you are the man to do it."

"Well, it helps me try to move on, if you take my meaning."

"A new chapter so to speak then?" Dylan's mobile plays a tune. "Aye. Excuse me but one minute, Timothy, 'tis our men on the mobile now; perhaps they are delayed."

Whilst Dylan talks on the phone, I ponder the twelve-day tour ahead and the story it will become for each of us on the wee journey. There never is a clean start or ending to a story in real life. So does the story of this journey start at the first site listed in the brochure? Or at the point where each traveler decides to come to Ireland and experience this particular coach tour? Or will it begin at the gathering scheduled to begin at 11 o'clock?

The group's story, of course, commences today here at Shannon. I know I got here to the Inn early, getting permission from the hotel to park near the entry. I put the big, fancy printed sign the trip organizers had brought all the way from America in the front window of the coach. *Celtic Spirit* it says in bright rainbow colors.

The first members of our group to find me were three chaps, all around me own age, who had stayed in the hotel the night before. They came over to me separately, but only a few minutes apart from one another, each seeking baggage-hold information for themselves and their wives. They were distinguishable in size and coloring, but all had the look of casual American professionals. For the life of me, I am unable to remember their names, but I checked them off the list. Twelve days hence, I have no doubt, I will know the names and their stories, for the stories are what make the enterprise worth doing.

I suggested to the second and third chaps that they might wish to seek out their fellow travelers in the dining room. No way from out here at the entry to see if they worked it out. But they seemed keen.

Dylan breaks into my train of thought saying, "Well, Timothy, all that goings on, just to hear that, indeed, my men have landed. I best be going to get a table. But first, tell me about this here Celtic Spirit trip. Is it one of those Yank last hurrahs? Or is it off to pubs and poet hideaways? I hope not gardens and castles!"

"So far, the only takers I have met are Yanks about me own age, but, nay, not a 'Last Hurrah' by intention, at least. The full title of the tour as written on the brochure is Celtic Spirit: *A Journey to Sacred Sites of Ancient Ireland.* A bit long-winded and too long for the window sign,"

"Abbeys and the graves of the saints, then? Or is it church relics you'll be after visiting?"

"Actually, the lass who leads the tour is deep into spirituality and wants people to see the likes of Newgrange and ancient stone circles, as well as the early Church sites. So Glendalough and Clonmacnoise are mixed in with Brede's Well and dolmens. She had me investigate the site of the Turoe Stone, some ancient thing I never even heard of meself. And she has included Yeats and a good deal of just soaking in the beauty and spirit of our Emerald Isle. She says 'tis every bit sacred and all meant to be transformational."

"Ach, to many of the thin places, then. Quite ambitious and intriguing, but . . .."

"Certainly of more interest than dropping a coach full of tourists off at Bunratty Castle or some fishing lodge. To tell the truth, I'm looking forward to it. The lass really seems to want to journey to the very heart of it all."

"Well, then, I better be about bank business. 'Tis good to know you have come upon a new endeavor for yourself, Timothy, after Sally's passing and all."

"Aye, the adjustment has not been easy."

"You are still in our prayers, you know. We miss you and are just waiting for you to visit us all. When you can, of course."

"I promise indeed, I will stop by the bank soon. Grand seeing you, Dylan. Cheerio, now, and God speed."

A bit of a lull in activity has occurred whilst Dylan and I conversed, probably partly due to the "FULL-UP: Pre-Booked ONLY" hand-lettered paper I affixed to the fetching American sign. So many people had been asking about joining the tour, that I was beginning to feel like the innkeeper in Bethlehem. Saying "no" is not in the Irish lexicon or nature.

But now I see a sour-looking woman, again about me own age. Looks like she can say "no" easily enough. Sure enough, she is to be one of ours. She gets out of a taxi she has insisted stop directly on angle to me coach. No concern for the traffic knot she is creating, she struggles with the Euros needed to pay the man.

"Would you be looking for the *Celtic Spirit* tour?" I ask.

"Is this the one the two Americans set up to visit sacred sites?"

"Aye, 'tis. And if you will give me your name and your bag, I will see to its loading. Meanwhile, a few of your fellow travelers are in the breakfast room if you would like to join them."

She does as I ask, then continues, "Breakfast was included at the B&B, so just direct me to the meeting room. What time is it, anyway?"

4

I bite me tongue at her rudeness as I answer. She is off whilst I note to stay clear of angering Ms. Mary Helena Moran.

Within minutes, I encounter the sour one's opposite. A lady of grace and ease with a smiling countenance, rolling her bag from the car let area. "Delighted to find this so easily," says she. She introduces herself as Kate. We begin to chat a bit about her few days traveling on her own and visiting the spa in Lisdoonvarna. I wonder if I should comment about Lisdoonvarna's being the site of the yearly bachelor fest, wherein matchmaking is done, but it might be taken as a bit forward.

At that very moment, the courtesy van from a posh nearby manor inn and golf club arrives with another woman looking for the tour. So 'tis no opportunity to comment on the matchmaking and I am saved from embarrassing meself.

This woman is tiny, well-heeled, yet casually dressed. She introduces herself to Kate and meself before worrying about the luggage. Rose, this one is called. She allows how the husband is off golfing with his firm and fishing with his clients. Talking so fast and with her accent, I have trouble making out all of it. But seems she is on her own abroad for the first time. She will be meeting up with her husband at tour's end for a trip around the Ring of Kerry.

The two women seemed to hit it off and head into the dining room for what I would guess would be more gabbing than eating.

After a bit of a lull, Herself and Himself pull up in a town car which I recognize as belonging to a small local establishment. They seem ready to meet and greet everyone. Half-jokingly, I warn them of "the sour one" who is lying low, waiting on them in the meeting room. We all give a nervous laugh and a prayer that all the personalities will get along as we travel. Then, Dorrie, who I see never likes a bad word said about a person, reminds us all, Herself included, that sometimes people are sour or crisp when they are nervous.

"If anyone could put a traveler at ease," says I, "you are the lass to do it. The luck of the Irish to ye," I add with a smile and a wink. Herself laughs, and they head off to set up the room and meet the lady under discussion.

Dorrie is the leader with the vision of the tour. Her boyfriend, my adult daughter tells me partner is the more modern thing to say, is called Gordie. As a bit of a joke, and to ease the tension that all beginnings have, I commenced to call them Herself and Himself when we sat for a coffee two days ago, finalizing the trip plans. 'Tis a classic West Ireland appellation and seemed in keeping with my role as the local on the team. If truth be told, now that I am retired from my position as a bank officer, I have slipped back into talking more like a Clare man than ever.

When we finally met in person, I was surprised to find Herself to be a wee slip of a thing. Himself is a tall, thin fellow with the look of a marathon runner. Ach, the wonder of pairings. They seem to be very earnest and intense, each in their own way, but they also seem to be full of fun, as well. Will I not be finding out more about them this fortnight to come? Already, I can see she clearly does the people–side and he the logistics. And their transatlantic call asking me to be "part of their team" was so bloody American. The deal was done before I had time to ponder it.

I still remember our first conversation with amusement: "It would be grand if you could also offer us some contextualization," she had said.

"Ach, would you be suggesting I provide a wee bit of local color?" said I.

"Perfect," was her reply.

"So then, would you ever be wanting me to relax into my true West of Ireland brogue, with all the flourishes, and now and again tell a wee story or two?"

"If you ever might find your way to do so, wouldn't it be grand?" trying her own hand at a bit of blarney.

Overhead, I hear the planes landing, one after another and know the overnight flights from America have begun to come in. Folks will be through customs and have money changed, and then find their way over to the Inn. I am parked where they will easily see me coach before needing to bother the hotel staff.

Soon a steady stream comes out of the terminal and a surprising number walk over here to the Inn. It is fun to try to guess which ones will be coming along on our journey. I realize there is to be more of a mix of ages and types than I thought and I am glad of it.

Finally, they all sort themselves out. The activity across the car park at the terminal quiets. My tally says we are still one person short, so I take me time locking up both the bus and the storage area. Still, the missing lady does not appear.

Normally, I just wait by the coach for groups, but Dorrie wants me to be part of the in-gathering. She has strong feelings about how the first coming together of people has the power to create the tone of the trip, giving a story its beginning, so to speak. She wants people to be in what she called "right relations" with one another, to feel safe to be themselves and encouraged to share in the richness of learning from one another. She wants me to be a part of that. I joke that "she likes to puff me up." But in truth, I do enjoy her confidence in me. Some guides treat us drivers as if we are *eejits*.

I finally have to tell Herself that the straggler is nowhere in sight and that we would need to begin right off if we are to keep to our schedule. I know she will be disappointed. At our planning meeting, she had talked about all the dynamics of group start-up, sounding like the training manager back at the bank. But, I know she is correct in her thinking.

Me own experience says that starting on time, setting norms of conduct and making people feel at ease are important, with or without the highfalutin language of behaviorists.

The lass also had pointed out that she wants us to do some up-front work loosening people up and encouraging them to get to know each other since many are traveling alone. She said we would need to be addressing three unstated questions that would be on everyone's mind: Am I safe? Will I be accepted? Will I like the experience? And she made Gordie and me promise to work especially hard the first few hours, even the first few days, till people could get beyond these concerns.

Now, her well-crafted opening is being derailed by our latecomer. Of course, she handles the situation with ease. Quick as a bunny, she rearranges the agenda, confirms that I keep a watch out for our lost one, and turns the program over to Gordie to kick off with logistics.

"Good morning, I am Gordie, Gordon Eaton, and this is my partner, Dorrie Donahue. We are so pleased to meet you and so look forward to traveling with you on this adventure to the Celtic Spirit: *A Journey to Sacred Sites of Ancient Ireland.* Is everybody in the right place?" he says with warmer tones than the crisp let's-get-it-done voice I had heard to date.

"We are calling this our in-gathering rather than orientation. We will hold the orientation tomorrow after breakfast when everyone is fresh. We know you are excited to get out into the countryside and see Ireland. Plus many of you may be experiencing jet lag. So I will try to be brief with announcements.

"First, if you have not already found out about him yourself, this is Timothy, Timothy Mulhearn, our bus driver. I will be handling logistics; Dorrie, the personal stuff; Timothy, the driving as well as providing local color and lots of tidbits. From what we have seen so far, he's an Irish treasure." He chuckles, looking and gesturing to me as he speaks whilst I squirm a wee bit at the attention.

"Please come to me with questions. I will try to keep everything coordinated and will negotiate for us as a group.

"Breakfast and dinner are included in your tour package. Timothy and I will find places for us to stop for lunch, for breaks and such, but you are on your own for those activities. Sometimes, we will stop in villages where you can more easily pick up snacks, personal items, etc., so be ready with your lists when such occasions come up. We won't be able to stop every time an individual thinks of something, as you might when traveling in your own family car."

I watch the faces as Gordie talks. Some are eager, some nervous, some already distracted. The older teenager has some electronic device he is fiddling with, texting, or the like. I wonder if he is going to say anything about electronics. They can drive you round the bend on these trips.

"You all received an itinerary, but let me pass out a summary sheet describing our three lodging sites and highlights of each day. You will probably look at it often. Do not concern yourselves with trying to remember it all; you can trust that we'll take care of it for you.

"When you check into your room tonight, I'll also give you a packet that includes more information about Celtic Ireland and a pamphlet of Dorrie's about spiritual transformation. These are terrific resources, but remember that, first and foremost, this is a bus tour and an experience of a lifetime. When questions do arise, we are more than willing to answer or get answers to your questions. So, please, ask away.

"Now, sit back and enjoy and, as the old expression goes, 'Leave the driving to us.' Timothy has posted a road map on the back of his seat, in case any of you would like to follow along our route.

"Timothy, is there a place up in the front of the bus to leave a clipboard and perhaps have a message board?"

Good thing I was listening attentively. "Aye, there is. Consider it done," I reply.

"Speaking of cell phones," Gordie continues, "we want to ask that ALL electronics be turned off at all sites and at all meals. If you are using camera phones or the like, please keep them off unless you are taking a picture. For one thing, it is just common courtesy. For another, it is a huge distraction, and thirdly, Dorrie is concerned it can disturb the vibrational energy of the place and the experience for those tuned in to such things.

"Today's plan is to head out ASAP, stop at a great little tea shop near Doolin, and then go to the Cliffs of Moher. Dinner will be at the Salmon Run Lodge, our home for the next three nights. It is a quaint, refurbished hunting lodge that I think you will all enjoy. There is a great pub just down the road that has live music tonight, if you still have some energy by then."

As he says the word music, in walks a tall, skinny, breathless, wild haired, flaming red-head with a backpack and what looks like a lyre harp in a nylon case over her shoulder.

"You must be Lily," says Gordie without skipping a beat. "Do join us. I am Gordie. My partner Dorrie was just about to begin introductions."

Lily takes a moment getting out of her gear and settling in. She reminds me of a cat, the supple way she moves and then wiggles into a small space on the floor, taking it over once there. The energy of the whole room shifts with her arrival. People readjust themselves, all smiles on their faces but with questioning and alert looks in their eyes. Twelve days is a long time with a group of strangers and folks seem a bit leery of one another.

Dorrie welcomes everyone in her own way and then invites them each to briefly introduce themselves and say what drew them to this particular tour. She assures them that there will be plenty of time to speak and listen to one another's stories, to more completely share their hopes, expectations, and intentions as the trip progresses, but that, for now, she is just looking for a quick hello from everyone.

She also assures them that there will be no pressure on them to bond as a community. People might not get to know everyone on the trip and she assures them that is okay.

She concludes by saying, "Trust that you will have conversations and experiences that will give meaning to your trip. Remember that this is not a contest or a course. You cannot and need not know everyone nor will you all get the same things out of the trip. Whatever happens is meant to happen. Whatever happens will be perfect."

With nary a pause, the sour one, Mary Helena, speaks up. "Well, we might as well go around the circle. I am Mary Helena. I have come to see the Holy sites and to honor St. Brigid and St. Patrick. It is these two Blessed saints who saved me from despair on more than one occasion. My daughters gave me this trip, saying I need more joy in my life. But, of course, they couldn't be bothered to come with me. My oldest who was supposed to come cancelled out at the last minute. So it was come alone or lose all that money." After a slight pause, she adds, "I am from Boston, a Southie born and bred. I attend mass regularly and I have never missed a St. Patrick's Day Parade."

After a bit of waiting, the young blond fellow takes a turn. "I'm Kevin. I'm an agency administrator for the State of Delaware. Personally, I am most drawn to the Yeats aspects of the trip, but mainly I came because I thought it would be something my son and I could share. This is KJ."

The son jumps in, instantly outraged in that way teenagers can get at the drop of a hat, "Dad, KJ sounds like the name for a toy store or truck company! I want to be introduced as Jackson, and I plan to only answer to Jackson. Don't you or any of the rest of you call me KJ. I mean it." At which point, he folds his arms, slouches back into his chair, and returns to fiddling with his handheld gaming device.

Dorrie and Gordie refrain from making eye contact with one another, but I know they are taking it in. I have a feeling Gordie's experience with teenage boys will be needed before this bus tour is over.

The next couple speaks up, "We are the MacAllisters. I am Peter and this is Penny," says the first gent I met this morning. "We live in Arnprior, near Ottawa, Ontario, Canada. We usually vacation in Nova Scotia. This year we wanted to go someplace new, but we didn't want to miss our summer 'fix' of traditional Celtic music. So here we are, eh? I try not to speak for Penny, but I will be the first one at the pub tonight, to be sure."

Penny cheerfully agrees, adding that she also has a deep interest in Irish folklore and feminist spirituality, as well as Celtic music.

"We are Sandra and Jake Monfredo," says the woman next to the McAllisters. "I prefer Sandra, but I won't bite your head off if you say Sandy by mistake. We have traveled extensively to some pretty exotic places and love learning about new cultures. I had breast cancer recently, though, and we wanted to visit someplace easy, you know, where the language and health system are not a challenge, but a place that still has character."

Jake adds, "We realized that we had only come to Ireland once as part of one of those packaged "St. Patrick's Day Parade" deals. The sacred sites aspect of this trip intrigued us. Like the lady from Boston, we, too, are Catholic. As a kid, I told everyone in the neighborhood I was Mediterranean Irish. Half said as a joke and half to fit in, since I was outnumbered."

The group continues the go-around, but it is too much to take in even though I got a head start by having loaded the luggage. Patience, I remind meself. In due time, I will know them all.

Then, Kate, the lady from the car let, speaks. She is a bit of a looker, especially for a woman of me own age. 'Tis not at all hard to tune back in. Seems she's a recently retired women's studies professor at a college in upstate NY. I have been told many a time that New York is not like the pictures of New York City, but I still find it hard to not imagine skyscrapers and rush hours whenst I hear the name. She quite concisely, but charmingly, tells the story of going to Lisdoonvarna for the spa as a gift from her son and then discovering it was the town of the matchmaking legend. She gets a bit of a laugh for that. She blushes a wee bit, which is even more endearing.

And, finally, Lily, our wild late arrival, offers in a wee whisper, "I just wanted to be here with all of you."

Folks are beginning to get restless. Is it the fey way wee Lily has about her or just that people are anxious to get up and move? Dorrie must sense it, too. She suggests we end for now and prepare to depart, giving people fifteen minutes for a last minute W.C. stop and a chance to settle themselves in. All agree and all manage to be in a seat and ready to go on time. Wouldn't it be grand if such timeliness continued?

Some exclaim delight and also a bit of panic as I take the first round-about just outside the airport "the wrong way" as they name it. But they begin to get more accustomed to cars passing on the right as we get on the main road. More than one expresses relief not to be driving themselves. I just chuckle to meself.

As we drive through the countryside, a quiet buzz is established. Folks start talking to their neighbors and settling in for the ride. All the couples and parent-child twosomes sit with their companions. 'Twas to be expected, but will probably change as we travel. Dorrie sits in the tour guide seat across from me and Gordie sits with Lily.

Lily booked at the last minute as a replacement for the sour one's daughter. Gordie wants to get her information and orient her a bit. As I glimpse them in me mirror, I chastise meself for thinking of that Mary Helena as the sour one and promise meself to use her name properly in the future. I see it was the lady professor, Kate, whom she latched onto as a travel companion. Happy am I to be away up here in the driver's seat.

Dorrie and Gordie and I agreed to mix the seating up, as well as separate during meals the first few days as part of encouraging folks to get to know one another. 'Twill be easy for all three of us as we all genuinely enjoy hearing people's stories.

Soon we approach the town of Doolin. I turn on the PA system and hand Dorrie the mike so she can tell them about this charming wee village, known for its traditional Irish music. Along the sea road, she points out the Aran Islands in the distance and explains that Galway City is to the other side of the Bay.

The ferry stop is abuzz with activity. I slow down as much as I can, whilst Dorrie points to the area out at sea where a ship of the Spanish Armada lies at the bottom.

The narrow streets of the village and the traffic give me pause as I squeeze the coach through and we head across the town. A number of folks exclaim how much they would like to put this place on their itinerary for their next visit, especially during music festival time. I, meself, never get enough of being here.

'Tis indeed a gem, this town: quintessentially *Gaeltacht* with the bright primary-colored doors on the front of the shops and pubs and the signage that rings true of an earlier time. My real dream is to be a publican with me own bar. I so love the *craic* of pulling pints and talking to the lads when it is slow and to the tourists at the height of summer. But there was no pub in me budget, not with high prices and the economic slump Ireland is experiencing. The wee coach is a grand second-best way to meet with a mix of folks. So here I am delivering the visitors to the pubs and places of interest instead of owning a pub meself. But, 'tis fine, I remind meself. I am blessed in many ways. Thanks be to the saints, a rainbow did appear.

I easily find the tea and gift shop Dorrie and Gordie had visited only by website. The real thing is even better than the advert. I hear the teenage lass exclaim to her mother, "Wow, just like in *The Secret Garden!*"

Indeed, 'tis undeniably resplendent in colors. There are more varieties of poppies than I knew even existed in all of Ireland: hydrangeas of all shades of pink, blue and purple, and trillions of wildflowers that blend in with the formal gardens beautifully. Me wife Sally would have loved this.

Everyone takes pictures and brings their tea out to the terrace to enjoy the vibrancy of colors and the variety of blossoms in what appears to be the most natural of settings. While some also visit the gift shop, others just soak in the sun. I tell them all 'tis important to appreciate the sun when 'tis above you. One never knows for how long 'twill last.

The younger lad, called Nathan, reminds me in manner and build of me own son at that age: small-boned, dark, and bright as a star up above. He and his table were watching a man in amongst the greenery, wetting one flower with a spray bottle. At that age, this is the kind of thing which would have gotten me own son's attention, as well. He comes and asks me what the man is doing. I have not a clue. Doesn't the lad, politely but unabashedly, approach the gent and ask him?

The fellow replies that he wants to take a picture of the morning dew on the petals. Since 'tis now afternoon, he is making dew. This sends Lily into peals of laughter as she comments, "The devas of form have a helper, making dew, making do," and laughs some more. Nathan now has questions for her about what she means, but she is laughing too hard to answer.

The older boy with the iPod-thing is off by himself, sulking. He has a copy of Joyce's *Ulysses.* Hard to say if it is to show off his intellect, to spite his father who described himself as a Yeats man, or because of genuine literary interest. Time will tell, will it not?

I go off to open the coach and give it a bit of an airing whilst Gordie gathers folks up. Then, as we drive back to the coast and up around the sea to the Cliffs, I put on some Celtic music, *Riverdance*, to keep the jet–lagged ones alert after time in the sunshine.

County Clare has been me home since me birth. Yet, I shall never get over the feeling of awe as I drive up and down the hills along the Galway coast. The water is so blue and sparkling as it splashes on the sandy beaches one place, and dark, powerful and foreboding as it pounds against the black rock of the cliffs in another. Promontories and sharp cut-outs vary the coastline to the left and green pastures both left and right are squared off by the slate grey of stone fencing. The fencing creates a ribbon-like effect across the vistas to the East that finally begins to give way to the bleak, stony Burren. With a chuckle, I take the mike and share me Uncle George's favorite line to visitors, probably not for the last time, "Sure, you have nothin' like this in America?"

We reach the Cliffs themselves, and are they not just as grand today as the first time I came here as a wee boy? Maybe grander, for today we have the weather. 'Tis an auspicious sign for the twelve days of touring that lie ahead.

As I sit here with me tea, I keep thinking about the words burned into the wee, thin oak plaque above the peat bin in me ma's kitchen when I was but a lad:

May yer clouds niver be without a rainbow

As a schoolboy, I cringed to see the misspelled words so proudly displayed by me ma, right when Sister Angelica was teaching us proper spelling of English. But now, I understand the meaning behind the words and what me ma was trying to impart upon us children. Sure enough, the clouds can become dark and the promise of a rainbow is all that keeps a man going at times.

This opportunity I have been given, me own business, mixing in with people and their stories, is one of the rainbows. I feel blessed to have it to keep me going.

With only one half of a day gone, I am already imagining this is to be the best of all the coach runs since I started up me business, though 'tis too early to really tell. And it may be that it is just the hunger I have to be around companionable people since me Sally passed to the other side. Me boy and girl are all grown now. He off to live on the continent as part of this new EU era, and she busy with her brood of little ones, right here in County Clare.

Herself and Himself must have got my name from Cousin Delaney in New York, for I haven't had the business going that long; executive tours mostly through referral from friends from the bank and short runs to Galway, the Ring of Kerry or even Blarney Castle. But these ones were looking for someone willing to do some planning with them, suggest eateries and the like, for a coach tour lasting just short of a fortnight. They want to be as far from the packaged American Express or Cook's Travel as they can get. And here I am, offering a fresh new business, unencumbered and ready for adventure, too. 'Tis a perfect match.

I call me wee buggy The Journeyer. My daughter said The Wanderer, my first choice of names, did not inspire confidence. Ironically, the tour flyer has the title Celtic Spirit: *Journey to Sacred Sites of Ancient Ireland*. This is, perhaps, a harbinger that a good match-up has been made.

One of the first things I learned is to hold back and stay with the coach a good bit when we first reach a stop. There is always someone returning for a jumper, a camera, or umbrella. They get all discombobulated if the coach is locked up and the driver nowhere to be found. Today's weather, however, couldn't be more grand, so I would doubt there will be anyone coming back for wraps and such.

Even though 'tis a beautiful day, I warned them to watch the wind. It can be fierce. I didna tell them me own story of almost being blown away over these very cliffs as a teenager. Perhaps over a pint tonight at the pub I will, but we all are just finding our way with one another and I didna want to take over the microphone from the lass.

The fear of falling is still with me as I see folks approaching that stretch of the cliffs. Doesn't it make me stomach turn over to this day? There is now a thin stone wall to keep people from charging right up to the edge, but still some heed no warning and get seduced by the beauty and the power of the place. The way the surf pounds the rocks and sprays up and about, you would think they would feel the fear, as well as the magnificence.

It is not just me that sees the fierce beauty of the Cliffs. 'Tis known world-round; more than a spot of beauty, more than one of the world's wonders. 'Tis a place of powerful energy. I am glad the wee girl plans to offer a ritual up on the top of the hill. 'Tis clever of her to open her tour here. Magic or not, 'tis special, to be sure.

The colorful goats, recently receiving their stripes of red and blue, are playing along the fence for me amusement and the amusement of any who stop to look. These wee animals make a mockery of the slides and tea towels for sale that pretend to capture the Isle with a few green shamrocks. While buses pull in and out, they skitter and scamp, putting on a show. The real Ireland is, indeed, still here for those with the eyes to see.

And by me meaning, it is the wee lambs and goats scampering around less than a meter from one of the wonders of the world that is our uniqueness. Sure Niagara Falls doesn't have a naturally occurring pasture or stretch of unmanicured grass within sight of it, does it now?

Indeed, the Yanks would have built some high-rise hotel and restaurant and an electric lift shaft down the side of the Cliffs if this glorious spot had had the misfortune to be situated in New York. I pray that with all this Euro tourist money, we keep our senses and resist such progress. And, I think, here in the West of Ireland, we will. For we have a proud story.

Yeats talked about the terrible beauty that is Ireland. He was talking about the rebellion, but his words speak to more. When I think about all the Irish-Americans who look out across the great expanse of blue sea and ponder the journey their ancestors made, I am reminded of what we lost in the Great Famine and beyond. Yet, we are a sturdy lot. We endure.

If we withstood famine and victimization by the English, we can withstand this wave of commercialism as well, can we not? And, hopefully, even this deep recession and debt problem.

Sure, we continue to hold the memory of the stories: stories of our ancestors, stories told by the bards, stories of the faerie folk, stories of Patrick and all our saints, stories of our struggles as a people to keep our own country, stories of those forced to leave for distant shores, and stories of those who stayed to eke out a living right here in this place.

They say that those in America who cite Irish heritage amount to two times the number of Irish people actually living here in Eire. 'Tis especially grand to hear the account of those who left these shores and made it to the Americas. Of course, now, not all the stories are of success and glory. The emigrant stories I hear are of both pain and joy, desperation and courage, opportunities lost and opportunities seized. Powerful like, every one of them. Sometimes, me questions stir the visitors to seek to know more about their own heritage; to appreciate their roots and the hardships faced by their ancestors.

Aye, the terrible beauty that is Ireland has generated more stories than I can even imagine. And, thanks to the beauty of this land, the Blessed Virgin and the legend of St. Patrick, I get to hear a good many of them.

Of course, not all the North American visitors come from Ireland, and not all are particularly interesting or interested in telling the story of their people. Yet, so many, whether there is any Irish blood in them or not, look beyond the cliffs to the West for hours, watching the sun on its journey until sunset comes and the winds die down a bit and the crash of waves against the rocks is less deafening. Others stop and buy a trinket and a wee card to post, perhaps have a coffee, and barely bother to look out and beyond at all. They seem to think that the refreshment building is its own destination.

I chuckle when I think of the man O'Brien, the landlord who built this here folly o'er a hundred and fifty years ago to woo tourists. Might he have had even an inkling of what would come, what with tour buses and charters? These "American Express tourists," as we call them, see only the half of it. They are on and off those buses so fast they often miss the ruins at the top of the hill, the green and white foamy wave surfaces, the birds nesting in the rock cliffs or flying with the currents, and the wildflowers popping up like wee miracles from amid the rocks. They certainly miss the magic.

That's why this trip holds such promise. It is not an American Express or Cook tour at all. 'Tis more, indeed, 'tis more.

I got a wee sense of all me passengers back at the airport hotel when we were starting out. There are stories inside them all, that 'tis certain. Indeed, it goes without saying that everyone has a story. And sure, there is no better place to be telling your story than here in Ireland, where people always have time for a yarn and the most pressing business is the present company we are with, and the best leisure activity a good *craic*.

And if your story is a sad one, we Irish will cry along with you. If it is a boring one, we will spice it up a wee bit as you tell it, weaving in tales of others in the same situation and the predicaments they got themselves in and out of. After a bit of time, even the dullest person begins to feel a part of something bigger and grander and livelier than ever before.

'Tis the real secret of Ireland and why people of all colors and backgrounds feel at home here. We may be an isolated country 'til of late, and most people in the West of Erin have never been beyond the neighboring village, but we Irish mean it when we say to visitors, *"céad míle fáilte"*—one hundred thousand welcomes.

"Timothy? Timothy!" I hear Gordie calling as he gestures for me to open the door. Doesn't he have a new *bodhran* in his hands?

"So you have bought yourself something, already a day into the trip. I thought shopping was what your American women did to distraction, not you gents," I tease as I open the door and take the bag from him.

"I've always wanted to have one of these handmade Irish drums. I learned a bit how to play one from my great uncle, but somehow the drum itself disappeared after his death," he answers to me teasing.

"Aye, you have a good one here. The lad who made it, did it well. And the stenciling on the goatskin is bold and beautiful," I add after looking it over.

He asks if I want to join the group for the opening ritual and meditation Dorrie is going to lead up on the hilltop. As he speaks, the wild one, Lily she is called, breezes back, wanting to get her harp from the coach. Tickled to death she is that Dorrie has agreed to let her play for the group up on the hill. Her enthusiasm is catching. I agree that I will lock up the bus and be right along.

As I walk in and along the path, I see some of the folks still sitting on the rocks and others making their way up the hill. Seems to me our folks stand out, even though at the moment I can remember not one name. Every group has its own chemistry. These folks seem to have enough lightness of spirit and readiness to be swept up in the music of the harp to suggest we have a good wee ride ahead of us.

On the way to the top of the hill for Dorrie's opening ritual, I am joined by one of the gentlemen who overnighted at the Inn. He reintroduces himself as Rob. We chat as people slowly begin to gather.

I ask him which one of the ladies is his wife. He points to the intense looking woman, over at the cliff's edge. "Her name is Peg," he offers, adding, "she's usually very outgoing and full of life, but this connection to her Irish roots has gotten hold of her. We went to *Da* at the Limerick playhouse last night and it really disturbed her. She tells me she just can't get past the thought of the thousands upon thousands who were forced to leave during the Famine. I understand, but am not really feeling it myself, so I thought I would leave her to her thoughts for a bit."

"Aye, a lot of Americans come here and stare out in like fashion. And yourself, now? Did your people come from Ireland?"

"No, and I guess that's why this doesn't touch me as deeply. Don't get me wrong, I see the Famine as horrific, like the Inquisition or the Holocaust, or the atrocities of Viet Nam, Darfur . . . well, you get the point. But these are not my roots. My own grandparents fled from Franco's Spain, so I get emigration. But, I also know they didn't have anywhere near as bad a situation as the Irish diaspora folks."

"Right enough. So you may be from a line of Spaniards who jumped ship during the Armada? The ones, you know, we call the Black Irish?"

"Now there's a thought; at the very least, I can use it to explain my love of Irish pubs back home. I am hoping to get a taste of the real thing here, with your help. How does that sound to you? Will we be able to go to some authentic pubs?" he asks, grinning widely.

"Do I look like a man who could refuse such a request? By the time you leave, you'll be singing so many songs and drinking so much stout that we will be needing to make you an honorary Irishman," I reply with a grin, as well.

"It's a plan then!" he shouts above the wind as he rushes over to give Peg a hand as she climbs over rocks toward our path.

Peg introduces herself and takes Rob's arm, giving him an Irish smile that would melt your heart. The man has good taste, you can say that for him.

Lily is toward the top and to the side of the well-worn path, sitting in a patch of shamrocks, playing her harp and calling everyone to gather together.

"It's just overwhelming," says Peg with a sigh, the sober look returning.

"Aye," 'tis all I say.

I hear more sighs as folks look out from the top o' the hill. This group could compete with the West of Ireland—the sighs are so long and deep. Indeed, I sigh, too, for the view never ceases to bring a leap to me heart.

Me wife and I took the balloon ride straight up once. From that vantage point, you see the flatness, a six or maybe even eight kilometer slab of grass and rock like a tabletop over six hundred of your American feet above sea level, with blue-blue water, green-green earth mixed with rock, pure air, and sky from horizon to horizon.

But from the ground, there is no end in sight; it is just a huge expanse. Kate joins our little group, saying she feels like a whirling Dervish, just trying to take in the scenery presented to her from this one spot. It would indeed make a brilliant 360 degree movie. And she would make a lovely Dervish dancer.

When we all are gathered, Dorrie asks us to form a circle. She invites us to be part of a ritual of Opening. She promises that she will talk more about the principles of transformation, Celtic spirituality, and sacred sites and that she will answer questions after breakfast tomorrow. For now, she encourages everyone to set their intellect aside and to enter their bodies, to breathe deeply and release their breath fully, and to feel their feet firmly planted.

And then she begins in a firm, joyful voice:

Ancient Ones of this Green Isle of Ireland, First Nations peoples of the Americas, and indigenous peoples throughout the world called to the Four Directions and asked the Spirits of the Sun and Moon, Sky, Earth and Water to join them as they created their sacred circles.

Here, at the first sacred site of our tour, as we gather as intentional seekers of the Mysteries these sites hold, let us do as they once did.

Please turn with me to the East, source of the morning Sun, symbol of Spring, and of the East Wind, which here in Ireland is gentle and light. We ask the Spirits of the East to join us in our circle and on our journey.

Turning to the South, source of the midday Sun, symbol of Summer, Fire, and of the South Wind, which here in Ireland is strong and warm. We ask the Spirits of the South to join us in our circle and on our journey.

Turning to the West, source of the Sunset, symbol of Water, twilight, change, and of the West Wind, which here in Ireland is a hard and wayward wind. We ask the Spirits of the West to join us in our circle and on our journey.

And, finally, we turn to the North, source of the Darkness of Night and Stars, symbol of the Earth on which we stand, and of the North Wind, which is fierce and bringer of magic and newness and the promise of spring and rebirth once again. We ask the Spirits of the North to join us in our circle and on our journey.

Would you now turn in toward the Center, joining hands?

We join hands and draw to our circle the Spirit of That Which Is Greater Than Ourselves.

We call that Power by many names and we gather for many reasons. But whatever our Beliefs and whatever the specifics of our Purpose:

May we open our senses to the beauty and wonder around us.

May we open our hearts to one another and all we meet.

May we open our minds to viewpoints and realms beyond our present knowing.

Thus, we ask to be open to Spirit for our Highest Good.

We ask that our bus tour be blessed with good health, sunny skies, and right relations.

Thanks be to the Universe.

Let us stand a bit longer in silence together and in gratitude for all we see and experience."

"May it be so," adds Rob.

Others chime in, as well.

"Halleluiah."

"Shalom."

"Salaam."

"Namaste."

"Peace."

"Amen."

"Blessed be."

"There you have it," I think, as Lily resumes her harp playing. "A start worthy of me Celtic ancestors. If they are not Irish, by the time this wee lass is finished with them, they will all be dancing a jig and praying to Brigid herself." I watch as folks stroll off, some to reflect, some to try to capture the place on film, others to buy souvenirs. We even have a sketch artist in our midst. Later, as people gather back at the coach, I see that tin whistles and journaling books are at the top of the list along with packets of materials for making wee Brigid's crosses.

Rob hustles to catch up to Dorrie, saying, "I'd like to apologize for taking the last line back on the hill. I lost myself in the moment. I forgot I was a group member, not the minister."

She laughs. "Actually, I'm flattered that you became so involved. It also is a wonderful way to empower other group members. I really want folks to bring their personal beliefs and individual faith language to this experience."

"You're very gracious to say so. As we told you by phone, both Peg and I plan to downplay our vocations while on this trip. After all, we are on vacation. But, I can tell you that I have a feeling that it's going to be hard not to pipe up with connections to our ministries. Already, the words of Emerson, Thoreau, and their transcendentalist friends are bursting to come out of me."

With a quick hug, they board and the rest of the group comes along quicker than I had expected. I get ready to pull out as Dorrie asks for the microphone.

"Well, our Celtic journey is officially beginning. It begins much like the story of Celtic spirituality. It begins with people high on a hill honoring nature, acknowledging forces more powerful than themselves, and accepting the beauty around them in gratitude.

"This direct connection to Nature, her beauty and her power is the first of a number of dimensions to the Celtic story that we will experience as we go. Already, I think you can feel the palpable energy of this land. I truly believe that the story of Celtic spirituality and its ability to survive into this new millennium has not only the potential to transform individuals, but to transform the world.

"I am so delighted you all are here to share this journey with us. Now, I will leave you to your own thoughts.

"Timothy, may we have a bit more Celtic music as we journey forth? And, Lily, thank you so much for playing the harp up on the hill. It was beautiful."

I put Orla Fallon on low like. There is silence for a bit, with me wondering how all this talk of journeys, transformation, and calling of the elements is sitting with the group. I hear murmurings and what I think might be early signs of discontent. Someone pipes up to ask about the sign to Brede's Well. I realize that accounts for the murmuring. These eager folks are afraid I am passing up the Well.

Before Orla gets through another song, Gordie comes up to the guide's seat and takes the mike. He thanks everyone for being so prompt getting back to the bus, then assures them that we will be coming back tomorrow to the Well after a good night's sleep.

He explains that he has just called Salmon Run Lodge and the rooms will be ready when we arrive. Dinner will be at

7 p.m. in the lodge's dining room. He says there will be reserved signs on the four tables that are for our group. It was already agreed that he, Dorrie, and I would spread ourselves out so we could answer questions and get conversations going about music. The man is so organized that he has now enlisted the MacAllister's, Penny and Peter, who know a lot about Celtic music, to sit at the fourth table.

Now, after confirming with meself, he adds that those wanting to go to "a real Irish pub" as a group should meet at 9 p.m. in the lobby. He lets everyone know that tomorrow, breakfast is from 7-9 a.m. and Dorrie will lead an Orientation Meeting at 9 a.m. before we leave for the Well.

He then assigns each person traveling alone to a roommate since there are no single rooms. I fear from what I see in the mirror that the poor professor, Kate, is getting paired with the sour one, I mean, with Mary Helena. Ach, well, the lady will manage. Maybe Gordie can switch them when we get to the next lodging place or maybe Mary Helena will relax a wee bit.

Harp music from my CD fills the air until we reach Salmon Run Lodge. Nestled between the roadside and a lively stream that still has the remains of a salmon weir, the lodge is warm and inviting. The bit of thatched-cottage look at the front gives cover and charm to the entire facility, balancing off the modern extensions to the original lodge. Well done, indeed.

I get down to dinner after a quick wash-up in time to save a place for Dorrie and Gordie at separate tables and to escort the MacAllisters to their table, as well. I, meself, take the fourth table. I am curious to see how folks will fill in and what form the music discussions will take.

Nathan, the younger boy who reminds me of me own son, purchased a tin whistle back at the Cliffs so he is nudging his mother to hurry up so they can sit with the MacAllisters. It seems Peter MacAllister, the Canadian, has promised to teach him how to play the wee thing. Boys that age are one minute adult-acting and the next minute still wee boys so 'tis grand to see him carried away in excitement.

Nathan's mother, Leslie, pauses to chat with me as the boy rushes over to Peter. "Excuse me but is there assigned seating?"

"Not at all, I was just seeing that someone with some knowledge of Irish music was at each table so as we could lead a discussion, if people wanted to go in that direction. Dorrie suggested it to get us eased into the first night."

"Great idea. We all know how awkward table talk with strangers can be. Certainly, if Nathan has his way, our table will be talking about flutes and whistles. But, mainly, I am relieved since I prefer not to have the children always thrust together. The other two are older and also, the other boy, Jackson, is so sullen and angry-acting. Back at the Cliffs when Kevin bought tin whistles for his son and himself, Jackson threw his to the ground and stormed off in anger."

"Missed that wee exchange," says I, noncommittally.

"So you find Nathan reminds you of your son?"

"Aye, though me boy is nigh on thirty now. You will be amazed at how fast they grow up."

"Mmm. People keep telling me to brace for the coming teenage years of sullenness, but I am hoping with Nathan it won't be drastic. Was your son a handful?"

"Not like some. He had lots of interests and goals that helped us all through it. And me wife, God rest her soul, was a very patient and calming force in our house."

"You lost her?"

"She passed on not long ago."

"I'm so sorry. I didn't mean to pry."

"Not at all, not at all."

"Kevin shared with me that his wife died a couple of years ago. My heart goes out to both of you and to Jackson, who seems to really be struggling. I wonder, Timothy, if you have some sort of Irish blessing or Celtic prayer that you find helpful. I would like to share it with Kevin and Jackson."

"Aye, Irish blessings and prayers abound. I have a wee book on them in the coach; remind me tomorrow to give you the loan of it. As a matter of fact, a particular blessing of me own mother's has been running through me mind all day. I will write it down for you, as well. So are you, yourself, a religious person?"

"Oh, God, no. Not at all. It is Nathan's interest in Harry Potter that brought us here. I wanted him to see some of the history and folklore from which the Potter story comes. I don't want him to go too far afield in fantasy. This seemed a good way to ground him. His dad is too busy to take much time off in the summer and there are not all that many things for a boy his age and his mother to do together. So finding something fun, and educational to boot, took a bit of doing."

"Aye then, we will have to see to the fun, as well as to the educational things that Dorrie will be providing."

"Well, I have kept you from your hosting functions long enough. Thanks, Timothy."

I scramble to remember names as I continue to greet people until Dorrie arrives and takes it on. I see two couples from early morning at the Inn are already seated at my table and that Rose, the lady with the husband on the business jaunt, is just sitting down. Thanks be to Saint Patrick, I know all these names and have a basis for beginning.

I see Kevin and "Jackson-not-KJ" come in last. They take the two open seats remaining at Gordie's table. Aye, but the saints are with us or Gordie himself is a wizard. It is important that the boy bond with one of us and I doubt very much it is to be me. I give the lad credit, though, for not bringing his computing device with him to dinner. But there is a book. Although in fairness, he has not opened it as yet. He is a broody and angry one, that.

Turning back to our table, I hear Jake giving his critique of the food. "This salmon is amazing, so fresh, and the roasted potatoes . . . I must say the food here in Ireland is certainly better than on our first trip, years ago. I remember everything boiled into one big mush. No offense, Timothy."

"None taken, Jake. You have the right of it. Irish food, especially at restaurants, is much improved. We have a fierce pride in using fresh local foods, like this salmon, and our duck and lamb are outstanding. Add to it that our cuisine has gotten much more international."

"I sure am enjoying it," adds Rob, "but I do hope the pub life is still traditional. That is the only thing on my wish list for the trip. You know, I practically lived in The Plough and Stars, an Irish bar in Boston, during my college years. I always wanted to experience the real thing."

"Rob has some romantic notions about us Irish, you see," laughs Peg.

"I was right enough in marrying an Irish colleen, wasn't I? But any more and I will make my Irish bride blush. Tell us about tonight's pub, Timothy."

I don't even have to be in me cups to carry on about the quintessential Irish pub experience. 'Tis a particular fondness of mine. So I regale them with stories and tidbits of information about pubs and pub music throughout dinner. I even suggest they look for two great pub signs to get as souvenirs for their home bars, if they had such things. The first:

There are no strangers here, just friends not yet met.

Rob quips that there was a similar sign in the vestibule of his church:

Let no one be a Stranger.

We all muse about the similarities between pubs and churches.

I go on to say that when I was a lad, no self-respecting Irish musician wanted to play Irish-American songs like *McNamara's Band* or the like. There used to be a poster that said IRISH ONLY PLAYED HERE. And we discuss the dispute over the originality of Danny Boy and how it goes to the tune of *Londonderry Air* which takes me into an explanation of Derry versus Londonderry. At that, I realize I am talking too much, not facilitating at all.

But Sandra hooks me back in and on me mark by asking, "So, Timothy, what was the second sign we need for our bars?"

"That would be the classic," says I: *Céad Míle Fáilte*– One hundred thousand welcomes. "Oh, and I should not be forgetting *Sláinte*, the equivalent of cheers to you Yanks."

At the end of this long rendition, I decide to check with Gordie and the other tables to arrange the pub visit before people leave the dining room. First, to Gordie, since he is the operations man.

"Timothy, we were just discussing U2 and wondered if you were a fan and what people think of U2 and Bono over here."

"Aye, indeed, our man Bono is an Irish treasure. I first saw him in Dublin when he was just getting known."

"Would you believe that everyone at this table saw him on the Mall the weekend of the Obama inauguration? We were all there and didn't even know we would be meeting each other…awesome…," pipes up the usually sullen Jackson.

"Were you ever, now? That is, indeed, a coincidence."

The lot of them nod in agreement.

"Over the days ahead I would love to hear the stories, all of them. But, Gordie, I came to check with you about our going off to the pub tonight. Is 9:15 too early?"

"Sounds good to me. How about the rest of you?"

Nods, again.

"So, Timothy, do you mind telling the other tables since you are already up?"

Dorrie's table also had questions about Irish musicians.

"Timothy, just in time," says Kate. "We were wondering whether Mary Black is more popular than Orla Fallon, or the reverse?"

"That was me wife's department; I only know that I like them both. This brings me to the reason I came over. We are meeting in the lobby by 9:15 p.m. for those going to the pub. I make no promise of a female vocalist tonight, but there may be one."

The sour one looks particularly sour but all the others give cheery assurance that they will be ready. So I go on to the MacAllister table for the same announcement. They are having a fascinating discussion of when Celtic music actually came to the Americas. But I do not tarry, knowing me own table is waiting dessert.

The blemish to a wonderful dinner comes as I am leaving the dining room.

"Just you wait up, Timothy. I want to tell you what I told Dorrie. I did not come all the way to Ireland to go pubbing or hang around with a bunch of pubcrawlers. I could do that at home. The drink has gotten the best of too many Irishmen already, and I will have no part of it. No part at all. Do you understand?"

I am so taken aback, I just stand silently.

Before I speak, she says, "Hmmpff," and storms out.

May the saints preserve us.

It is always fun to see who shows up for the amusements, was me thinking as I wait for the pub goers in the lobby of the lodge. Peter, Rob and Jake arrive first, with their respective wives, Penny, Peg, and Sandra next. And me, so proud of meself for getting the names straight.

Then, come Kate and Rose, the other early arrivals this morning. The boy, Nathan, and his mother join us as I assure them, again, that pubs are family friendly. Next is Kevin, without the teenager, Jackson. Then, Himself and Herself and some of the others, still nameless to me. We are off.

And lucky we are to leave when we did. The premises are near full-up. Most of the men go to the bar while the women take up the tables. I let the women know that the place has no table service and offer to take their orders.

"Merlot would be nice, thank you, Timothy," say Kate.

"The choices at an establishment such as this will be red or white, and it will come with a screw top. Not at all the quality of a wine bar, you should be told."

"Thanks for the warning; I guess I will go with a light beer, then."

"Harp, then? And the rest of you? We also have shandies that many ladies like. It is a mix of beer and lemonade. And, Nathan, I will bring you a lemonade."

Taking the orders to the barman, I see the men are making their choices: Rob, a Guinness; Gordie, a boilermaker in the same spirit of adventure; Peter, a Bushmills Irish. Stouts for the rest and, meself, I add a Jameson to the list.

Leslie comes up to the bar to request some nuts or wafers and asks me, "Now, what exactly is the difference between your Irish whiskey and Scotch or bourbon?"

"Let me first bring our man Rob round to this discussion. He has a fierce interest in all pub information."

Rob turns around at the bar to face us.

"The main distinction between Scotch and Irish whiskey, she asks now? We thought of it first, don't you know? In point of fact, in Gaelic the word whiskey means 'water of life.' Also, Irish whiskey uses barley (which you will hear called corn, or barley corn), just as American whiskey differs because you people use rye. And, you will find that Kentucky bourbon has but one go of the distillation of the mash, Scotch has two, but our Jameson has at least three. There is nothing can compare to a single malt, twelve year-aged Irish whiskey," says I. "And, there is the Orangeman's whiskey, Bushmills. Peter can tell you more about that, I believe."

Leslie just grins and says she is glad she asked an authority on the subject, to which we both laugh.

After a bit of time we hear, "So we'll have a bit of a hush," from the barman. "In addition to our regulars tonight, a wee lass called Lily will open with a Gaelic tune."

Sure enough, there is "our" Lily with her lyre harp, singing what seems an original tune, though none of us are sure. At the end of the performance, Peg goes to the back to encourage her to join us, but the wee lass disappears too quickly. Fey one, that.

The "regulars" take over. I am ever so proud: fiddle, flute, bodhran, uilleann pipes. Their singer begins with *Carrickfergus* and then livens things up with some classic Irish sing-along tunes, probably playing to their American visitors. They only play one fiery Irish rebel song, at the request of our Kevin. Few Americans realize how explosive this rebellion music can be in these parts even given today's improved political climate. The hardcore songs are seldom played these days, except in very rural pubs among neighbors who share the same sensibilities. I would have to explain that to Kevin. At which time, I also would confess to him that I love to hear these songs meself.

Many Americans still think of the IRA as romantic and supporting it is akin to supporting the Irish Republic. But, if the truth be told, celebrating the rebellions and troubles are hardly romantic or strengthening to the country when everyone alive today knows someone killed and maimed by violence. 'Tis not history yet; 'tis raw memory still. Most of us in the Free State wish to avoid rehashing and stirring it all up. No one needs to get in the crosshairs of a gun or a fistfight; and so these songs are best left alone. But 'tis another story for another day.

Sally Gardens, one of me very favorites, comes next. Our group gets a second wind as I encourage them to get with the *craic* of it. Pretty soon everyone sings the choruses, especially the Clancy Brother songs, *Wild Rover* being the group favorite:

> "*No, Nay, Never (clap clap, clap, clap) No, Nay,*
> *Never No more, will I play the wild rover, No,*
> *Never. No More.*

Whiskey in a Jar, another good sing-along tune follows.

After a few more . . . songs not rounds . . . we all feel the weariness of a long day set in. After the set finishes and the lads take a wee break, people decide to make their way home, home to Salmon Run Lodge. 'Tis a wishful lot, some weaving a bit, and all in good form.

Rob pipes up, "Three cheers for Timothy for giving us an initiation to the real pub life of Ireland."

And they all cheer as me countrymen look on with bemused faces and I feel meself blush. Great fun this, me job of providing local contextualization, is going to be.

DAY TWO

St. Brigid's Well *Poulnabrone Dolmen* *The Burren*

Our second day in County Clare begins with a visit to an ancient well
sacred to Irish people for centuries. Some still call it Brede's or Brigid's
Well in honor of the Celtic goddess. It has since become a holy site named
for St. Brigid of Kildare. Here you will see all the
layers of Celtic spirituality.
This afternoon we travel through the Burren, visit the Poulnabrone Dolmen,
the interpretive museum of Craggaunowen, and the Caves of Alliwee.
The evening is free, with the option of going to hear traditional Irish music
at a nearby pub.

DORRIE

    I wake up to find the pillow next to me empty, and my heart skips a beat. Then I see him, quietly doing his yoga practice by the faint light of the window. Shaking my fear of losing him, I lay there quietly, just watching the movements of his tall, agile frame. I'm so grateful that our first day on tour went so well. Ah, how perfect, to be doing what I love, with the man I love, in a place I love. The Universe is, indeed, good to me.

My mind floats back to our free time before the bus tour began. We spent a truly magical day along the Shannon biking through the lush countryside of rhododendrons, wild lilies and roadside lupines, accented by the occasional magpie sitting on the stone fences along our way. We laid out a mid-day picnic of freshly baked Irish soda bread, Dublin cheddar, and oak-smoked salmon. A feast worthy of a Celtic king or Druid high priest, but instead, spread out on our plastic rain gear and shared between just the two of us. Secluded as we were up a farmer's lane off a country road, protected from the wind and prying eyes, we fed one another the strawberries that I'd tucked away for dessert.

Our intimate afternoon was finally interrupted when a huge lorry came barreling along, like it was on the expressway, not an old, narrow country road. Out of the corner of my eye, I noticed a warren of bunnies scurry up the lane beyond us. They, too, had been startled. They were running like mad, up and over a small rise in the grassy field; I suddenly realized they were running over a fairy circle, a ring of grass covering an earthen circular rise about fifty feet in diameter. So amazing. If not for the truck and the bunnies, I would have missed it completely. They say the reason there are still so many fairy rings here in Ireland is because the farmers were too superstitious to remove them. Most of the modern Irish people don't hold as strongly to superstitions as their ancestors, but the culture still includes an honoring of the tradition and legends of the Fairy Kingdom. And no one wants to tempt fate or the fairies.

I coaxed Gordie up and over to the fairy ring. Reverently, I asked the Spirits of the place, whomever they might be, to bless us and bless the bus tour we were about to lead. I can still feel the answer, *"Yes!"* inside myself.

A feeling of being suspended in time and place overcame me, like we were circled in enchantment. Even Gordie, the skeptic, seemed to feel it, pure Emerald Isle magic.

Now though, I have a weirder, stronger feeling. I am so confused. Someone is shaking me.

"Earth to Dorrie! Earth to Dorrie!" Gordie is standing over me, already showered and dressed. "I have been trying to wake you! Thought you were awake before I showered. What happened, sleepy head? If you sleep any later you won't have time for morning meditation. I have a bunch of billing things to take care of with the lodge staff. I'll see you for coffee."

He's out the door before I can say anything. I immediately get out of bed before I fall back asleep again. Hard to believe, on a day as important as this, I would have nodded back off.

Within fifteen minutes, I am dressed and out to the stream behind the lodge for my deep breathing meditation.

The misty morning is perfect for a "soft eyes" meditation. I sit with my back to the lodge, looking out at the water and letting the Spirit of the Place calm me and fill me for the work ahead. Tomorrow, we will lead morning spiritual practice sessions for any who want to participate, but this morning is mine, mine alone.

My role in the tour is most critical today, framing the trip, trying to convey the universal meaning I see in the Celtic experience, and inviting individuals into their own spiritual journey. Yet, my monkey mind is full of thoughts of Gordie and our relationship. I know I need to let go of outcome about it, that is what I teach and what I know to be true. It's just living it is still hard sometimes. Perhaps that is why I teach and coach, to reinforce my beliefs so I'll follow them myself. The journey for me on this trip is exactly that lesson. May Brede, Brigid, St. Brigit guide and support me.

I so admire Gordie's work, his passion for kids, his sensitivity to the pain of teens in trouble. But, are we right for each other long term? He sometimes resents my wanting so much meditative time and mocks my intuitive leaps. In turn, I sometimes become judgmental about his busy-ness, his intense need to be working all the time, and his difficulty expressing his feelings for me, his feelings period.

Breathe deeply, I remind myself; let go of anxiety, let go of attachment, let go of insecurity. I am calm. I am relaxed. Universal energy is pouring over me and through me. I am embraced in Love and supported by Spirit.

It is time. I am ready. So I take leave of this beautiful place and head in to the breakfast room to meet Gordie and Timothy. I chuckle when Timothy greets me, "Herself, is it, here at last and looking ever so beautiful." I love that he calls me 'Herself.' What a dear man. Gordie and I are so lucky we found him. He seems to get and respect what we envision on this tour. That is so important.

For me, this bus tour is so much more than just a visit to sacred sites. It is an invitation for people to embrace these sites as part of their personal journeys of transformation. Not all came for this, not all who were attracted by the idea will follow through. Yet, I feel called to create the space for people who do want that opportunity.

My own journey, both my career path and my spiritual path, have brought me to this point of guiding others. We joke that Gordie is the *sherpa* guide, seeing to the logistics of the climb up the Himalayas trip and I am the *bodhisattva*, the spiritual guide. It is a private joke, though. I am just humbled to have the chance to share what I have learned.

While I have designed the trip to create space for Spirit to enter, I have only outlined the program at this point. I am waiting because I want to learn the wishes of each individual and hold them in my heart and mind as I craft the details of our meditations and workshop sessions. I hope it will be a transformative experience. The key, of course, is the sacred sites themselves. They hold the power beyond time and space to transform all who enter with right intention.

Gordie, Timothy, and I will get to see how each story unfolds. Yes, we guide them to these sites and free them from the hassle of hotel choices, etc., but it is their work to do. Each must find their way on their own journey. Empowerment, infusion of spirit, and lots of affirmation are the tools we provide.

Gordie keeps reminding me not to front-load the experience and overwhelm people. I know he's right, yet I so wish for everyone to get all they can out of the trip and to be prepared for each site. Today is especially heavy with me providing both information and ritual, because at the beginning, there is just so much to impart. I still feel the creative tension in my body, even after meditation. It's okay. The tension is here to help me keep my balance.

I discovered the sacred sites of Ireland when I was twenty-five, jilted and heart-broken. I had just suffered a breakup from the love of my life and was finding myself very alone. I knew how important Celtic spirituality had become to me and I had always wanted to visit Ireland. So I packed up and spent six weeks here.

I heard Timothy describe me as 'a tiny wee slip of a lass.' With my fire-red short-cropped hair and a wiry body, I often have been called a wee leprechaun. What he doesn't know, but might very well sense, is that I have always been fascinated with my Irish heritage, skipping along talking to my leprechaun friend, watching *Finnegan's Rainbow* over and over, getting neighborhood kids to look for the pot of gold rather than play hide-and seek, and humming *too-ra-loo-ra-loo-ra* as I did my chores.

But unlike Peter Pan, I succumbed to the world of grown–ups, rationality, and fitting in. I gave up my fairy friends, my imaginative life and the stories of my childhood. I did well in school and was considered well-adjusted and on the right track. But in my heart, I knew something had been lost. I sensed something was missing. As those here in the West of Ireland would say, I could no longer see the "mountain behind the mountain."

The summer of my senior year in college, my grandmother took me to Iona, Scotland. A life-long Episcopalian and journal writer, Gran sensed this lack of faith and loss of spiritual optimism that I felt so deeply inside myself, but had not articulated. As she put it, she "was distressed that her favorite granddaughter had no religion, not even a spiritual practice." She designed the trip to give me a chance to find my spiritual roots and to find my way in the world. What a wise woman. She also introduced me to a little book that became my spiritual primer. I still have its lovingly bedraggled pages.

The experience changed my life. It was my first journey to a sacred site and my first adult experience with transformation. Its lessons would help me on my personal journey and become the foundation of my professional work, as well. Gran, I love you. I am so grateful to you.

Now, here I am back in Ireland as a guide, partnered with Gordie. We are calling it, both our working together on the trip and our relationship, an experiment. Clearly makes sense for the trip. And it fits for the relationship, too; I think we both wonder if we are just a passing thing. When it is good, it is so very good, but....

Both Timothy and Gordie remind me that this is just the second day and to go easy on my expectations of telling folks "everything you need to know about Ireland and personal transformation but were afraid to ask." It is perfect advice because trying to do and say it all is a trap into which I easily fall. Thankfully, I have the two of them to keep me from going too far.

Everyone seems in good form and ready to start the day of touring. A full Irish breakfast of eggs, sausage, rashers of bacon, and broiled tomatoes is offered, but I take the oatmeal. If I don't start out eating sensibly, I'll gain ten pounds in a fortnight and be disappointed in myself. Besides, Irish oatmeal is the real thing.

I enjoy sitting with John and Melanie, Trish and her daughter Megan, and Rebecca, who had taken a workshop from me at Omega. It is the first I have had a chance to talk with any of them at any length and I am delighted to hear more about their interests.

After breakfast, Gordie rounds everyone up for our quick orientation.

I begin, "Yesterday, at the Cliffs you were introduced to the importance of Nature in Celtic spirituality. As many of you know, the Celtic calendar is based on the seasons of the year and the elements. The cycle of day, of month, of year were at the heart of the direct experience of ancient peoples everywhere. In Celtic tradition, it is still a fundamental aspect of consciousness. There is a handout in your packet on Celtic spirituality that gets into this more, if you are interested.

"Today, I would like to lift up four more aspects of Celtic spirituality that will be demonstrated in the sites we visit. So, together, the five I have identified are:

The Beauty and Power of Nature at the center of our
    interconnected lives.
A sense of direct experience of Spirit enhanced by visible and
    accessible places of sacred ritual.
The co-existence of truths and worldviews honored side by
    side with others.
The continued presence of the Divine Feminine.
The celebration of Mystery and Wonder.

"You'll see that Celtic spirituality is layered, like striations in rock formations that hold and leave visible the story of geologic time.

"All of this is extremely well, oops, no pun intended, illustrated at Brigid's Well, our first stop of the day. This ancient site is in Lisconnor and is one of the best known of the sacred wells here in Ireland.

"You will find the names Brede, Brighid, Brigid, and Brigit all used in connection with these wells. The name Brede was given to the ancient triple goddess. Brighid and Brigid were both then used to represent the Celtic goddess of water, serpents, and fire; fertility, creativity, and inspiration; mothers, poets, and metal workers; fire, light, and healing. Notice, everything is in threes.

"Brigid was such a key figure to pre-Christian Celtic Ireland that in the fifth century, she either reappeared or was reconfigured to be St. Brigid. St. Brigid is the nun who founded the first cloister in Kildare. In some legends, she is at St. Patrick's right hand. In another, she is in confrontation with him. In yet another, she is at Mother Mary's side for the birth

41

of Jesus. She and St. Patrick are the holiest of saints here in Ireland.

"Over time, the Celtic celebration of Imbolc and the Christian Candlemas merged. This is St. Brigid's Day on the Roman Catholic calendar. On it, the Catholic rite of the Purification of Mary follows a tradition of both Jews and early Christians to wait six weeks after a birth to cleanse the new mother before allowing her back into temple or church. This, of course, fits with Brigid's role.

"So, many paths lead us to Brigid as a sacred figure who protects and heals, particularly women and children.

"You probably have often heard people, even scholars, refer to Ireland as Christian or pagan. In my view, that is a limiting, Christ-centered paradigm, suggesting there is only Christianity now and there is 'whatever was' before it.

"In point of fact, there is much more to the pre-history than we can include on this trip and still much more to be uncovered. I will break it into three periods, but even that is insufficient. Let's look at three major layers:

Ancient Ireland—which most of us learned as the Stone Age or, you younger folks might say Neolithic Period. We are learning through most recent archeological and new historical perspectives that Stone Age Man (SAM) was more complex than realized. Rather than characterizing these folks as primitive savages, we will see what might be just a glimpse of the complexity of their world.

A Middle period of Celtic tribes—characterized by an extensive oral Druidic tradition, what became known as the Celtic pagan religion and led to a rich mythology of place.

Christian Ireland—where the legend and real-time work of Patrick and others create a Celtic Christianity that never completely gives way to the strictest forms of Roman Catholicism.

"That should be enough background for now. I do hope, though, that you will take the time at some point to read the packet of materials. But for now, I just want you to have an appreciation of this context before we go over to Brigid's or St. Brigid's Well.

"Given this history, you can see why the Well has many names and why it is considered a sacred place by so many, a place for pagans and Christians alike. It was an ancient site of ritual, which has both changed and remained untouched over the ages.

"Perhaps, this is the magic of Ireland. Perhaps this is part of the magic of threes.

"When we get to the Well, you will see some people praying to the goddess, others to the saint, and even others to the element of water; some will simply be appreciating the archetypal meaning of the Well, not calling it prayer at all. As we all know, there are many forms of prayer. One might kneel at an altar, lay prostrate on a prayer rug, or cross one's self when heading into danger. Sometimes prayers come from a psalter or memorized liturgy, some are silent and others are a repetition of a simple phrase; the list of variation goes on. But the point is, we do not know how the Ancient Ones prayed.

"We do know that sacred wells were part of Celtic mysteries. In fact, wells were sacred in many ancient cultures.

"We also know from wisdom teachings that the power of intention is one of the most powerful gifts we were given.

"I first learned about the power of positive visualization and intention through motivational psychology. Remember the Olympic American gymnast Mary Lou Retton and her mantra 'Need a Ten, Got a Ten'? She and her coach credit that repeated visualization and statement of positive intention with winning her the gold.

"Then I began learning about how intention fit with spirituality and religion in its earliest forms. I want to share it with you and invite you to consider at least trying out this form of prayer, if you do not already.

"Ask yourself what your intention is for this trip or perhaps for your wider life journey. I realize not all of you came for this transformational aspect of our time together. Certainly, you may choose not to participate. But I hope you will at least enjoy exploring the questions and ideas with us, taking it all to whatever level you wish.

"If you are so inclined, I suggest we take a little time in reflection and meditation. This will allow you to formulate a prayer of intention for our visit to the Well. You want it to be a clear, positive statement of the future state you desire. You all know the expression, 'be careful what you wish for,' so think it through. You might also want to add the request that whatever you put forth be for your 'Highest Good and the Highest Good of Others.'

"If you feel ready by the time we reach the Well, you can then lift this intention up to Brede, Brigit, or St. Brigid, or whatever form these energies might take in your worldview. If you are not ready, you'll have the memory of your experience at this sacred well to call upon when you do find yourself wanting to connect with it.

"Lily has agreed to play for us for the next fifteen to twenty minutes to give you time to begin contemplating what you want from the visit to the Well. We will prepare to leave ten minutes after that. Let's begin."

Inviting people to do this is always nerve-racking for me the first time. I don't want to impose; yet, I know a gentle framing and nudge can lead folks into amazing journeys.

Over time I have learned to initially close my eyes and do my own meditation, holding everyone participating in my thoughts and heart. Once everyone is engaged, I open my eyes and begin watching. There are always a few fidgeters, occasionally someone walks out, some read or doodle quietly, and the rest go deeply into meditation. There is no right thing. I'm not watching to judge but looking to catch who needs support, encouragement, direction, or affirmation. Most surprising today, is that it is Peg, the minister, who fidgets the most and then slips out right after Jackson. It's not a surprise that he leaves. I can see the poor kid is really struggling. Everyone else seems engaged in the activity until it is time to begin the day's journey.

Timothy, of course, has the bus ready. We have to wait for Lily, but it is hard for me to say anything to her when she had been so generous about playing for us. She finally hops aboard and we are off. We arrive at the Well in no time.

Oh, drats. Two big tour buses of people are already here and another bus, a local one, is stopped to let off more people. How will we sense the sacred with a bunch of people distracting us with chatter and camera clicks? The small group of women walking in from the bus stop reminds me that this holy place is powerful and to let go of my concerns.

Nonetheless, I suggest everyone explore on their own until the bus tours leave. These tour groups tend to spend no more than ten minutes at a stop like this. All agree to meet me at the Well for a short invocation when we have more privacy. The site is small enough that I know people can just keep an eye out for the right time.

If I weren't group leader, I would chat with the local women first and then go directly to the Well for prayer, but I don't want us all to be in a bunch, waiting on the leader. I hold back a bit so people can go their own ways.

Mary Helena and a number of others gravitate to the statue of St. Brigid where the Rite of the Holy Well is performed. This is where the local women immediately congregate. I stand with our folks, quietly in prayer, in what becomes an outer circle. Mary Helena edges in closer and closer to the statue until she blends in with the circle of Irish churchwomen. She pulls out her rosary beads and joins them in their Latin prayers.

A heavy-set, yet spry, elderly woman in a black dress and cardigan speaks to Mary Helena when the prayers are finished.

"So it looks to be you're from America, are you not? And what part of America might that be?"

"I'm from Boston, the South End," Mary Helena says in the softest of voices. "Brigette is my confirmation name and is the given name of my middle daughter. I told Sister Mary Clare when I was just six that I would come to Ireland some day. Thank You, God, here I am."

"Fiona! Fiona, come up, Fiona. Fiona has relatives in Boston, don't you now, Fiona? Come here and speak to the American lady."

A younger woman with red hair scurries over. "Aye, two of me uncles went off to America as lads and have families there now. Would you be knowing the Callans or the Flynns over there?"

"I know a Cory Callan and a Donald Callan was in my parish."

"That would be me uncle. Would you tell him that Fiona, Fee to him, sends her love and will say a prayer here at the Well for them all?"

"Sure. I would be honored to."

"And *céad míle fáilte*, one hundred thousand welcomes, to yourself and your friends all around."

"Hi, I'm Trish, and it is so lovely to meet you all here at the Well. Do you come often?"

"Once a week, by the clock, we do, indeed. We make up the women's prayer circle from the chapel, just down the road a wee bit."

"I just wanted to add that Briget is my confirmation name, too. Patricia Brigette Cassidy. But I don't think I spell it like you do here in Ireland."

"Ach, dearie, so many spellings of Brigit here. One more doesn't matter. I feel the Irish connection and your line to St. Brigid no matter your spelling."

"She watches over you, my dear, just pray to her when in the need," offers still another.

"Sure there are more Irish in America than here in Ireland. Would I be right in guessing that more of the group have the blood of the Celts flowing through their veins?"

Many nod, myself included.

"Well, then, may Jesus, Mary, and St. Brigid herself bless you all."

After a bit more conversation, Melanie asks the ladies about the rites of the church and St. Brigid's power over fertility. She listens wide-eyed as one woman tells of becoming pregnant at 40, and "thanks be to St. Brigid," birthing a healthy baby boy. Another tells of the brides who come before the wedding with their mothers and aunts to bless the marriage and ask for it to be fruitful. Another of the elderly women says that she came out today, despite her achy rheumatism, to pray for her granddaughter whose pregnancy is in danger.

Trish, Megan, and I move into the grotto which gives cover to shelves of votive candles, rosaries, and icons. Another segment of our group is there. I join Rob, Jake, Sandra, and Trish in lighting candles. Megan waits, watches and then finally repeats what she sees her mom do. I assume she is not being raised Catholic. Rose also hesitates, but I have no idea why. Peg looks grim and distant, and wanders off.

Trish interrupts my thoughts about Peg, saying, "I am really surprised at how connected I feel to the Catholic legacy of Ireland. When I heard Mary Helena say she had taken Brigitte as a confirmation name, I was floored; I hadn't realized how much I've blocked out my Catholic connection. I was just so hurt when the Church would not support my divorce. I never connected any of that to our decision to come on this trip. I totally saw it as a chance for Megan to see a bit of another culture that was easily accessible. Dorrie, I keep thinking about what you said about the power of prayer. I can better understand now why my grandmother and her friends were so bitter when the Vatican did away with Latin mass. The rituals of the mass had been an embodied prayer for them, not just a rote recitation. I am realizing I miss that kind of ritual in my life. And regret I have given Megan none of it."

"Sometimes the Universe brings us what we need before we even ask."

Jake and Sandra move on, with me tagging along. We come across Nathan and Leslie looking at the little trinkets that have been left along with "clooties" (strips of cloth) and ribbon and strings tied to bushes. I explain to Nathan that these are left in gratitude and/or in petition. Jake adds that it was similar to a tradition at Shinto shrines they had visited in Japan. Rebecca offers that a similar tradition exists in her Jewish faith. She tells Nathan of having visited the Wailing Wall in Jerusalem and of finding slips of paper under small stones in old Jewish cemeteries in Prague. They are all such touching Universal expressions of remembrance and blessing.

Finally, the tour buses leave and I go over to the Well. Everyone meanders down to join me, being guided, if not called, by the gentle sound of the water amid the stillness and peace of the setting. Some have already bowed their heads or kneeled in prayer. I see the local women are being urged to join us as others get tiny water samples or take pictures.

Now all are gathered around the pool of water in front of the Well. I lead a short invocation:

> Brede, Brigid, Brigit
> Protector of Women and Children, Holder of the sacred powers of pregnancy and birthing, and source of healing energy for our world. By whatever form you take, we are grateful to you for the Flow of Nurturing Love, the Spark of Creativity, and the Light of Inspiration we experience in our lives.
> We ask that you hear our individual prayers of Gratitude, Intention, and Petition. Help us to birth these intentions and manifest our gratitude in the world.

I back away, wondering what each will say and do when they have their private moment at the Well. Some speak out loud, others silently. I wish I could hear everyone's prayer. And I pray for the Highest Good for each and every one of them, us.

The coach and spiritual guide in me want to assist, whether with resource information, a directed visualization exercise, or just holding their desire in my heart. But what I am meant to know and do will become apparent. The stories will unfold as the trip unfolds, and the lessons will be learned, or not.

I'll do my part to put people into a place of safety and openness. Ireland and all its energies will do the rest. Transformation will happen for sure. Not sure for whom or when, but there will be changes coming. I've known that from the beginning. That knowing was what made all the work of presenting the tour worthwhile; it is at the heart of what gives meaning to my own journey. Thank you, Brigid, for the opportunity.

Rebecca tells us she has been taking it all in with a strange sense of *déjà vu.* The sacred well is also important to her Jewish ancestry. She tells about being named for Rebecca, mother of Jacob and Esau. She reminds us that in the *Genesis* story, Rebecca is found at the Well of Aram. Our Rebecca shares her awe at the power of the well with the women around her.

Rose reminds us that both Jews and Christians share the stories of Jacob's Well. Angie adds her memory of the first pictures she saw in church school of Mary, Mother of Jesus, and the women around the common well of Nazareth. Someone else reminds us of the Biblical story of the Sumerian woman. The well is archetypically the Source of Life, or Mystery and Miracle, adds Kate. Then Rose offers a Yeats poem she has just read that morning:

> *I know you now, for long ago*
> *I met you on a cloudy hill*
> *Beside old thorn trees and a well.*

She adds, in her own words:

> May all people—all sentient beings—simply understand
> the universality of all our experiences.
> Amen, Blessed Be, Shalom, Salaam, Peace.

Megan gives me a big hug. "This is all so new to me, but it totally feels right. This is what interfaith stuff ought to be. I mean, if people would only admit that the things they worship are the same as those other religions worship, too. Did you hear Rebecca talk about being Jewish? Then there was Penny, the Presbyterian, Angie of some other Protestant group, and Kate is into feminist spirituality." She takes a breath and continues, "Dorrie, you probably know all this, but where do I go to learn it all?"

I notice the smile and color return to Peg's face. What's up with her? Don't know, but I turn directly toward her. "Megan, the people on this tour are a treasure chest of resources, starting with Peg. I bet if you ask them for some of their favorite books and pose your questions one by one, you will have the equivalent of a college course."

Peg jumps right in at the invitation. "For certain, Megan. I would love to help. You have great insight and those are great questions. I think you are exactly where you need to be, doing exactly what you need to do to learn, my young friend. I was standing here thinking about interfaith possibilities, myself. In fact, I was thinking about how disappointing it is that the title of the book I would like to write is already taken. There are so many books you might enjoy. I'll be glad to provide a list."

"What's the name of the title you wish was yours?" Megan asks.

"*One River, Many Wells*. In fact, I recently gave a sermon *Sources from Which We Draw* that used the theme of drawing from the well. I'll give you my congregation's website and you can check it out. Also, email me when we get home and I'll send you bibliographies on comparative religions and on feminist spirituality. Of course, you might prefer to just go to Google to research these things yourself."

They're still talking when I notice that most of the men are up in the old cemetery behind us. Gordie taps his watch and gives me a questioning look. He's right to suggest I round people up. Also right to leave the timing to me, so I can gradually wind this down. Not all sites will have the same meaning to everyone. It makes perfect sense that a feminine archetype, dedicated to a goddess and first female saint of Ireland, would have more meaning to us women.

I give the signal to head back to the bus. Then I see that someone has circled back and is prostrate at the level of the water source. Tears roll down her face as she prays in supplication saying, "Brede, Brigid, Brigit: Maiden, Mother, and Crone…Midwife…We seek your help… Creator of Life… hear my prayer. Bless us with a child we can raise in love…I beg of you."

It is Melanie. John comes up behind her. He reaches out his hand and pulls her up and to him, holding her long and hard.

I leave them alone, starting back to the parking lot, giving them a few minutes. They walk arm and arm through the grove, back along the bush-lined path. Melanie stops and ties her exquisite Armani scarf to the brambly bush near the votive display.

Now, only now, it is time to go. I thank Brigit and St. Brigid for the gift of their wisdom and pray for Melanie.

On the bus, I sit back in my seat and give a deep sigh. People are getting "it." Of course, the power of place is at work; it is not my doing. I am like the Reiki masters who say the healing energy comes through them, not from them.

Timothy puts on a wonderful James Galway CD so we have wordless, quiet airs floating through the bus. I let my mind wander to my own prayer for my relationship. While the professional and spiritual aspects of my life have a nice flow to them, I don't seem to make out so well in the relationship department. No one since Charlie has truly felt right, and Charlie went and "felt right" into the arms of another woman! So I sometimes wonder if a life-long love is really in my cards.

Charlie left me, not quite at the altar, but nearly that. He wanted to go into politics and wanted someone who would play the dutiful role of social secretary and charming hostess and confidante within the wives' group at the country club. He was right that I wasn't that woman; I realize that now. Back then, I was devastated.

Gordie has the same drive to make the world a better place as Charlie had, but he does it on the street, not in the country club. And he doesn't need someone at his elbow. As a matter of fact, part of the problem is wondering if he needs me at all.

I also wonder, sometimes, if I am being too cautious. Maybe, I really want to marry this guy and am afraid to admit it. So I asked Brigid for the Highest Good for us both, and I set my intention to be present in the relationship and let go of trying to figure it out. Hmmm.

A nice long walk with an ice cream, instead of lunch, will give me time to finish up my own thinking and be ready for the full afternoon ahead.

TIMOTHY

James Galway was just the tone we needed. My, but these people are serious-minded and seem to go deep. We are just a short ways from the town Gordie and I have chosen for lunch so I am going to liven up the music and bring people back from their reveries. The Dubliners are just the ticket.

As we approach the town, the wee lass yells, "Mom, Look! Ballykissangel!" In the mirror, I see the joy on Megan's face. I smile at the memory of me own daughter when she was that age. One moment sophisticated, the next childlike. And sure enough, this wee town does look a lot like the town in the BBC series. With the river meandering through, the arched bridge with the bus stop, the stone church with spire at one end, whitewashed walls along the road separating it from the school yard, and the wonderful row of colorful shop doors beckoning, it has the look of it.

"Sorry to disappoint. The telly series *Ballykissangel* was actually filmed in Avoca, a town in Wicklow."

"Oh, too bad. Can we go to this Wicklow place?"

"Afraid it is not on the itinerary but do enjoy this one for today."

"Yeah, so Timothy, lots of towns are called Bally this or Bally that. What does it mean?"

"As you might guess, Bally is the word for village or town. And now, before we pass all the eating establishments on the way to your drop-off spot, let me point them out. We are just passing the town pub with its great carved sandwiches. The fish and chips shop is down this lane toward the river and a Chinese sit-down restaurant is next to our stop right here. I can only stop the bus for unloading, so gather your things if you will. I will meet you back at this exact location in one hour."

"And just how far do you expect us to walk to get a sandwich for Heaven's sake?" It is Mary Helena.

Dorrie starts to speak but, thankfully, Trish steps in, "Why not join me right here for Chinese? The kids are going to explore the town. We can talk more about our confirmations. Besides, it'll be fun to see what Irish-Chinese is like. I've tried Chinese in Spain and Japan and Latvia as well as variations around the US and Canada on Congressional trips with my boss. It's become a one of my travel traditions. Anyone else want to try it out?"

Kate is the last to get off the coach. She turns, "What about you, Timothy, should we save you a seat? You are not eating alone I hope."

"Me plan is to go down to a wee café with ease of parking. I would be glad for company though—if you would consider joining me?" I surprise meself by the invitation. But it is all right.

"Sounds fun," she responds. So off we go.

We have a delicious home-baked beef-in-whiskey pot pie and apple tart with custard for dessert. Kate comments on the custard. I explain to her about Bird's Custard and that at home it was put on everything. "Me ma used to say the 'wee envelope of Bird's was the key to her kitchen. If visitors came unexpectedly for tea, you could always find something to put beneath it."

We converse with the lads at the next table and then relax into easy conversation between us. On the surface, we have little in common, yet we could have talked for hours. And 'tis so much easier without the noise of the pub.

GORDIE

I try to meet up with Jackson and hang together over lunch, but he's already split. He can't get into too much trouble in this small town at mid-day. After all, as Timothy says, "what's in the cat is in the kitten" and the boy may be troubled, but he's got more of his father in him than he wants to admit.

I get some fish and chips and go it alone to a table in the riverside park. The last couple of days have been great. Dorrie and I arrived two days early to get our bearings, meet with Timothy, and have some time to ourselves. It had been an intense time for each of us at work. I had horrendous budget problems involving my board and a teen suicide that left my staff at the drug center reeling. I was pretty wiped out by it, too.

Dorrie had a corporate client that had announced an early retirement incentive, bringing her a flood of referrals for lifework planning/coaching. We hadn't had much time together. Some relaxation before the group came was much needed.

The night we arrived, we had dinner and a relaxing night at a small inn along the Ennis Road, a short taxi ride from the Shannon airport. The next day was caught up with logistics. It started with a fantastic meeting with Timothy for a get acquainted and go over the itinerary meeting. He's great. What a relief. Twelve days is a long time to depend on someone to keep the atmosphere of openness, cheer, and safety we require.

Later, I followed up on lodging and meal plans and finalized the participant list; Dorrie worked to customize her sessions and meditations to meet the needs of the individuals on the tour. I took all the concrete info like food allergy information and sleeping preferences while Dorrie looked at the psycho-social, spiritual aspects.

We are still trying to get a general sense of folks and their needs and interests. Still there are not a lot of surprises. After all, the responses came from advertisements in a few key magazines: *Yes!, Utne Reader, UU World, Spirituality and Health,* and from Dorrie's extensive email list from workshops at places like Omega, and Consciousness and Spirituality in Business. The upshot, I would say, is that they are mostly progressives looking for purpose and meaning as they explore a different culture and dabble lightly into its history. Also, mostly East Coasters like us.

The beauty of Celtic spirituality is that there is something for everybody. Like the Sufi story of *The Blind Men and the Elephant* which I use with my teen groups, it is a matter of attention. You can define Celtic spirituality through a number of lenses, all equally valid, yet none complete: Catholic Ireland, generic Christianity, paganism, goddess worship, Gaia/Mother Earth stuff, pantheism, humanism, magic, Other World realities. It's all here; each person, scholar, or cleric seeing it quite differently than the next. None are entirely right or wrong. I, personally, come down on the humanist side of life—give me a book or time to walk in nature, that's my religion and the kind of spiritual renewal that works for me. I took the *belief.net* quiz on-line once and no surprise: Humanist, Unitarian, and Buddhist came out about even. I could do without the mystical and theist parts. But that's the point, isn't it? We don't have to hold the same beliefs to honor the land and its messages. That's how I hope we learn to build the global village.

In that respect, I think Dorrie is right when she says Celtic spirituality and the culture of this land have profound tenets that can and should be applied to twenty-first century challenges. She expresses it better than I do. But, how can anyone continue to think religion can justify dominion over nature after coming here and seeing beauty all around? How can anyone think that there is only one religious truth? Beats me.

That's the paradox for me, how to honor religious freedom and yet address the values questions. A religion that breeds hate or victimizes people or destroys the land is not a religion to honor, to my way of thinking. Too much blood has been shed in the name of religion.

I also find that some of Dorrie's transformational stuff, though, is a bit much for me. But she has quite a following. I have to respect that she helps a lot of people through their own personal forty days in the desert.

Coming on the tour as a co-leader was my idea. I see it as kind of an experiment in playing to each other's strengths. I didn't say straight out that it is also a test of whether we can do a long-term relationship, but I think we both know the bottom line here—leave committed to being together or break up.

Oh good, the bus is right on time. Folks pile in, all but Lily who is nowhere to be found. Already, she is beginning to test my patience. Finally, someone sees her waving from across the river. Wet through and through and laughing as she skips up to the far side of the bridge once she sees that we are coming for her. Fortunately for Timothy, she's waiting in the direction we are headed. She jumps aboard, gives Timothy a quick peck on the cheek, and thanks him sweetly. No apology, no explanation. Then again, she doesn't complain about being all wet. Cool it, Gordie, I tell myself. Cool it.

The Burren, a unique geological phenomenon, came into being millions of years ago. Situated in the Northwest section of County Clare, we had been driving in and about it for two days but now we are going into the thick of it. Burren means "stony place" and that is certainly a no-brainer to remember. It is so barren. Burren, barren, not hard at all to remember its name. I read that in Cromwell's time, it was said about the place that "there is not enough wood to hang a man, not enough water to drown him, and not enough earth to bury him." Then it got worse. Sadly, one can still see remains of villages lost to the famine. But, one also can see scores of ruins from Neolithic times and beautiful wildflowers pushing through the rock. That's why we are here.

As we ride through the midst of it, I find new meaning to the words "eke out a living." It's not hard to see why Ireland endured so much emigration. This bleak, barren, rocky landscape is like something from a space walk odyssey. I've never seen anything quite like it. Scientifically, the place is a rarity, too. Archeologists, geologists and botanists from all over the world come here to study its unique features.

Timothy stops and folks get out for a bit. I announce that there are numerous hiking trails and that Timothy will bring folks back tomorrow who choose hiking the Burren as their optional activity.

The wildflowers grow straight out of what looks like pavement. Sandra, who knows a lot about flowers, points outs flowers that grow in the Grand Canyon, the Arctic Circle, the Alps, and Mediterranean islands. But, she tells us she is surprised to find them all growing here. I don't know much about flowers, but I am surprised anything grows in this wasteland. Go figure.

Timothy offers some bits of information he remembers from his son's school field trips. The vertical cracks in the limestone slabs are called *grykes.* They allow the rain to seep down and thus have created hundreds of caves like the one we will be seeing later. These *grykes* leave isolated rocks called *clints.* Between them grow more grasses than you would imagine and that is what the sheep, goats, and donkeys eat. He lights up his little recitation with the crack that if anyone ever has use of that information, they should ring him up immediately and he will buy the smart devil an Irish Sweepstakes ticket as a prize.

Our first official stop of the afternoon is Poulnabrone Dolmen. We choose it from among many in the area. I've been using a picture of it as my screen saver over these months of trip planning. Yet, to see it in person. Wow. I can't wait.

As we ride along, I decide to give folks a sample of my glossary of terms related to stones and the Stone Age. I can fall into the same trap as Dorrie wanting people to know everything. But, it made me crazy to hear words bandied about that were unfamiliar to me. So I added a handout to Dorrie's packet on terminology. Here are the ones I chose for today.
Megaliths: large standing stones. Dolmen: special configuration of three stones; a capstone resting on two end stones. Cromlech: another name for dolmen, as is table stone, altar stone, or portal stone. Henges: standing stones arranged in

a circle or an earthen embanked enclosure, broad ditchless banks, inward orientation.

We arrive just as I finish the abbreviated list. We all are spellbound that such a configuration of rocks was placed in this desolate place so long ago and that it has survived. Seems like an impossible engineering feat in the midst of a farmer's field, and a stony, uneven field at that. It is truly amazing and magnificent in its simplicity.

Dorrie asks everyone to gather at the dolmen. She begins, "Well, here we are at a quintessential portal stone. We have no documentation to tell us how ancient peoples viewed or utilized these specially situated stones, but one theory is that they were gateways or portals. Only later were they used as sacrifice tables or shelters. I have a focused meditation and ritual for us. But, first, I want to share this reading that appeared out of nowhere this morning.

"Last night at the pub, some of us began talking about leprechauns. Many of you got a kick out of the fact I always put a pint on the table for 'the wee men.' We had a great discussion of our views and beliefs, and about imagination, the Other World, the unseen. As you may know, fairies are known in legend and custom not only here in Ireland but also in cultures around the world. Many of these cultures also describe portals or gates between worlds."

"Like *Star Gate*," Megan whispers to her mother.

Dorrie continues, "Keep all this in mind as I read you a letter that I found on the table back at the Lodge. It was with the notes I made in preparation for today's sessions. I have no idea where it came from or who wrote it. It just appeared. So I think I am supposed to share it with you.

"First, let's gather in and around the dolmen and just experience the mystery of the place. Feel the energy and imagine all who have stood on this ground over the centuries. Think about what you have in common with those who have come before, think about what is different and why. Let's be silent together, and then I will read the note.

The Leprechaun Message
Whether you know it or not, all of you
have been called to be here.
Some of you by your ancestors.
Some by us, for we need co-workers in
the human race to help us learn to be creators
with free will.
Some of you to heal the planet and some
to be healed by the planet whose hands and
heart are here.
We will take you on a magical mystery
tour full of fun, spontaneity in the moment, and
openness to being.
Surrender to the experience and you will
enjoy yourself and be transformed. Resist and
you make yourself miserable;
This is a healing journey...

Silence. Then she adds, "Please, take those words in as you wish and do with them what you wish."

I'm a little nervous about how this leprechaun thing will go over with people and annoyed she didn't ask me for my opinion about including it. But that's Dorrie. Seems to be OK, still... as long as she doesn't go over the top with the mystical, esoteric, other kingdom stuff. But after all, this is Ireland. At home, people might think of angels leaving messages, here I guess it is kind of normal to think about leprechauns and fairies.

She keeps going, "Now, to the part I planned for this afternoon. Here are three questions that I invite you to think about:

If I could walk into another time and place, what would I like to see and experience?
If I could leave behind something or release myself from something while there, what would it be?
If I could bring something back from this Otherworld, what would that be?

59

"When you are ready, walk in through the portal and return, holding these questions and your answers (if you have them already) at the forefront of your mind.

"You may want to write down what images, words or feelings came to you. We have plenty of time. You may get something right away; it may come over the twelve days of our bus tour, or long after your return home. Don't force your answers. Trust that they will come.

"The bus will leave in about thirty minutes which will give all of you who wish to do the exercise a chance to do so. Lily has offered to play for us during this time."

People mill around, taking pictures, pacing. I can't concentrate on the questions since I still am concerned people will think Dorrie is too woo-woo with the leprechaun stuff. But, I get over it when, with great enthusiasm, Nathan makes a ceremonial pass through the portal, giving a dance on the other side and returning with a look of wonder. Ah, the lack of inhibitions and the flexibility of youth, and this kid, especially. He has no trouble at all answering the questions or picturing himself able to pass into another realm. I don't remember ever being that sure of myself or as comfortable with uncertainty as he is. Then again, I didn't grow up reading Harry Potter.

The reactions among the rest of the group are varied, but not what I expected. Rose finishes in tears but with a bright smile. John, Sandra, and Angie are visibly moved. Amazingly hard to anticipate what will touch whom and when. I know Dorrie keeps praying fervently that at some time and place on the trip all will be touched by the spirit of transformation, as she calls it. More power to her, as long as she doesn't go off the deep end. Me, I just want us to get comfortably through the itinerary. But, I have to admit, this other stuff is fascinating to watch.

I also notice Mary Helena sitting on a rock making one of those Brigid folded-reed crosses she got kits for at the Cliffs. The buzz was that her ankle or leg was bothering her and that is why she pitched a fit about where the bus stopped for lunch. But she hadn't asked for help, so I was leaving it alone. Dorrie, on the other hand, goes over to check it out. I hear her ask Mary Helena if she needs anything. Mary Helena's reply is negative in tone, but I missed the words...something about the uneven ground and walking through pasture. Then, Dorrie asks if she wants us to take her to the ER or stop so she could buy a cane or an Irish walking stick.

The farmer at the next croft could have heard Mary Helena this time. Her reply: "No, and I am not going over to go through that rock in some pagan ritual either. Just leave me be."

"Well, then, do let me know if you need anything, I will respect your wishes to be left alone. But remember we are not mind readers. We can't help if we don't know what is wrong."

Mary Helena gets in the finally punch, "Why aren't we at St. Brigid's Fire, you know, the place with the eternal flame, instead of this pile of rocks? There is nothing spiritual about a Stone Age pile of rocks used for blood sacrifices."

"I am sorry you feel that way. Not every site will be for everyone. But look how many are enjoying this place. Thank you for not ruining it for them. As for St. Brigid's Fire, it's in Kildare, way south of our route; its monastery and sacred well were never on our itinerary."

Dorrie is so more tactful than I would have been. I figure I have to take a turn at this portal thing just to show support. After going through the motions, I look around to see who is where. Nathan has discovered donkeys in the field across the road. I stroll over. Peter and Timothy are there, too. We watch the boy try to pet the donkeys, warning him of their kick.

Timothy points out the cuts in the earth where the turf has been farmed. Peat, he tells us, is still used for fuel by the locals. In fact, one of the donkeys has a two-sided straw basket over his back to hold peat and it is partially full. I swear we're having the luck of the Irish with all these serendipitous extras. Maybe the peat farmers will come back to finish while we're still here.

I cross the road to see how Dorrie is doing getting folks through the ritual. Rebecca is leaning against a rock, sketching away. She does nice work. I'll have to ask her if she wants me to put some of it online after the trip.

Jackson is into a book, again. This time it is *Portrait of a Young Man*, even darker than *Ulysses*. I'll find out later from Dorrie if he did the portal thing. I need to keep an eye on him. Some people just have a darker nature. But given his age, the recent death of his mom, and his level of anger at his dad, who knows where he's at.

Just then, Lily finishes playing, puts her harp down, goes through the portal and trips through the fields with lightness and joy. For a moment, I wonder if she will just disappear right before us. But she bounds back, just as light and happy, if not more so. Jake gets her picture, but I wonder if that *lightness of being* she has will show up on film. She sure is a mystery.

Our next stop of the day is Craggaunowen, an open air interpretive museum. Even though the day is pretty full, we wanted folks to have a sense of how it is thought the Celts of pre-historic times lived. We are only going to visit to see the reconstructed *crannog*: a tribal lake island dwelling place from the Iron Age, a ring fort, and a Bronze Age cooking site. Tomorrow, the medieval castle is an option for those who don't want to hike. Or folks can just hang out at the Lodge.

Timothy says he actually has stopped in here. He whispers to me that "the best of it is the cheeky lass, dressed in costume, giving the interpretation. She is a looker." I keep patting myself on the back for finding this guy. And I kind of envy his spontaneity.

Megan, who by now I expect to compare everything she sees to a play or movie, proves me right, "These round huts with the dark thatch roofs look like coolie hats or something out of *South Pacific* or *Joe, the Volcano.* Weird."

Trish, the mom, adds, "It's also weird to see all the wood made into a ring fence of the fort and the bridge made of logs. How incongruous after the bleak and barren landscape of the Burren."

Nathan, of course, is the first to discover the replica of the boat. The young Irish guide tells us about St. Brendan, the Navigator, who is reported to have sailed to America in the sixth century. She describes an adventurer in modern times that made the trip in a boat built like this just to prove it was possible. Rob tells us of a place in New Hampshire called the American Stonehenge. The curators there purport evidence that both Leif Eriksson and St. Brendan came to North America by way of Greenland. But the guide needs to move on, so the group agrees to table this discussion with so many others for dinnertime. And I get concerned that people will get bored with all this stuff.

Our final stop of the day is Alliwee Caves. There are a number of caverns connected by tunnels which go back at least one third of a mile. The many passages include an underground river, waterfall, stalagmites, and stalactites. Reminds me of visiting a cave on the way to Florida when I was a kid, in Virginia I think it was. Some of the group have never been in a cave so, even though it isn't particularly spiritual or Celtic, it's a hit.

Situated directly under the Burren, this too is a fascinating geological phenomenon. Also cool to think we will be hiking above it tomorrow.

I particularly like the fact that remains of a black bear, extinct in Ireland for thousands of years, were found inside when the entrance was rediscovered in the 1940's. Megan is quick to imagine a connection to *Clan of the Cave Bears.* Her niche sure has become established after only two days. I'm going to start calling her our goddess of book and film.

Dorrie, my own Celtic goddess, makes another connection, one to bear totems and myths. She regales everyone who is interested with information on the caves in France and the origins of the labyrinth. I gently suggest that we move on. I, for one, am weary of all this intellectual chatter. I just want to have the physical experience—sights and sounds and silences that are surreal.

She keeps going, suggesting people consider how natural caves might have led to the construction of places like Newgrange, promising that when we go to Newgrange we will really enjoy the comparison. A small group continues to talk about the ways the symbolism of womb-like structures have been the theme of the day.

Nathan slips away. I do, too. We leave the never-ending discussion of matriarchal culture, the Divine Feminine, and archetypes. We follow the light to be outdoors. Immediately, Nathan yells out that he sees a farm market across the parking lot. Just the break we need. I'm going to have to put this kid on staff, finding all these tidbits of local culture that weren't in my playbook at all.

We haven't stopped for snacks at all, come to think of it. A few Irish boiled sweets, a.k.a. hard candy, have been the only thing passed around so far. This is great. And the guy is even selling this amazing local soft cheese in a waxy covering that is delicious; the cheese that is, not the coating.

Dorrie gives me a big squeeze from behind, "How you doin', stranger?" she asks with that grin of hers I find irresistible.

"'Tis what I will be doin' with you tonight that matters," I reply in my best imitation of an Irish brogue.

"Well, then…." says she, with her best imitation of a West Irish sigh.

It's the first laugh we have had together all day. "Still trying to get a handle on who's who," I say, getting back to business.

"I know what you mean. The dinner last night gave me a chance to know Trish and her daughter a bit. Trish is a single mom working in PR for a US Senator; Megan, is a high school junior. If I remember right, at our in-gathering Trish said the trip was meant to help Megan explore what she liked to study. You know how intense some families get about college decisions, majors and all. But at the Well, this whole other theme of being reared Catholic emerged. Isn't that fascinating?"

"I guess. What about the other two women? They're a couple, right?"

"Oh, you mean Angie and Rebecca? Yeah, they talked openly about when they moved in together. Angie is divorced with a son who lives with his dad. She is the one who has been sketching. Rebecca is the one who took my Omega workshop. She's a writer. I think she was with a big name magazine but now freelances."

"Leave it to a group of women to find out all about relationship stuff."

Dorrie laughs. "Well, talking about the soulfulness of Irish ballads and about Mary Black, relationships are bound to come up. But I can't deny it."

"Speaking of music, I had a great conversation at my table last night about Bono and U2 and the soaring, worldwide interest in today's Irish music. I'm going to download some songs for Timothy to play on the bus. He says people were upset that they had missed the talks at other tables, so we thought we would expand his sampler of Irish music for the bus."

"Great. But, I thought you planned to talk about the bardic tradition and the old songs of Ireland."

"Well, I can be flexible when I need to, you know," I say with all the charm I can muster and not a drop of defensiveness.

"Indeed, you can." she says, giving me another squeeze, and following it with a real kiss.

"Also, last night when Bono came up, I discovered all of us had been at the Obama Inaugural."

"Us and how many thousands?" she laughs and adds, "seriously who all went?"

"Well, Trish and Megan, John and Melanie, Kevin and Jackson said they were there. I'm not sure who else."

"Did you notice Melanie at the Well? She was very emotional. I want to reach out a little and make sure she knows I'm available if she wants to talk. This reminds me, some people have already approached me about one-on-one coaching. I thought I would set them up tomorrow during the hike."

"What about our time to go off hiking together?"

I never get an answer as people hop back on the bus for the return to the lodge.

Dinner is a choice of pasta primavera with a couple of big Irish prawns added for good measure or duck with a nice medley of vegetables. Jake compliments me on the food. Whew. Glad we got it right. Nothing makes a tour go sour faster than bad food. Classic trifle is for dessert. This particular trifle has vanilla pudding with pieces of sponge cake that have been soaked in whiskey, with both strawberry jam and orange marmalade marbled throughout. It's served family style so each table has a lovely glass bowl to see how an Irish family would serve it. Reminds me of Gram's house. The wait staff announces that anyone bothered by the whiskey, even though it is a small amount, could have apple tart instead. I avoid looking at Mary Helena. But I am relieved when no one raises their hand. Hopefully, that means we don't have any recovering alcoholics feeling the pressure of all the pub talk. I make a mental note that if we ever do this again, we need to consider some social activity alternatives. And what about Mary Helena...could it also be that she's mellowing? Doubt it.

After dinner, folks meander out to the stream or head back to their rooms for a bit before Dorrie's evening session. Hope it isn't too long. I want to get to the pub and relax.

I go into the lounge to set up. Peg and Kate are in heavy conversation but say I won't be interrupting. The gist of it is that Peg wants to know all about Kate's visit to the Famine Museum. We've passed a number of signs for it, but Dorrie and I chose not to include it even though it is nearby. Seeing the remains of abandoned cottages is hard enough to swallow.

"The hardest sites I've ever visited were Dachau concentration camp, Wounded Knee, and this Famine Museum. The inhumanity, the purposeful policy of extermination . . . from seemingly civilized people." Kate stops. All three of us are silent.

"My, but being here and hearing it from someone who has actually visited the site makes it so real. . . still though, it is so utterly unbelievable."

Kate renews her narrative, "Peg, did you know that within the five year period of 1845-50, one quarter of the population, over two million people, either died or emigrated? The potato blight itself might have been an unavoidable act of Nature; but the lack of help and the harsh policies of landlords like the one who owned the Museum manor house were inexcusable."

"Isle of Tears; Trail of Tears," Peg murmurs.

"Yes, and I think the workhouses and orphanage buildings were the hardest to see, so hard to think of all the losses those folks endured. At the Well, I was thinking about a novel I read on the plane about the suffering of the families and the women who no longer even had the strength to 'keen' or perform the ritual cries of mourning. One of them leaves something at a sacred well. I now realize it was a reference to Brigid's Well. I couldn't help but wonder how they continued to believe in any god, or goddess, after what they experienced."

Beats me, I think. But then, that is part of the story, I guess.

While we wait for everyone to gather, I start an informal feedback session just to see how everyone is doing and if there are any problems. Mary Helena complains about there being too much walking. I note her concern and remind her to specifically tell me when it's a problem and we will try to fix it. Ugh. But, everyone else seems happy with everything.

Dorrie and I had debated what piece of info needed to go next and how to condense it. She opts for talking about the Celtic mysteries. I think it is the right decision. I so often hear the term "the mysteries" bandied around and never really know what that means. I asked a workshop leader once and got a lame response, "It is a mystery, so how could I possible explain it? Ha. Ha." So, go Dorrie!

She begins, "Well, today you have seen the five aspects of Celtic spirituality that I lifted up: Nature at center, direct experience of Spirit through visible and accessible sacred places, co-existence of different culture periods and beliefs, the continual presence of the Divine feminine, and an appreciation of the mystery and wonder of the Universe.

Let's look at this last one a bit more. Using the spirit of threes, so ingrained in the Celtic culture, I will suggest three levels at which one looks at the Celtic mysteries:

The What—Physical observation either in person or by media description of those places and things which seem to defy logic or nature. *The visit to the sacred sites themselves.*

The How—Exploration and theories to explain about how these places, things or stories originated; how they were created or came into being; and how they impacted the lives of the people. *The information we learn or hypothesize about these places.*

The Meaning—The search for the original purpose, as well as finding one's own message, often the experience of being changed or transformed by the essence of the place. *Our experience as we visit with the intention of opening to the message of the site.*

"Inherent in the idea of mystery is the sense of something hidden, something deeper in structure and pattern, something that draws you in to its center.

"You can watch the Discovery Channel or read a book about Ancient Mysteries, say, of the Egyptian Pyramids, the Delphi Oracle, or the Anasazi Native American Cliff Dwellers. You can listen and wonder how it was possible. However, most people can't, or don't take the time to, get their arms around that third level. Likewise, when people talk about the mystery of the Holy Grail, there are three levels:

What is the Grail?
How does one find the Grail?
What is the meaning of the Grail?

"You might remember that Perceval has to 'pierce the veil' by asking the question 'whom does the Grail serve?' to unlock the mystery.

"Tomorrow night, we will look at the Celtic cross. You will notice through the trip that the Celtic cross and the Celtic tree are both symbols that hold a great deal of meaning and power. They each open people to the mysteries of Celtic spirituality. But enough for now.

"Oh, I also wanted to remind you that you have handouts and worksheets on *The Steps to Spiritual Transformation* in your packet. Like the ancient mysteries, these steps are profoundly simple but are challenging. Let me know if you have questions.

"That's all for tonight. Please join us in spiritual practice in the morning if you are so inclined. Again, there is a handout describing spiritual practice that I commend to those of you who are new to the concept."

I take over announcements, telling them about tomorrow's options and encouraging folks to come to the pub if they wish.

So, off to the pub we go, a place where music and dance can transport a willing body to places of sacredness or fancy, the sacred and the profane as they say. More of the group come along with us tonight. I guess people are getting over jet lag and settling in. Mary Helena let me know, in no uncertain terms, that she would not be coming to any "drunken brawl." I told her that it was much different than a tavern at home but, of course, she didn't want to listen. Come to find out, she had given Timothy a tongue lashing last night on the subject of "drink." I guess now it was my turn.

"So are you ready to be off again?" asks Timothy, sporting his warmest smile and an Irish cap of a beautiful woven pattern of grey and teal wool. "You're in for a special treat tonight. Come along now. We probably will just have to find seats catch as we can tonight, me friends. But, ladies, we will see what we can do. Gents, we may be lucky to find a place at the bar to lean our elbows on."

There's Lily again, only this time she is already playing. How in the devil she got there so fast I do not know.

Folks are mesmerized by her songs; she smiles in our direction and keeps playing. Her sound is actually hauntingly beautiful. The combination of harp and voice seem to create an Other World feel. At the end, she tells us the songs she played this evening are *Sounds to Heal the Earth;* she calls it interdimensional music, whatever that means. She invites everyone to think of what we each can do for Mother Earth while she plays a final song. Wow, mighty that.

The woman gets a standing ovation, people standing in tears, clapping and clapping. Lots of locals are out of their seats, too. You just couldn't plan this stuff, I think. Peg goes to bring her back to us. But like last night, Lily has slipped away.

Soon we are on to more rowdy stuff: the drum, pipes, flute and violin players are the same as last night, but they are joined by a banjo, concertina and a small accordion. Timothy is all proud, telling us about the concertina. Seems tonight we are getting a special treat, a musical style unique to County Clare. Whatever. I love it and so do the others.

Many of the tunes are kind of familiar, but none of us know any words. Then, they get into *The Wild Rover*. We can do this one! So with the place packed and the beer flowing, we all sing along.

Timothy shouts above the din: "Getting the luck of the Irish tonight, are we not?"

Yeah. We sure have been lucky, so far at least. *Sláinte.*

DAY THREE

A Day of Options

Hiking the Burren   *Craggaunowen*

Quiet Time   *Shopping in Town*

Since this is a trip to the sacred and spiritual aspects of Celtic Ireland, we want you to have time to rest, reflect and be with the place. This a day for you each to choose what is best for you.
We will open the day with optional spiritual practices:
Sound toning, yoga, journaling or your own choice.
Group activities from which you can choose include active options like hiking the Burren, visiting the mansion at Craggaunowen or exploring the adjacent town.
If you choose to be solitary, Salmon Run Lodge and its surroundings also offer a beautiful slice of the Celtic landscape.

ROB

After thirty years together, you begin to know something about one another's rhythms. Early in our marriage,

71

Peg and I developed an unwritten rule not to talk with one another until after our teeth were brushed, so to speak. Today, I'm especially careful not to disturb her. She tossed and turned all night. Since she usually sleeps like a baby, I want to give her time to sleep in as late as possible, process her dreams, and wake slowly.

I've actually been dressed, sitting reading and writing for quite some time just wishing for her to wake and get beyond the "brushed teeth."

I'm concerned about what is going on with her. Plus, this book I'm reading is gearing me up for a full-blown theological, philosophic discussion. For now, I have to make do with jotting a few things down in my journal. I had had this revelation about the difference between men and women based on Dorrie's talk about the Grail mysteries and my experience at Brigid's Well. I really wanted to sort it out with her, but I retreated to my journal instead. I wrote: *Unlocking the Mystery of Mysteries: male and female energies. Men search for the Grail, the Holy vessel. Women* are *the Grail. They are the chalice, the container, the well and source of life. The Mother, the divine feminine is within them.*

Watching the different reaction of the genders to the Well yesterday, I was struck by how taken the women were with the whole experience. We guys appreciated it, but it wasn't such a big deal. Of course, I know about Jungian archetypes (well meaning female, mountain meaning male symbology). Dan Brown has even brought it to the movies. And with a wife like Peg, daughters, and a divinity degree from Andover, I thought I understood feminist theology. In fact, I have bragging rights among male colleagues in this area. I even read Merle Stone's *When God Was a Woman* before I entered seminary. I intellectually "got" that it is hard to feel validated and find God within if that God is always depicted as a male, Father God, and you are female. But, yesterday, I saw something that took me deeper or kind of turned the concept inside out. Now, I have even more questions...

I write down some things I still need to think about: Mother/Father God means both men and women need to acknowledge the Divine Feminine. Both the masculine and feminine faces of God have to be experienced by all of us, male and female. But how does it relate to gender???????? and identity??? Men reject the Divine Feminine thinking they need to grow up, separate from their mothers, become a man. Patriarchies deny or suppress the feminine. Why? We all lose.

There is kind of a yin/yang mirror images thing going on with this. Jung's Animus and Anima and how we have both in us and maybe, like right or left–handedness, one is more dominant. Lots to think about.

My mind hits a brick wall. I return to my book, *Anam Cara,* a gift from my men's group at church. What a thoughtful choice it was. This guy O'Donohue expresses himself beautifully and writes about Ireland and Celtic spirituality in ways I appreciate more and more with every step we take here and with every page I turn. I'd love to be able to write like that.

Peg woke while I journaled and now emerges from the bathroom ready, at least, to say, "Good morning. You're up and about early."

"And ready to go. I gotta say I'm really pleased with this tour you chose for us. I especially like staying in one place for a few days like this and having variety in our daily routine. I was afraid we would have one of those 'today is Tuesday, it must be Belgium' experiences."

"I'm relieved you like it so much."

"Yup. In fact, I like the fact that we have choices today. My first choice is to find a spot to read *My Soul Mate.*"

"Read? But I was planning to go to the sound meditation Dorrie is leading," she replied groggily.

"Not read with you, but read *Anam Cara.* Certainly you are my one and only soul mate, my dear, but I mean the book I'm reading. The title means soul mate in Gaelic, remember?"

"Ah, yes, the John O'Donohue book your men's study group gave you. Is it really about soul mates? And are you thinking lovingly of me as you turn each page?" She is showing less sleepiness and teasing me a bit.

"That, and much more. It's extraordinary. He puts heart and wisdom into his exploration of Celtic spirituality. Ties in beautifully to what Dorrie has been saying and what we have been seeing. PLUS, it's nice to get a male voice into the mix."

"You poor dear, are you feeling outnumbered?"

"Let's just say, I need to hear more male voices in the choir as we sing in Celebration of the Divine Feminine."

"Well, it is way too early for you to wax poetic, dear, way too early."

Now, I can broach the subject of what's going on with her. I go gingerly by first asking how she slept. Most women like you to ask about their emotional states, but not my Peg. She only shares the real big issues when she has already wrestled them to the ground. She was the first woman I ever met who didn't act all needy and frail around me to get attention. After four sisters and a mother who were all highly dramatic, Peg was a breath of fresh air. Except, if I am truly honest, for the occasional time I feel shut out and insecure when she clams up.

She puts me off, as I expect. We agree to meet at breakfast and I head downstairs. I cajole an early mug of black coffee from the breakfast staff and find a cozy overstuffed chair near a window looking out at the salmon stream to read.

Before I reconnect to my new muse, this amazing heart-centered Celtic mystic by the name of O'Donohue, I start thinking about spiritual practice. As a minister, I am always looking for new ways to encourage and engage people in finding a spiritual practice that fits them and will stick. I give Dorrie and Gordie a lot of credit for committing to lead these pre-breakfast options. As the Nike folks say: *Just Do It.*

I was thinking of my first spiritual practice, yesterday, at the Well. I learned to pray to Mary at an early age. As they say, St. Brigid is the Mary of the Gael, and the Well yesterday so reminded me of my own mother and Sister Magdalena. My spiritual path began with these two deeply spiritual women. From their example and urging, I learned the discipline of a daily spiritual practice and the importance of ritual as an expression of faith.

The journey from Catholic altar boy to Unitarian Universalist minister may seem like a strange one. But, the story is not all that different from most. I took incremental steps on my search for meaning and purpose. Often, I didn't realize at the time which steps and choices were the defining moments. I think that is why I'm such an advocate of spiritual practice: centering, listening for guidance, and opening to possibility certainly help me find my own truth.

I stare out the window with the soft eyes of meditation. Is that Lily, sprite-like, across the stream, skipping in the mist? The wind stirs the trees and the image is gone. I quickly lose myself in imagining the Spirit of Celtic wisdom, dancing and laughing in the light of this new day. Mindful, or is it mindless, meditation? My own little joke.

When I emerge from my reverie, I hear Gordie checking the sound and electronics for Dorrie. I'm tempted to help, or at least to participate in one of the sessions, but my book's call is greater. I just keep thinking how rich the options are in my world. I am a man blessed with so much I tell myself as I sink back into my comfy, overstuffed chair. I am lost in my book until the smell of bacon grabs my attention. I wander toward the breakfast room. On my way, I peek in on the sessions that seem to be wrapping up.

Dorrie is using a Goldman CD for her sound work. I can't catch the exact words of the mantras, but each note on the scale has its own word, that I can tell. She summarizes that now that they have cleared and opened their chakras, breathing deeply, they can practice the toning without the aid of the CD. They try it and I am amazed to hear them come into pitch together just by humming together—even my wife, who can't carry a tune in a whiskey jug. Just then, Lily lets loose with this vocal rift that sends chills to my spine. The whole room seems to vibrate to the sound. Wow.

I'll have to get this CD for our meditation room at the church. We have one of Singing Bowls and another of some Gregorian chants but this one is great. I've read about sound therapy as a treatment modality for both mental and physical healing, but had not realized how accessible it is for meditation.

I also decide to join them tomorrow.

Gordie had mentioned to me that he had been faithfully doing yoga as a spiritual practice since college. His athletic coach had suggested it to help after an injury. Now I get a glimpse of him in action. I never could get interested in yoga so I take special note of what he is doing. Maybe, there is something to draw me in.

As I watch him lead the group, I can tell he really knows what he's doing. If I watch closely, I can even separate those who do this regularly from the occasionals and the novices. I am impressed that he seems to know how to engage and challenge them all.

It still isn't for me, but that's OK. Not all options work for everyone; that's what choice is all about.

I get myself more coffee and take a seat where I can watch everyone enter the dining room. I love watching the dynamics of groups. Who sits with whom and how those choices are made was actually the subject of a paper I wrote on non-verbal communication in grad school.

Some of the couples like Jake and Sandra, John and Melanie, Peter and Penny stick together. Others, like Peg and me are less predictable. So far, the young people are sticking with their parents and the single travelers are mixing it up. It will be fun to see what subgroups develop over the remaining days and whether folks make an effort to build community. So far, at least, there are neither cliques nor isolates.

Dorrie stops by all our tables to say there would be no session after breakfast today so the hikers could get a full day of hiking in. She reminds everyone that traveling can be grueling, especially for those who are afraid they will miss something. She encourages everyone to listen to their bodies— the choices really are about different levels of physical and group activity. Then, with a smile, she bounces on to the next group.

Peg and I quickly agree we want to go to Craggaunowen. I want to spend more time hearing about Brendan the Navigator, and she wants to see the mansion and its antiques. We have lots of time. The museum doesn't open until ten so Peg goes back to the room while I hang out in the lobby. Timothy is about to take the hikers to a trailhead and then return for our group. I tag along, just for the fun of seeing the village come awake with activity.

Gordie has arranged bag lunches and water bottles for the hikers. He gives out maps with directional and geological info. I take one just to read. There are a number of trails and options. As we ride along, the group chooses a common starting point that still gives individual hikers some freedom. Everyone promises not to hike a trail alone and to always be in communication with one other person for the sake of safety.

I guess people come from all over the world to hike here, but it is too rocky and desolate for me to get jazzed. I keep my opinions to myself and enjoy the ride. It's fun to watch deliveries being made, people buying "petrol" and running in for a newspaper as we drive through town. Just reading signs like "Telly Repair" makes me chuckle and appreciate that I am in a *somewhat* foreign culture.

Timothy stops to point out their chosen rendezvous spot and announces pick-up time as he drives the group to their starting place. I'm curious about how their day will go and who will connect with one another, but not curious enough to join in.

Driving back, I sit in the tour guide seat and chat with Timothy. "Would I be right in noting that you are a man who enjoys observin' people and culture?" he asks me.

"I certainly do. I love to see the choices people make."

"Aye, and as a man of the cloth, you would be having a front row seat for that, would you not, now?"

"You're right. I do see a lot of folks at turning points and when they are dealing with the ramifications of choices they have made. But, sometimes I am even more fascinated by the little choices people make, like who extends their hand to a stranger and who makes eye contact when sharing of themselves"

"Aye. When I was a banker, I saw more of the big choices, too. But, now I see the patterns of the smaller daily choices people make. 'Tis why I enjoy the bus drivin' and pullin' pints."

"Pulling pints?"

"Aye, you would be callin' it bartendin'."

"Of course . . . Speaking of bartending, are we on for the pub, again, tonight?"

"Saints willin', we are, indeed, we are. I see you are spending a good bit of time with our man O'Donohue?" His statement was a question.

"Say, again? I don't get what you mean," I reply.

"Did I not see you reading O'Donohue's *Anam Cara?*"

"Oh, of course, and I love it, too. Did you ever run into him over here? That would be an enviable pub conversation."

"Ach, afraid I have not had the pleasure, but I have heard him a time or two on the radio. I have been told he divides his time between the West of Ireland here and then over in America."

"Well. I would love to go to a reading or get a chance to talk with the guy. I want to explore this whole concept of the Divine Feminine more and what it means for men and how we embody it as men. I think you Irish have a head start on embodying it, having kept Brede and Maeve and all these female goddesses and heroines alive through the ages. "

"Aye, you have something there, and, wouldn't I like to be present for the conversation the two of you would be havin'. Two insightful men such as yourselves trying to sort it all out. Powerful conversation, that would be: you, the man of intellect with heart, and he, the man of heart with intellect."

We pull up in front of the lodge to find Peg and the others waiting. So many conversations left unfinished, but there is plenty of time.

Peter and Penny, Sandra and Jake, Mary Helena, and Peg board the bus. Mary Helena complains from the start, although I don't really pay much attention. I'm on vacation and lost in my own thoughts still. We visited the pre-historic part of this interpretive museum, yesterday. The visit today is meant to focus on the restored sixteenth-century castle and the renowned Hunt Collection of medieval art which is also part of the fifty acre site.

None of that interests me, but it is what Peg wants to see. My fascination is with the story of Brendan the Navigator. So Peg and I plan to split up when we get there. The men hear us talking about our choices and decide to join me. Timothy joins, too. We all agree to meet back at the tea shop when we finish.

Timothy drops the women off at the Castle, taking them directly to the door. Giving Mary Helena her due, she does thank him. Maybe the poor woman is grouchy because she is in pain.

The castle or mansion or whatever you call it was built on a crag overlooking the lake in 1550, we were told. It is considered an excellent example of a fortified Tower House, quite typical of what was built by big landowners of the sixteenth century. It was abandoned about one hundred years after and not restored until the twentieth century. That's enough info for me, that period of history never interested me much.

As Timothy suggests, we go off to find the "wee slip of a lass who would tell us more about St. Brendan and his sailing trips." We find her and wait patiently until there is a lull in bus tours. That way we have her full attention and ask a bunch of questions about this guy who probably truly discovered America. Peter, maybe because he's from Ontario, seemed to already know more about these Greenland-Icelandic explorations. Jake and I are floored by the accounts. Even though I had already stopped celebrating Columbus Day, I have to say it is hard to let go of the idea that the Spanish might not have been the first to explore the New World. Another paradigm bites the dust.

When we exhaust our topic and maybe our guide as well, we walk up to the tea room to meet the women. Our first stop is the gift shop; the second stop, coffee. When we realize that not all the women are done, we take our own table. Mary Helena and Peg seem to be getting on famously, to my surprise. I pull out a deck of cards with Celtic knots decorating the back that I just purchased. We amuse ourselves until the women are ready for lunch.

Penny and Sandra finally appear and now we can eat. A round table for eight, overlooking the lake, provides the perfect setting for a delicious High Tea. Peter jokes that the empty seat is for Dorrie's leprechaun.

Rose is in the lobby when we return and sort of gives us a rundown of who's where and what's going on. Dorrie's doing one-on-ones with folks who want individual coaching and Rose is waiting for her turn. Some of the women went shopping and had tea in the village. Now Kate and Rebecca are meeting to discuss some project they might want to work on back at home. As I recall, they started talking about feminist spirituality the very first morning of the trip. Rebecca was talking about a magazine piece she had recently done and Kate about the course she used to teach. They sound excited about the idea of collaborating.

Rose said they all had cream tea at the local hotel. Seems cream tea means scones, jam, and cream with a cup of tea. Glad we had the High Tea with real food. Megan had gotten permission to join them, rather than hike with her mom, so she is the one providing all these details. I see Peg getting antsy. As soon as Megan finishes, Peg excuses herself for a nap. I stay behind. Megan starts up with another burst of enthusiasm about their trip to town and Rose taking her to a shop where they have locally hand-tied flies for fishing. I can't resist asking them if they think American fish will want to bite on such foreign substances.

Just then, Nathan comes wandering in, looking kind of bored.

"So Nathan, what have you been up to?" I ask.

"Oh, texting friends, sending pictures to my dad, and looking up stuff about some of the places we're going. Mom and Dorrie said it would be okay to stay behind as long as I didn't leave the grounds of the lodge. And Gordie arranged this box lunch for me," he answers politely.

"What are those cards and sticks you have?"

"Oh, my grandmother got me these things for the trip. They're really awesome. The wooden sticks have ogham symbols and names and this book explains what they mean and how they might have been used by the Druids."

"Ogham?"

"Yea, like, it's like an ancient alphabet, but each symbol represents a tree and has stories with deeper meanings. Want to see?"

He hands me some of the sticks and shows me a picture in his book of a long vertical line with hash marks going up and down. Kind of like ladder rungs but some slanted and some on one side of the vertical line and some on the other.

"So what do you do with the sticks?"

"You are supposed to be able to use them kinda like tarot cards. But I have just been drawing one out of the bag at a time and reading about it. I haven't gotten too much into the tarot set yet."

"May I?"

"Sure. I'm keeping a record of what stick each person draws. Is it okay if I write down what you draw?"

"Let's do it." I draw a stick.

"Awesome. The hazel . . . that is really cool. And the old Gaelic name actually is *Coll*."

"You know all about them already without even looking in your book?"

"I know this one because it is really special. It was a wood used to make Druid wands and has wisdom and magic in it. Besides, when I use the animal cards and read the tarot cards, I keep coming across it. Hazelnuts fell into the pool at the Well of Segais and are what gave the salmon wisdom."

"Very interesting."

"Yeah, it also says here that they were used for divining rods. Do you know what that means?"

"Divining rods are made from lightweight branches with a fork in them. You hold the two forked ends and point the single end straight ahead. Then you walk around looking for water or gas or whatever. It dips down and points to the ground when you find it. Farmers used to use them in colonial days."

"Way cool. Maybe Timothy will help me find hazel wood so I can make one," Nathan says excitedly.

"They say you have to have a gift for it for the divining rods to work."

"You mean like have magic in you?"

"You could put it that way, I guess."

"I tried scrying at Brigid's Well—you know, like Harry Potter in *The Goblet of Fire*. But I didn't see anything . . . Do you know anything about that?"

"Can't say I do. Maybe Peter or Timothy will know. I do know something about tarot, though; if you want to learn more about it, I can help with that."

"Thanks, that would be great. When would you want to do it?"

"Let's give you a couple more days with your ogham and your Druid animal cards. When you are ready to add tarot just let me know. This looks like a great Celtic deck. We can even talk about it during a bus ride, but we also will want to spread the cards out on a table to do an actual reading."

"You can do that?"

"I've dabbled with them, for fun–just for myself and my family. I don't believe they predict things, but they can offer ideas to ponder. Peg and I started teaching our kids about indigenous cultures using different decks of animal cards and then tarot cards. I made it kind of a hobby to collect all different kinds. I'll gladly teach you what I know."

"Wow, thanks."

"Here come the guys, now. Earlier we were thinking you might like to play a game of cards with us, but actually this is more interesting. Maybe you can try your readings out on them."

"Thought you could do with some crisps and a real American soda," offers Timothy.

"Chips and Coke, wow. For me, really? Thanks." He dives into the potato chips like he has been starved all week.

"Won't you all join us in some crisps or biscuits, cookies to you Yanks. I bought enough for everyone. Particularly since no one wants to spoil their dinner," Timothy says with a wink to Nathan.

Rose strolls in and we invite her to join us.

"Nathan was just telling me about the hazel tree and the Well of Segais and I drew the hazel ogham. Nathan, tell the folks about it."

"I wasn't sure if I should tell about somebody else's stuff."

"Oh, no worry, I'm an open book, but good of you to be thinking along those lines."

"Tell them mine, too, if you want," offers Rose.

"Earlier, Rose drew the salmon card in my animal card deck so I read more about the Well of Segais. The legends say the salmon is the oldest animal. The Well is supposed to be 'the well of wisdom and the source of life.' See the hazel nuts on the card, falling into the pond with the salmon jumping! Timothy, it says here that the well is at the beginning of the Boyne River, near Tara. Isn't that where we are going tomorrow? Can we stop there? Please?"

"Aye, we will indeed be at the Boyne, but finding the well is another matter. I've heard tell of the place, but never have heard of anyone going there. I'll talk with Gordie and see what we can do, lad. You have the right of it. It would fit right in with this tour."

"Do you guys believe in magic? Do you think the fact that we drew cards and sticks about the Well and might go there tomorrow is magic?" Nathan asked.

"Probably just coincidence, but it does make you wonder," Peter offers.

"My take is the Jungian idea of synchronicity," I say and then realize I am probably talking over the boy's head.

"Maybe it is magic. Maybe it comes from the Faeries or our guides from the Other Kingdom," speculates Timothy.

"Do you believe in fairies, Timothy?" Nathan asks.

"We Irish have never really given up on our belief in the Little People. I can tell you that, now."

"What about you, Rose?"

"I had a little fairy friend as a child . . . My parents kinda made me grow out of it, but now that I am here in Ireland, I'm intrigued again."

"Really? I sure would really like to know how all this stuff fits together–magic, story, fairies, religion, nature, and science? Sometimes it makes perfect sense; other times it just feels weird," admits Nathan.

"What do you think?" I ask him.

"I really don't know. I've tried to talk to my dad about it all. He's a surgeon who trusts only in science and technology. He just shrugs and says it's 'above his pay grade.' Once in a while, though, he gets a far-off look in his eye and says 'there is more out there than science, I felt it today while operating'—but he never can say what it is."

"But what do you think?" asks Peter, echoing my question.

"Well, I think they all fit together somehow but, like, I don't have the words to say how and I never find anybody who does. That's why stories are so cool. They kind of put it all together. But they really don't answer the question."

"Aye, the power lies in the stories, does it not?" puts in Timothy.

"What about you guys, what do you think?"

"Well, I like what the poet says about living the questions and I think you, young man, are on to the right questions. I think mystery and wonder combine and then transcend science and religion."

Nathan nods.

Peter continues, "There is a revival of interest in the ancient mysteries and some new wisdom schools that intrigue me. You know, like the popularity of the Dan Brown novels such as *The Lost Symbol,* weekend retreats, and certificate programs. Nathan, you'll get a kick out of knowing the Harry Potter books were really an important part of this trend. Who knows where it all is leading us?"

With that, folks descend on the lobby, the doors to the dining room open, and our little group disperses. Peg comes down looking refreshed and joins a table with John and Melanie. I bet she wants to hear more about Melanie's school. I seek out Gordie and some of the hikers to hear more about the Burren.

After dinner, the group gathers in the lounge for Dorrie's talk on Celtic spirituality. Everyone seems to be talking about tomorrow's visit to Clonmacnoise.

Emboldened by Timothy, who said Megan and Trish need to tell the story they had shared with him, Trish begins, "By now, most of you are aware that Clonmacnoise is considered to be the center of the monastic life. You may remember the book *How the Irish Saved Civilization* that made that case a few years ago. Well, this story is about Megan doing a school project based on that concept. Forgive a proud mother for bragging, but the story does fit with what we are doing."

"Mom was reading that book when I got this assignment to take a moment in history and write how changing that moment could change the world. Mom let me read about how the Irish monasteries were responsible for keeping the Latin Bible and reading and writing in general alive during the Dark Ages. The author was saying they had saved us all from ruin." Megan says as she takes a deep breath and continues.

"So I decided to write about what would have happened if St. Patrick and Ireland's version of Christianity beat out Rome's. I had gone with a friend and her family to their small Irish church in our neighborhood a couple of times. It was way different than the Catholic church that my Gram and Gramps go to."

"In fact, it had broken away from the Catholic Diocese a number of years ago over an issue of liturgical difference. It changed its name to St. Kevin's Holy Celtic Church," adds Trish.

"So I wrote that what if Dublin became the city center of the Church and that instead of a pope the Church was run by a group of Celtic elders. What if no Protestant Reformation happened and the Crusades ended with peace being achieved with the Muslims. Christians would then share Jerusalem with Jews and Muslims. The Jews would have a home in Israel and there would have been no Holocaust. Italy and Spain would not have been the center of Christian Europe and the focus would have been to the North not the South. The fighting between the religions and countries therefore would have stopped long ago.

"I wrote that since the Irish lived in such a natural environment and loved Nature, we would have all learned to respect the planet more. Now that I am here, I truly think that could have been true."

What a great question. It could have been my thesis in divinity school. What a bright and creative kid.

I knew it, here goes Peg, "Megan, you are in very good company. Two women theologians I know and respect have written extensively about the difference between Jesus, as pastor, and Jesus, the victim of suffering. They note that the crucifix, the symbol of suffering for our sins never even appeared in the early Church. In fact, their research finds no written reference, art, or Church artifacts showing anything but a pastoral Jesus, a shepherd with his lambs, a teacher surrounded by his disciples up until the year 1000 CE. It gives me chills to think what might have been had that change not happened."

Kate and Rebecca jump in to get more information and Peg suggests anyone wanting to talk more about this meet over coffee. I can see Peg getting self-conscious about cutting into Dorrie's time.

With that handoff, Dorrie stands up and leads a final round of applause for Megan.

"What a great segue into tonight's session on Celtic spirituality. The Irish monastic tradition, especially the monastery at Clonmacnoise, played such an important role in the early Church and, in those days, the Church was the depository of civilization. We can't do justice to describing it.

"In your packet, there is a page that gives an overview of Celtic spirituality and one that describes a bit more of the Celtic calendar and such. Also note that I have put *Anam Cara: A Book of Celtic Wisdom* by John O'Donohue on your reading list. If you were to read only one book on Celtic spirituality, this would be the book. The man is a modern Catholic, Irish-American who captures the Celtic soul and demonstrates a deep appreciation of their ancient story, as well. I really think you'll like it.

"Let's arrange our chairs in a circle so I can introduce you to another facet of Celtic spirituality, lighting a ritual candle."

Everyone moves their chairs while she drags a little table to the center and throws a green cloth over it and places a green and white candle with three wicks in the center. She begins the ritual:

"Let us open the circle starting with the four directions and their corollary elements. This is similar to what we did as an invocation on top of the hill at the Cliffs of Moher. It is about connecting to Nature—so vitally and vividly important to the survival of ancient peoples.

We begin in the East: Element of Air, represented by the spear.
> Bring us focus. May our minds be sharp and our imaginations directed to making sense of our world and making a better world in all we do.

And then to the South: Element of Fire, represented by the sword. Bring us the cleansing and recharging energy of your flame. We need your warmth, light, and protection. Remind us that passion is a two-edged sword.

We now look to the West: Element of Water, represented by the cauldron. Speak to us of healing, transformation,

and inner wisdom. May our journey across the water
aid our search for intuition, inner knowledge, and self-
healing.
And to the North: Element of Earth, represented by the stone.
Bring your strength, wisdom, and magic to connect us
to the material world. Give us simple abundance and a
reverence for all that is our home.

"And now we light the three-fold flame.

For the three worlds of Celtic spirituality: The Mundane
World, The In-Between, and the Other World.
For the three forms of the Goddess: Maiden, Mother, and
Crone.
For the Christian Trinity: Father, Son, and Holy Ghost

"We ask that our circle be empowered by all these
triads represented and enriched by our expanded consciousness
toward each and all together.
"Our reading is a Celtic prayer from the time of
Clonmacnoise. It has many variations. This version is the one
used by Donovan, the first singer whom I heard put the prayer
to song:

> *Deep peace of the running wave to you;*
> *Deep peace of the flowing air to you;*
> *Deep peace of the quiet earth to you;*
> *Deep peace, deep peace.*
> *Deep peace of the sleeping stones to you;*
> *Deep peace of the wandering wind to you;*
> *Deep peace of the flock of stars to you;*
> *Deep peace, deep peace.*

"Let us be silent together."

After a few moments, she asks someone to turn the
lights up and hands out blank pieces of paper, also making sure
we all have pens or pencils.

"I thought it might be illustrative and fun if we each drew a Celtic cross. You will be seeing dozens of them tomorrow and they each tell a story. This exercise will help you to get the story on a deeper level than perhaps you would have otherwise. To begin, draw a vertical line down the center of your paper. What comes to mind?"

"North-South."

"Earth-Sky."

"Transcendence."

"Mother Earth-Father Sky."

"Up-Down."

"All great answers," Dorrie reflects. "Now draw a horizontal line that intersects that line mid-way. What comes to mind here?"

"Right-Left."

"East-West."

"Start of Day-End of Day."

"Timeline."

"Again, all great answers!" Now, before you draw a circle, what does a circle represents to you?"

"Sun."

"Moon."

"Circle of Life."

"Cycle of Life"

"Gathering around the fire."

"Connection"

"All are One."

"Community."

"Infinity."

"Ultimacy."

"Now, draw a circle whose center is at the point where the two lines intersect and whose outside edge touches all four line segments. No surprise, we have a Celtic cross. What do you see in it?"

"Connects the four elements and cycle of the year."

"It's the cycle of a person's lifetime in dimensions of time and space."

"It is like the zodiac."

"The Tree of Life and the Sacred Oak are similar in shape to it."

"It is like our circle and the candles to the four directions."

"It combines pagan and Christian symbols."

"Again, great answers. All are part of the speculation around the origins and meaning of the cross. Like most things, it is subject to interpretation. I had you start the model with the vertical line because all cultures have a symbol of connecting earth to sky or reaching up to the sky—the Egyptian obelisk, standing stones, Tree of Life, all are images of this up/down axis.

"The most noted legend in Ireland regarding the origins of this cross is that St. Patrick took a round symbol of sun or moon and placed the Christian cross through it. One way or the other, the message is one of both rather than either/or. The message of male and female integrated in family; Mother God/Father God as One; Past, Present, Future and Infinity. All are apparent for all to see.

"So, that is a bit of an introduction to what you will see at Clonmacnoise tomorrow. I am deeply grateful that so many sites were protected over the centuries and that we are able to visit so many.

"Lily has agreed to sing the second verse of *Deep Peace* as our closing. Join her, if you wish, as I extinguish the three-fold candle and we silently thank the directions and elements for their presence with us:

> *Deep peace of the Eastern wind to you;*
> *Deep peace of the Western wind to you;*
> *Deep peace of the Northern wind to you;*
> *Blue wind of the South to you;*
> *Pure red of the whirling flame to you;*
> *Pure white of the silver moon to you;*
> *Pure green of the emerald grass to you;*
> *Deep peace, deep peace.*
> *Deep peace of the running wave to you;*
> *Deep peace of the flowing air to you;*

Deep peace of the quiet earth to you;
Deep peace, deep peace . . .
Deep peace, deep peace . . .
Deep peace, deep peace . . .

After two nights at the pub, many of us have gained confidence enough to come and go without Timothy. But, in the spirit of things, most of us go as one big group.

"Grand altogether," says Timothy, as the main group goes to stake out some tables and have them pull us some pints. I am getting such a kick out of this. Tonight's music is a little different—three men; one with a fiddle, one with a squeeze box, and one with a banjo playing a round of jigs. Dorrie and Gordie lead the dancing; Penny and Peter are right behind them. When Timothy asks Kate to try her hand at it, I figure Peg and I can give it a try, too. Why not?

When the boys break after the first set, I tell Peg that's all for me and I sink into the chair like a man who just ran a marathon. The table talk is about some promotional contest Guinness used to run back home. The idea was to write no more than two hundred words on why you should be given an Irish pub here in the West of Ireland. Penny and Peter say they had entered the contest, as had Kevin.

Kate allows that she would never have thought of it then. But if the chance came again, she would jump at it. She adds graciously that if she won, we all would be invited over for an annual reunion, with drinks all around. Everyone laughs at the notion of her behind the bar, pulling pints. "If they could see me now," she sings and gestures like a Broadway star, adding "my colleagues and friends at home would never believe it."

Kevin then tells us the story of when his wife and he were in Connemara and traveling from small town to small town around Clifden. "We followed the music to a different pub each night. Then we found we were not alone hopping from place to place. At the first pub, we met a real character—a white–haired, slightly bent old man in an even older, thread-bare tweed coat and a black walnut walking stick which he placed on the bar to the right of his elbow. He had a stout or two stacked up and was downing a whiskey when he began to tell a tale.

"It, as they say, was a long story, but he told it with such charm and blarney that we were spellbound. We added to his line of drinks in thanks. Next night, new pub, same gentleman. What surprised us was that it also was the same story. And, you can guess, third night another pub and the same again.

"Janie's urging and a few whiskeys emboldened me to go up to him. 'I wonder if you would mind me asking why you tell the same story every night,' I asked. Then I added, just to dilute my bold query, 'you seem like a very accomplished story teller and we can't imagine you do not have more stories.'

"He laughed the heartiest of laughs and his eyes twinkled reminding me of my childhood image of Santa Claus. 'Aye, I know many a story, probably enough to last me a lifetime or until I no longer want the drink. But, you, lad, are not a seasoned pubber, or you would know that in these parts, you have your pub and you are loyal to it. See, the clientele stays put. I change pubs every night, but change stories only once a week—a bit like taking a bath.'"

Everyone in the place looks over at the noise our laughter is making.

"You should leave the state bureaucracy and be a story teller in Kate's pub when she wins it," quips John.

"You are on!" replies Kate enthusiastically, adding, "and maybe Timothy will take charge of getting the music."

Wild Rover and *Whiskey in a Jar* bring us to our feet as we clap and shout out the choruses. Then we close the place, singing *I'll Take You Home Again, Kathleen* in the pub and along the path back to the Lodge.

Timothy, Peter, Penny, and Kate harmonize as if they have sung together for years. Peter says it is the Jameson making them so mellow. Even Peg and I, who admittedly can't sing worth a plugged nickel, join in until I stop to give her a light kiss in the moonlight. "What a good day, my *anam cara*, what a good day. *Sláinte.*"

DAY FOUR

CLONMACNOISE
THE BOYNE VALLEY

We leave Salmon Run Lodge and travel to our next lodging, The Bend of the Boyne, a conference center within a convent run by local nuns.
Our main stop for the day is the famous Clonmacnoise whose iconic High Celtic Crosses stand as testament to the importance of the site. The monastery and scriptorium of Clonmacnoise were key to the preservation of the Church not only here in Ireland but throughout Christendom.

KATE

Travel and packing take their toll on some more than others. I've always been someone who could pick up and be gone in a moment's notice, even when the kids were little. Mary Helena though is the kind who makes a federal production out of it. I like to keep chores like this sweet and simple. Perhaps, I'm even quicker today knowing Gordie has a single room for me at our next stop. Hallelujah.

If truth be told, Mary Helena is irritating but also sad. She is so filled with self-pity and submerged anger. Maybe I'm being too harsh, but her negativity is infringing on this special time I've worked so hard to create for myself, time I need to adjust to retirement, and time I want just to relax and play. Uncharitable, maybe; but I have finally learned to set some limits.

I'm spending a lot of time talking to Timothy just to avoid continually being paired up with her. Sharing a room was one thing, but sitting together on the bus and being sought out at every bus stop and at every meal was just too much.

Dorrie's site meditations and rituals have really spoken to me: opening to Spirit, opening to the Divine Feminine, setting intention, embodying prayer, being willing to walk through a portal into a new stage of life, finding deep peace in oneness with nature. Hmm . . .

I've always responded more to invitation than criticism. Mary Helena is like the strict Zen teacher with the stick and Dorrie like the Zen master with gentle voice and embrace. Mary Helena may be giving me a lesson in keeping my heart open, but I prefer Dorrie's way.

Here's Timothy, now. He gives me his lovely smile and takes my bag. I go for a last walk along the salmon stream before sound meditation. County Clare has certainly been good for me. Still, I'm walking with Mary Helena on my mind, remembering my own dark night of the soul. The haunting questions that Angela Arrien lifted up pierce through my reverie.

When in your life did you stop singing?
When in your life did you stop dancing?

I found my voice along with many of my sisters during the women's movement. I learned to get back in touch with my body through yoga and dance.

When in your life did you stop being enchanted with stories?

Here in Ireland, that question might better be, "How can you help but become enchanted with stories?" These people and this culture live an enchantment. I envy them that. Take Timothy; his laugh, his joy for life, his gift for gab are all delightful. He never trivializes anyone or their story, but he knows how to lighten it. What a gift.

Finding a perfectly flat natural stone tablet on which to steady my journal, I stop, deciding to skip sound meditation so I can spend some time writing. I write and write and then hear Arrien's fourth question in my mind.

When in your life did you become uncomfortable with the sweet territory of silence?

I laugh to myself thinking that I always have been blessed with the ability to be alone with myself. My challenge is to risk, to reach out, to open my heart and soul the way I have always easily opened my mind.

I get back as breakfast is being served and slip into a table with Melanie and John, Rebecca and Angie, and Leslie, who's without her son this morning. I'm glad there's space at their table since I really haven't had a real conversation with any of them.

Melanie is speaking to Rebecca, "At our in-gathering, you mentioned that you saw yourself as here on a pilgrimage of sorts. I'd love to hear more, if you don't mind sharing. Like why are you calling it that and what do you expect from it? Do you mind my asking?"

"Don't mind at all. Talking about it helps me get clarity. I once read that pilgrimage is 'seeking what the heart holds sacred.' Isn't that beautiful? I kept thinking about it at the Well. As a freelance writer, I have traveled a lot and even written about places considered sacred by many. You know, Native American sites, Japanese temples, and even Jerusalem. But I was always an observer, an analyst, and a recorder. I never truly experienced the sacredness of any of those places, if you know what I mean."

Angie encourages her to go on. "Tell them about your workshop with Dorrie at Omega."

"Well, let's see, how can I give a short version? Basically, Dorrie told me that I was living in my head. At first, I had no idea what she meant. Then I began to think of all the times Angie would ask me things like 'how is your heart?' or 'how do you feel about this or that?' and I couldn't really answer her. I finally understood that I wasn't living from my heart-center. I talked and wrote about feelings and experiences rather than felt and absorbed them. So folks, in a nutshell, I came on this trip to practice living from my heart-center, being in the moment, and connecting to the sacred. And, I have to say, I am so blessed to have Dorrie and Angie, both here encouraging me. This whole trip is, well, amazing."

"Thank you for sharing that," Melanie says with a tear in her eye.

"Yeah, wow," John adds. "I guess I have always thought of a pilgrimage as being like a trip to Mecca or Jerusalem. I never thought of it as the inner journey that comes from the travel. I can see what you are saying. Thanks for explaining it and in such a personal way."

"I know a lot of people who have visited specific sacred sites with none of that sense of experiencing it in their heart-center, as you called it. I'll be thinking a lot about this whole conversation. Thank you." Leslie comments.

"It has become a pilgrimage for me, too." This is the first I have heard Angie say anything about herself. She continues, "When I got on that plane and then, again, when I went through that portal stone, it was like I was embarking on a journey of personal discovery. Like the Fool in the tarot, I was stepping off into a trip of a lifetime, a trip to find meaning and the true purpose of my life. Does that sound corny?"

"Not to me," Melanie says softly.

"I am so happy to hear you say that," Rebecca adds. "You have been so quiet these last few days; I wondered sometimes if you were just indulging me."

"I'm just taking it all in, sketching and thinking, and sketching some more. I've already sketched some of the iconic items: Brigid's Cross, the salmon and the Celtic Cross. But I can't begin to capture the scenery, the beauty . . .

"It's a wonderful trip and we're not even at the half-way point," Angie replies softly.

"I like the idea of a pilgrimage being intentional and proactive. Not sure I would come up with an image like a fool walking off a cliff." John chuckles a bit. Then he adds, "But a little spontaneity might serve me well. I like it."

"I guess I've always thought of transformation as something that just happens—grace—or else the extreme opposite—a horrific struggle," comments Leslie.

"Like Christians who walked the marble labyrinth floor of Chartres Cathedral on their knees or traveled the *Camino de Santiago* in chains?" Melanie asks.

"Yeah, like that. Or, you know, like working out at the gym. No pain, no gain," Leslie admits with a thin laugh.

"For me, places like the well and the dolmen are more sacred than any cathedral. I hadn't really thought of this trip as a pilgrimage per se, but I guess it really is for me, too. Melanie, thanks for asking the question. You know, one of my fears of retiring was that I would miss out on conversations like this. You all remind me that there is life after leaving academia. Thanks for that." I add, "There's a quotation by Joseph Campbell in my journal that comes to mind,

> *Your sacred place is where you find yourself again and again.*

"I am beginning to think it applies to this whole trip, for me at least."

"That's beautiful," murmurs Leslie. "You know, I came on this trip for my son, but, each day, I realize I am getting as much out of it as he is."

At that point, John asks, "So does Ireland have any particular pilgrimage traditions or sites? Like maybe going to Saint Patrick's Cathedral?"

"Well, the cathedral is on our itinerary, but Croagh Patrick is the place to go, I hear. It is a 'mountaintop pilgrimage' on our list of options when we come back west to Sligo and Mayo. Irish people go there on one of the Celtic holidays, though I can't remember which one. Dorrie will know more," answers Rebecca.

"Interesting you say that because I keep thinking about the rituals we did at the Cliffs, the Well, and the dolmen. They were so powerful. I had never done anything like that. Most surprising is how easily I now can transport myself back to those moments," Angie comments.

"I've had a similar sense during the tonings." I offer.

John then adds "You know, working out is my daily practice, but these last couple of days, I figured I'd try out the yoga. In college, my basketball coach gave us yoga as part of training. I've been thinking of these three questions coach used to ask us during centering: What do you think the Universe is telling you? What is your gift? What interferes with you being all you can be? They're great questions, huh?"

Soon, we're being rounded up for Dorrie's morning talk. I've never cared much for medieval history and would much rather just continue our table discussion, but it would feel mutinous to suggest we just stay put. So as a courtesy to Dorrie, I get a final coffee refill and saunter into the meeting room. Fortunately, Dorrie does the Cliff Notes version, sharing just a few key facts with us: Clonmacnoise was at its height during what we call the Dark Ages, before all the great struggles of papal successions, before the Protestant Reformation, and even before the English crown started using Ireland as a staging ground for its own wars.

Until *How the Irish Saved Civilization* came out, common thinking dismissed the period as one of invaders and marauders and not much else. It'll be exciting to walk the ground where old wisdom was held and cherished during dark times. And I will think of Megan and her essay and commit myself to tracking down those theologians Peg mentioned.

It really is just a short drive inland to Clonmacnoise. Gentle rolling green hills made me even more aware of how bleak the rocky Burren is. The site itself sits on a huge piece of property by Irish standards. It rolls down and into the wide, watery meadows along the Shannon. It is hard to say where its boundaries are and where the neighboring farmers' fields begin.

I try to imagine these green acres once were abuzz as a flourishing monastic complex. Ringing the monastery grounds would have been a whole town, housing craftsmen and their families as well as stores and transportation to provide food, supplies, and commerce to the monastery. I use a scene from a movie about Merlin I had once seen to conjure up the picture. Can't remember the name of the movie, though. Where is Megan when I need her for movie trivia expertise? Actually she's at the back of the bus, chatting with Peg, but it isn't that important.

I spy an intriguing little gift shop on the other side of the parking lot. Some Celtic window stencils catch my eye. I'll stop on the way out.

Dorrie begins again, "There's a lot to see in the visitors center, but I would like to ask you to walk right through and gather at the foot of the first High Cross on the grounds itself. Gordie will explain to the guides that we want to take a few minutes for centering and prayer before we start the tour. The guide will then walk the grounds with us and provide more detail than I possibly could give you.

"I would like to suggest that as you look over the five High Crosses and the fifty-some in total, you notice their evolution. Note that only in the very latest Celtic cross do we see a crucifix symbol in the center. Also, watch for the Egyptian symbols and Phoenician boats depicted on some. The notion that everyone but Columbus thought the world was flat and that you would drop off it outside the gates at Gibraltar is easily debunked at just one of those crosses. It points out how much information and understanding of earlier cultures was lost during the Dark Ages."

We get off the bus and hurry in to avoid the gusts of wind that want to blow us away. But then I stop short. There is this life size wooden sculpture of a cloaked monk or priest that I find simply chilling. Most people walk right by, but I just stand there. The figure is facing forward but bent over with the face hidden by a cloaked left arm. It's primitive, archetypal, and mysterious. But what is the meaning and why is it here? I quickly take a picture of it and rush to catch up with the group.

Sure enough they are waiting for me and, of course, for Lily who has wandered off.

"Thanks for gathering so quickly, Isn't this magnificent? For our centering prayer I have chosen words of Saint Patrick that have come down through the ages in many forms. Note how similar they are to *Deep Peace* which we read and sang last night.

This is a classic prayer called *St. Patrick's Breastplate*. It is believed he was under attack when it was first used. This version is also a song called *Deer's Cry*.

> *I arise today, through the strength of heaven;*
> *light of sun, radiance of moon,*
> *splendor of fire, speed of lightning,*
> *swiftness of the wind, depth of the sea,*
> *stability of earth, firmness of rock.*

> *I arise today, through God's strength to pilot*
>   *me;*
> *God's eye to look before me, God's wisdom to*
>   *guide me,*
> *God's way to lie before me, God's shield to*
> *protect me, from all who shall wish me ill, afar*
> *and a-near alone and in a multitude.*

> *Against every cruel merciless power*
> *that may oppose my body and soul,*
> *Christ with me, Christ before me,*
> *Christ behind me, Christ in me,*
> *Christ beneath me, Christ above me,*
> *Christ on my right, Christ on my left,*
> *Christ when I lie down, Christ when I sit down,*
> *Christ when I arise, Christ to shield me.*

Christ in the heart of everyone who thinks of me,
Christ in the mouth of everyone who speaks of
me.

I arise today.

I would have liked at least ten minutes to walk silently in meditation; however, the guide leaps into action after about 30 seconds of silence. To be fair, he joined us for the prayer. Then after what he thought was a long enough pause of respect, he made eye contact with Dorrie to get permission to proceed.

He introduces himself as Ian and says he taught Irish and English literature at a local university until retirement. Now he is a docent here. I keep thinking of my wooden monk or priest at the front entrance. What was his name? What did he represent?

Ian drones on in one of those singsong voices of a too well-seasoned guide, "There were nine churches, two round towers, a nunnery, a scriptorium, hundreds of early grave-stones, and crosses. Of special significance are the High Crosses and the samples of how the simple Celtic cross evolved over the years.

He points out similarities and differences among the fifty-plus crosses on site; thankfully, in broad strokes. He shows us where the land divided the consecrated ground from the non-consecrated. I see little difference but he says the High Kings paid handsomely for the privilege of being buried in the consecrated ground. I guess consecrated ground, a High Cross, and bags of money got you into heaven.

We walk over to the churches and ruins of churches, with Ian explaining the origin and time period of each. My attention is starting to wander back to my mysterious wooden carved monk. Maybe it is referencing the High Priest, like the tarot card, the way he seems dressed in ceremonial robes and sitting on a throne.

Ian says something about a pope. No, I think, the statue unnerving me was neither priest nor pope. Ian gestures down the grassy slope, past the nunnery and to a wide area where he is talking about the Pope's visit to Ireland. He half-jokingly remarks that the American, John Fitzgerald Kennedy, in 1963 and the Italian, Pope John Paul II, in 1979 had done more to lift up Catholic Ireland than any Irishman since St. Patrick himself. I'm amused that he uses JFK's full Irish name.

With that, the tour finally ends. Everyone thanks the guy, some with more sincerity than the rest of us. After waiting for Mary Helena to ask him what seems like a zillion (my granddaughter's number) questions about the Pope, I ask about the statue. He barely acknowledges that he knows where it is, let alone what and why. Odd, but, oh well.

I lose myself among the High Crosses and then in a ruin of a small chapel looking out at the grassy meadow of the Shannon. I watch the swans in the distance and marvel at the sunny, albeit windy, cloudless day.

Rebecca calls this trip her pilgrimage and that sounds kind of true for me, too. I came to have space and a place to consider my recent status of retiree and what I will do with the rest of my life. My years as director of a women's studies department at a university ended naturally and with a gentle fanfare befitting my tenure. There was enough pomp and ceremony to feel affirmed in my life's work, without it going over-the-top and becoming an embarrassment.

The kids are all grown and established in their own families. I always feel welcome, yet I have enough sense not to test their hospitality. We are all connected by our own family website and Skype. I don't think I will want to change our patterns of interaction now, even though with retirement I have more time. I've been mulling Mary Oliver's famous question over and over, the one that asks:

What is it you plan to do with your one wild and precious life?

Somehow, amid all this history and faded glory, it seems like a small question, but it is huge for me. I ask the wisdom of this sacred place to assist my knowing.

There have been a few small grant projects connected with a local women's institute, but the work of these projects doesn't really engage me beyond their specific deadlines. Not since my divorce twenty years ago have I felt so unsettled. Yet, this time, there is a sense of openness to new possibilities, self-confidence, and a spiritual optimism that I sure didn't have then.

So when a friend told me about Dorrie and handed me the flyer about this trip, I said "yes" right away. It was a good fit and a perfect time. I am so grateful I came.

I have studied some of the wisdom school mystery materials, have friends who had morphed their clinic practices to include transpersonal psychology and have been part of a Unitarian Universalist WomenSpirit group that had been meeting for years. Beyond that, I always put exploring my spirituality on the long, rather than short list of to-dos. I suppose if I were to join a congregation, it would probably be UU or a Quaker meeting group.

Some folks, especially men, thought our WomenSpirit group was a Neo-pagan group, even a witch's coven. But that was not the case. We were mostly academic women who got tired of critiquing religion and theology and sought to embrace spirituality. As Dorrie had said in describing Celtic spirituality, people have practiced some form of circle worship for years. In fact, when I was a guest faculty member teaching organizational behavior to MBAs, I would test them with the question of what is the earliest form of organization. When I asserted that it is not the military, but the family/tribe, the brighter ones would groan in recognition that the lens of domination and power are so omnipresent in our culture.

I'm so glad I chose a trip and a group that doesn't want to focus on battlefields or talk about how one giant is said to have killed hundreds or even one of the king's men, etc. I'm with stimulating people who are genuinely seeking to integrate spirituality into their lives. I so appreciate that. Maybe, that's the meaning of the statue—at least, for me. The monk is hiding from seeing the world outside his walls. In separating from the world, from family and the circle of community, mankind lost its way; separating religion from experiencing life, from spirituality. Perhaps that is why he seems almost sinister to me.

I am becoming clear that I am here, by that I mean both on this trip and in this lifetime, to experience the sacredness of nature, of the Celtic heart and soul that connects to nature in powerful and real ways. Perhaps, the experience will transform me, perhaps not. But I know I need to embrace it. I'm not sure what I am to do with my "one wild and precious life" as I age, but I give thanks each day for my health and the opportunity to continue the journey.

I exhaust myself in all this contemplation and realize it's time to get lunch and see the exhibits and also get those window stencils. As I walk back, a clear picture of the Hermit comes to me. He is another of the major arcana of the tarot. His message is to stop midway on the journey, listen to your spiritual guide, reflect, and go within. I do just that. I stop at the foot of a High Cross, sit at its base, and reflect some more.

At Brigid's Well, I had prayed for grace, particularly the grace to grow old naturally and to have a meaningful life until life was no longer in me. Like Mary Travers belting out *And When I Die,* I want to go naturally. At the dolmen, I had practiced stepping out and into the new, and probably final, phase of my journey with joy and courage. Now, here I am reminded that I have the trait, the gift, really, of contemplation. I should not waste it.

At some point, everyone visits the cafeteria for lunch. Not the greatest food or service, but a good way to accommodate the fact that different group members want to spend differing amounts of time at the site. Now I watch the waves on the wide Shannon this windy day as we head across the middle of Ireland to the Boyne Valley. We're going to stay three nights at a place called The Bend in the River Boyne Conference Center. Hope it is even half as nice as Salmon Run Lodge. The lodge and its setting were wonderful. Timothy tells me the conference center is run by a local order of progressive nuns to whom the property had been given in the 1960's. Sounds like no pub tonight. The Center will be our base for Dublin, Glendalough, Newgrange, and Tara.

The Shannon is the Mississippi of Ireland. The part most North Americans see is the part near the airport, an estuary actually that comes inland about sixty miles. But, I was surprised to learn that the entire river is 240 miles long, with its source to the north. Folks rent canal boats and take them up and down one section of the river and this could be seen as they headed East across Ireland. I was reading up on it because I want to bring the kids over sometime and rent one of the boats.

Timothy puts on a CD of ancient chants. Except for the music, the bus seems unusually quiet. Dorrie had talked about the fact there always comes a day on a bus tour when everyone has said and heard all they can retain of one another's stories and choose to simply stare out at the scenery. And in Ireland what could be more appealing—not a bad view to be had as we look out at the purple-shadowed Slieve Bloom Mountains. After a while, Timothy changes to a mellow Mary Black CD, turning the sound down even further so it won't disturb those who are dozing off.

Sometimes, even the extroverts need to be alone with their thoughts and this was one of those afternoons. Glad to see Timothy gets it and likes quiet in spite of his own extroverted nature.

Mary Helena found more of the packets for making Brigid's cross pins and some needlepoint kits, too. Some of the other grandmothers plus Trish liked the idea and joined her in buying more. She is showing them how to do it. Megan's working with a set of colored markers and Celtic knot patterns on stencils that she found. Nathan's busy with his ogham sticks, engaging people individually. I guess the idea is you pull a stick or a card and then he reads a little ditty about the meaning it holds. Jackson is slumped in his seat with Joyce's *Portrait of a Young Man,* hardly a light read or an inspirational read for a boy already alienated and depressed, but then sometimes one does need to go into shadow. May he and his dad find the healing peace they so need if they are to move on with their lives.

Angie is next to me and is quietly sketching as I journal. Rebecca is playing cards with John and Gordie. Angie turns to say, "There is just so much to take in. Do you think between your writings and my sketches that we are capturing it, at least a little? The energy from the hills themselves, the lilt to the voices of the proud guides sharing their country's treasures with us, the memory of all who were lost in the Famine and the memory of all of value that was saved in the Dark Ages. It's all amazing."

"It is, and it evokes so many thoughts and feelings in me."

"Yeah, not the least for me is the idea of how crazy it is to think that in the midst of all this, people who look alike and share the same god have been fighting, killing, starving, or raiding each other for centuries. What was that Yeats quotation someone used at the Cliffs? Oh, yeah, 'the terrible beauty that is Ireland.'" She just shakes her head. "I'm trying to capture this sometimes eerie, other times blissful beauty, but I'm not even close."

"But your sketches are wonderful. In fact, if you ever have prints made, I'd love to buy a couple as mementos."

TRISH

Megan and I purchased a beautiful t-shirt of flying swans that reminded us of those we had just seen on the Shannon and in the *Children of Lir* storybook I bought for my niece. I hadn't known the story, but I see Megan has pulled it out to read as we travel along this stretch of highway.

"Mom this is awful. There is no way you can give this to Chelsea."

"Why, what's wrong with it? The illustrations are wonderful."

"Yeah, the pictures are good, but Mom, it's the story of four children being turned into swans by their evil stepmother and living like that for four hundred years. Then when they are finally released from the spell, they age really quickly and die."

"I had no idea. The colors are so peaceful."

"Sure, Mom, but no little kid needs to read this stuff."

"I agree, although old fairy tales and legends are filled with wicked stepmothers, mean trolls, and lots of evil things. I used to have nightmares about burning in an oven as a kid, from *Hansel and Gretel*. I guess that's why I never read them to you."

"I don't get why they were even written."

"I'm not sure, but I guess it was an attempt to prepare children for the dark side of life."

"And adults get weirded out by our music. Which, by the way, I am going to escape into for the rest of this boring ride."

Speaking of music, Timothy has *Celtic Woman* on and I am transported back to the words Dorrie read back at the High Cross. That experience really pierced my armor. The feelings of unease began at St. Brigid's Well and the stirring of unsettled energy was evident at the dolmen, but I pushed both feelings aside. I didn't come for any kind of personal transformation like some of these folks. I simply wanted to see around Ireland with my daughter and share in some of the magic and beauty of the place. I have too much on my plate. Until Megan is off to college, maintaining the status quo is all I can handle.

I work as a public relations specialist for a U.S. Senator from the Northeast. I dropped out of college and went to D.C. to be a torch singer with my jazz musician husband. D.C. was the place we first landed a gig worth staying for, so we set up house there. I've always loved the city and still do. It's so stately, yet youthful; so full of promise, yet very real. Audiences seemed to get into our music. We had quite a following at one of the established gin mills in town. Then Mr. Blues, as I call him, got pretty heavily into the drug scene. I discovered I was pregnant and things went downhill from there.

The only choice I felt I had was to pack up, close out the bank account before he totally emptied it and head back home to stay with my parents. They were really great about it all. They encouraged me to finish my last semester of college and stay with them until I found the right thing. I started working part-time as a receptionist at the field office of a Senator Dad knew quite well. I liked the guy and his positions; I loved the staff and was able to write two papers on media issues under consideration for his communications director in D.C.

By the time I walked across the stage at graduation, I knew I would be OK. Three hours later, my water broke. And from the beginning, Megan was a wonderful baby. When she was only two months old, the Senator asked me to brief the Washington staff on Gen Xers. A year later, we moved to D.C. where we found a walk-down apartment in an old brownstone just a few blocks from the Hill.

There was a Catholic church in the neighborhood, but I never went or took Megan. Except for getting Megan baptized in Mom and Dad's church, I never went to church at all. Father Joe's advice to go back to Mr. Blues and the Church's general stance on divorce didn't sit well.

Meggie and I have managed well on our own. We have such a very special bond. I can already see that it is going to be difficult when she goes off to college. In fact, I chose this trip to give us some quality together time, knowing that later Megan will be off on her own journey. It's working out well . . . time away from Megan always texting friends and from both of us running from event to event, squeezing in a slice and a Coke, rather than dinner together.

I recently passed up a promotion to press secretary so I could continue to have flexibility and time to be with Megan. Maybe in a few years, I'll welcome such responsibility or, who knows, maybe I'll drop out and become a singer again. You never know. Hearing these soulful Celtic tunes and listening to Lily on the harp stirs me, that's for sure.

The idea to come to Ireland had been Megan's. We were curled up on the sofa watching *The Secrets of Roan Inish*.

It is such a captivating and eerie flick. We both fell in love with the West Coast of Ireland. So often it's hard for parents and teens to find common ground. I'm so grateful Megan is so bright and curious and open and interested in everything. My heart goes out to Kevin, with Jackson sulking at the back of the bus.

I read an article once about children coming into the world who are really old souls, here to help us with our evolution in consciousness. Sometimes I see Megan in that light. If truth be told, I have an extraordinary daughter.

Millennials and NetXers, the new focus of my senatorial communications assignments, are a new breed. They really get systems thinking and technology and are pushing us all to look at the intersection of worlds and to see constructs we older folks have bifurcated or put into boxes and specialties. Chaos theory, fractals, sacred geometry, quantum theory all are in their repertoire.

Megan has started researching the ancient mysteries online and keeping a list of books people have recommended. She is always ready to talk and listen to adults that engage with her on a serious level and don't talk down to her.

What a wonderful way for us to explore these questions of religion, spirituality, and meaning together. I am so grateful this is all happening, and we haven't even gotten to the west coast and the roans, yet!

The other thing I bought at the gift shop was a card with a wonderful Irish Prayer.

As the rain hides the stars,
As the Autumn mist hides the hills,
As the clouds veil the blue of the sky,
So the dark happenings of my lot hide the
shining of thy face from me.

Yet if I may hold Thy hand in the darkness,
It is enough...Since I know
That though I may stumble in my going,
Thou dost not fall.

I think I'll give it to Mary Helena. But first, I'll copy it into my journal.

Timothy announces we are approaching County Meath and the Boyne Valley. He invites us to listen to the Celtic Woman welcome us to the Boyne with:

Red is the rose that in yonder garden grows
Fair is the lily of the valley
Clear is the water that flows from the Boyne

I always feel disloyal to the Irish when *Loch Lommond* comes to mind. But after today, the tune will remind me of Ireland, for sure.

When the song is over, Dorrie gets back on the microphone to tell us a little bit about the Ancient Kingdoms of Ireland. "Although Ireland is now officially divided into counties, people still refer to the provincial names of these kingdoms.

"Connacht is to the west, where we will go the last few days of the trip. It is known as the territory of Queen Maeve and the land of Druids and magicians. Ulster, which is now Northern Ireland and part of the United Kingdom was known for its fierce warriors. Then there is Leinster to the east, where we will be going tomorrow. They say it's known for prosperity, nobility, and hospitality. Munster is to the south, known for grand fairs and for its harpers, horsemen, and the arts. The Fifth kingdom, called Meath, was rather like Washington, D.C., in that it was a small area, and yet the seat of power and government. It contained Tara, the Court of the High King. As you will see when we visit, all roads led to Tara and its processional entryways are magnificently laid out.

"You also may have noticed a sign to Kells, the little village where the monastery that gave its name to the *Book of Kells* is located. You have heard all about the monks working in scriptoriums to produce those magnificent Celtic manuscripts with beautiful calligraphy and illuminations or decorative illustrations. Well, the most famous and probably the most beautiful is the *Book of Kells*. There is a copy in Kells, but we will be seeing the one in Dublin instead. It's displayed beautifully in a lovely old library that you won't want to miss.

"Do you see we are near the road to Drogheda? Megan, can you tell us why that name sounds familiar?"

"Um . . . I got it! It's the homestead in *The Thorn Birds*."

"Good job, Megan! This Irish Drogheda was the commercial center of medieval Ireland.

"This area is also famous for the Bend of the River Boyne, *Brú na Bóinne*, which we are very near. This is the spiritual center of Ireland and where we will find Newgrange, Knowth, and Dowth. There is also an ancient path connecting Tara to Newgrange. Many of the most legendary stories of Ireland happened in this area.

"You may have heard Nathan ask Gordie if we could visit the site of the most famous well and sacred site in all Ireland, the Well of Segais. If you don't know about the sacred well and the salmon, get ready. Nathan has been reading about it in his cards and books so we asked him to tell us the story tonight as part of our program.

"Unfortunately, the well's location has been described differently by so many and the river has shifted so often over the years that no one knows for certain where the well is or was. It also was sometimes called Connla's Well and we looked for that also. Sorry, Nathan, we did not find your well, but we found a poem by George William Russell about it.

The Nuts of Knowledge
And when the sun sets dimmed in eve and
purple fills the air,
I think the sacred Hazel Tree is dropping
berries there
From starry fruitage waved aloft where
Connla's Well o'erflows;
For sure, the enchanted waters pour through
every wind that blows.

"And, would you believe? Here we are."

Timothy turns into the lane leading up to the conference center, our home for the next four nights.

The Center is a rambling old stone mansion to which solariums, terraces, and skylights were tastefully added to give it a light, open feel. Combined with the beautiful formal gardens and well-kept grounds, it has early twentieth century charm. Gordie shows us the dining room and tells us we will be sharing the facilities with members of the order and another tour group. We are free to use the parlors, the honor bar, the piano, and the library.

Dorrie cautions that some of the nuns and visitors might be on silent retreat and to watch for signs indicating reserved sections in the dining room.

A few of the rooms are on the third floor and there is no elevator, so Gordie sorts out assignments.

The Center's director says there is a Road Scholar (formerly called ElderHostel) group staying tonight that arranged for a local dance instructor and his students to perform. We're invited to attend the program.

After getting things secured in our rooms and freshening up a bit, people meet in the dining room. The food's not as elegant as at the lodge, but it is good, hearty, and plentiful. The salad, which consists of an orange square of Jello with carrots in it and a green square with pineapple, reminds Megan of my mother's fare. The meat eaters have beef stew and we vegetarians have a stew with mushrooms and tofu replacing the meat. It looks a little grey, but tastes fine. There are homemade scones with the stew and then more scones with jam and butter.

At dinner, talk turns to tomorrow's trip to Dublin. "Does anyone want to go to the General Post Office tomorrow when we have free time in Dublin?" Kevin asks.

"Why there?" John wants to know.

"It's the site of the Easter Rebellion," Penny jumps in enthusiastically.

"It's akin to going to the site of the Boston Massacre, isn't it?" suggests Rob.

"Is that like in the Liam Neeson movie about Michael Collins?"

"Leave it to you, Megan to know your movies," Kevin chuckles. "Now do you also know the Yeats poem?

Was it for this the wild geese spread
The grey wing upon every tide;
For this that all that blood was shed,
For this Edward Fitzgerald died,
And Robert Emmet and Wolfe Tone,
All that delirium of the brave?
Romantic Ireland's dead and gone,
It's with O'Leary in the grave.

"Wondering how I know it by heart, aren't you? It was the subject of my senior thesis in college."

"Kevin, we know you come at this from literature, but, Penny, are you an IRA rebel inside that quiet exterior or are you a history buff?" asks John.

"I took a survey course on the History of Ireland—a Cambridge Adult Education class—many, many years ago. I was looking to meet an interesting, educated Harvard grad as much as also wanting to get a better handle on the origin of 'The Troubles.' My grandfather who immigrated to Canada from Northern Ireland always referred to the Catholic-Protestant, North-South struggles as 'The Troubles.' Boston pubs like the Plough and the Stars ennobled the IRA in the 1970's when I frequented them as a Boston University student. I had mixed feelings about it all and wanted to know more. My grandfather would not have been pleased with the Irish-American bar crowd or me for frequenting such places. So the course taught me about the rebels and how folks like O'Connell, Parnell, and Collins fit together."

"Were they part of the Easter Rebellion?" Megan wants to know.

"Collins was. It was in 1916. The other two were earlier leaders," Penny explains.

"Is that the same as Bloody Sunday?"

"No, Bloody Sunday was actually two years later. Collins orchestrated a retaliation strike, simultaneously assassinating British Secret Service officers stationed throughout Dublin to keep control after the Rebellion."

"In the Michael Collins movie, someone was jailed in England. But, I didn't understand a lot of the story," remarks Megan.

"Michael Collins and Éamon de Valera led groups that believed in different strategies and tactics regarding independence from Britain. You need a storyboard to keep track," Penny explains.

"All I know about Irish history is that Éamon de Valera was born in the U.S. and had a Latino father," Rob pipes in. "And by the way, Penny, I frequented the very same pub in Boston. Think we were ever there at the same time?"

"Wasn't Parnell Protestant?" Jackson jumps in, to my surprise.

"Right, I've never understood all that. I thought this was civil war between Catholics and Protestants?" I admit.

"Parnell actually stood for Home Rule, and you are right he was a member of the Anglo-Irish gentry. England liked to think of Ireland as a bunch of unruly, Catholic peasants. Made it easier to subjugate them and use their resources to maintain its empire. But, in reality, there was a tapestry of differences in class, religion, and identity to the land that played out over the centuries of English rule.

"Parnell lost favor over the issue of compromise. More radical elements said his willingness to compromise was because he really wasn't Irish—that he was Protestant, gentry, and had cultural roots tied to Britain. Then he got involved with a married woman, Katherine O' Shea, as the song says, and his enemies used that to destroy him along with the Catholic villagers who had trusted his leadership." Penny shares all this with continued enthusiasm.

"To me, these folks all look alike; how can there be such a deep hatred among some, when they are all Christian and all Caucasian?" I comment.

"Good question. If you know or have noticed, much of the violence in Northern Ireland peaks in July. July 12th is the day of the traditional Orangemen's Parade in Northern Ireland. Good King Billy, or William of Orange, came into Londonderry as part of his plan to take back the British Crown for the Protestants. Celebrating his invasion is akin to Confederate flags waving at a civil rights day event in Washington.

"This fight over control of the English Crown often was played out in both Scotland and Ireland, but more so in Ireland. It was, after all, a separate island and easier to demonize and victimize the 'savages.' A lot like what happened in the colonial Americas, both how the British treated the settlers and how the settlers treated the First Nations Peoples.

"Protestants from Scotland, solid Presbyterians like my grandfather's ancestors, were given incentives to come to Ireland, especially the area around Belfast in Northern Ireland. The idea was to stabilize the political situation and keep the Irish from wanting independence. Belfast became an industrial and shipbuilding center and remains the seat of British rule in Northern Ireland. If you want a good read on this whole part of Ireland, try Leon Uris's *Trinity*. It is all about this issue and the lives of nineteenth and twentieth century Northern Irish Protestants and Catholics, alike."

Dessert arrives at the table; a sponge, the Irish name for white cake, with chocolate frosting. We dig in, leaving The Troubles for another day.

"Now, if you all are finished with your dinner, I would personally like to invite you to the parlor. I have a wee surprise for you before the evening's actual program commences." Timothy is grinning and teasing us as we follow.

"When I last went for petrol, a wee leprechaun whispered in me ear that you were in need of a drop of ambrosia. 'Tis a drink of the gods, from the Other Kingdom altogether. Mead is a honey wine known to be the world's first alcoholic beverage and 'tis just as good today as 'twas in the days of the Druids and bards.

"So I stopped at the chemist to pick up some plastic medicine cups for sipping, this way the young people and non-drinkers can enjoy a wee sip. The heartier drinkers are then welcome to finish it off after the dancing program.

"You will be tastin' some apricot in this one; the bee hive was placed amid a grove of apricot trees to make the honey for this variation, sometimes spices and other fruits are used. The word honeymoon is believed to have come from its centrality in medieval nuptials. *Sláinte!"*

Dorrie makes a lovely segue as always, "What a great setting for a bard to tell a story. Thank you so much, Timothy." The group claps and cheers . . . then Dorrie continues. "As you may have noticed, our own Nathan has been reading up on Druid tradition in his cards and books and sticks. We have asked him tonight to tell the story of the Well of Segais. Are you ready, Nathan?"

"Aye, I am", says Nathan in his best imitation of an Irish brogue, which, thankfully, he does not try to use further in his presentation.

"As we all are discovering, most Irish stories have a number of versions. The story of the Well of Segais that I will tell tonight is about the time when Finn MacCool–that's the English version of his name, I can't pronounce the Gaelic one, *Fionn mac Cumhaill*–was a boy and how he came to have the wisdom of the salmon.

"You see, there were nine hazelnut trees growing around the sacred pool of water created by the well. Nine is a magic number and hazel wood is the ninth tree of the ogham. These were the trees of wisdom. They say the purplish nuts dropped into the pool and the shells came off, leaving 'kernels of wisdom' for the salmon to eat.

"Some say there was also a beautiful fountain created by the well as the water surfaced. As the nuts dropped into the pool, the salmon ate the nuts and grew wiser and wiser. Now the salmon is the oldest of animals so he has accumulated the most wisdom.

"One day a boy seeking to learn poetry finds a giant, who is also a poet, by the banks of the Boyne. The giant had been seeking the salmon for seven years. Now he has found and caught it and is going to cook it. He allows the boy to stir the cauldron but makes the boy promise not to touch or eat the flesh of the salmon. It is for the giant only to eat.

"But while stirring the pot, the juice of the salmon splashes out onto the boy. The boy licks his thumb to soothe the burning feeling. As he does so, he unintentionally breaks the rule. And, by tasting the salmon, he is the one who gets the wisdom. The giant is really mad. But he is also smart. He accepts that it was meant to be. He names the boy Finn, meaning the Fair One. And so it was that from that day forward, Finn could put his thumb in his mouth and foresee the future.

"The rest is a story for another day, as they say."

We all cheer, clap, and heap compliments on him. His storytelling, his poise, and his research were all great. Seeing this kid and thinking of Megan and her friends gives me hope in the coming generation, something I need given how negative Congress is these days.

Bards and Druids and storytelling would likely also stir up a great discussion among us, but the dancers have arrived and the Road Scholar group is waiting for us.

We quickly head back to the dining hall where chairs have been arranged to create a mini-stage.

"Céad míle fáilte or one hundred thousand welcomes," begins the dance coordinator/instructor. "Me name is Liam Mulligan and the young dancers and I are so pleased to have the opportunity to be with you tonight. Traditional Irish dance has had a grand resurgence in Ireland since *Riverdance* and the brilliant reception you Americans have given our dancers. We thank you for that. You will see the renewed interest reflected here tonight.

"While the monks who held primacy over the history of early Irish culture seldom made mention of dance, you will not want to assume that we spirited Celts did not frolic with the fairies and dance the night away from the beginnings of time. Not all of history is writ.

"I believe we danced and danced and then danced some more.

"There are three major categories of Celtic dance:

Step dancing, which you will see tonight. We will do both the Hardshoe which produces the additional treat of sound—like clogging mixed with softshoe which is more like modern dance and ballet.

Set dancing is usually a couples' dance with four couples making up a square and including rings where men go one way around the circle and women the other. A group of our older lads and lasses will demonstrate that, as well.

Céilí dancing or dancing at local parties is the dance of the Irish reel, jig, and polka. We will not be doing that, but 'tis up to you and the nuns what you all do after I have taken the young ones home to bed. Let the dance begin."

The costumes are intricate in design and extremely colorful, with the boys in waistcoats and the girls in dresses of brocade, velvet, and other fancy fabrics. They dance to recorded music with amazing precision and energy. They hold their spines and upper bodies rigid as they do some really fancy footwork with speed, and still the precision is there. They are so alive.

I want to start dancing with them. I want to sign Megan and me up for lessons. I am juiced by the whole thing. Dance, one more facet of the Celtic spirit, embodied with lightness, beauty and joy. What a trip.

DAY FIVE

DUBLIN
Saint Patrick's Cathedral
Book of Kells
Abbey Theater

Today is our day to visit Dublin.
We start at Saint Patrick's Cathedral. The bus will then take us to Centre City Dublin where we will enter Trinity College to see The Book of Kells. The remainder of the day is yours to choose among the many sights of Dublin: the museums, shopping on Grafton Street, the Poet's Walk, Deer Park, Guinness Brewery, the General Post Office, St. Stephen's Green. We will then meet at the Abbey Theatre for its evening production before returning to The Bend of the Boyne.

MARY HELENA

The drive to Dublin is mostly highway. Thank God, we are going to a city. If I see one more sheep and hear everyone's "oohs and ahs" about how cute they are, I might scream. I thought this was going to be a religious trip, but it's a pagan trip with a gratuitous peppering of Catholic places just to look balanced. My girls should have known better than to send me off with a bunch of pseudo-sophisticated atheists and pagans. They question and critique everything and believe in nothing. Hmmpf.

I just wish I were home. My leg and ankle are killing me. I'm afraid of phlebitis setting in. My circulation isn't good to begin with, my cholesterol is probably higher than a kite with all this rich food, and the long plane ride wasn't good for me. I pray, Jesus, just get me home okay.

There probably won't be decent parking and even more walking today. But no one cares about me. That roommate I had was off to the pub every night, coming in at all hours. At least I have a single room, now. We are staying with a wonderful order of nuns. No pub around, either.

I told Gordie I was not paying extra for the single and that he better see to it that I had some transportation today. The only one who watches out for me is the sweet senator's assistant who shares my confirmation name, but she's always busy with her daughter. As for the rest of them, they just use all the right buzz words like healing, spirituality, and transformation. What happened to putting words into action? What do they think they are going to transform? That's what I'd like to know.

Gordie gave us an overview of logistics for the day; we're starting at St. Patrick's and Trinity College, then we have free time until we all meet at the Abbey Theatre marquee at 8 p.m. He had more maps and brochures about the city and a number of folks made plans over breakfast or already knew what they wanted to do.

I want to know what I am supposed to do with myself all day when it is so difficult to walk. The best I get is that I might want to take a book and stay at the famous Bewley's coffee shop in between events or take a bus tour. As if I want to pay extra to get back on a bus. Hmmpf. Gordie did give me the money to get a taxi from Trinity or Bewley's to the theatre. Big deal.

Dorrie's at the mike again. That girl can talk.

"Someone asked about the term, Celtic Revival, in the Abbey brochure. As you will see firsthand today, Dublin has been strongly influenced by the English and English culture. The Celtic Revival was an effort in the first two decades of the twentieth century to strengthen and lift up Irish culture. It really was as much about identity as a people as it was about politics, borders, and governance.

"The Gaelic language was dying out, and when a language goes, the culture often follows. When we go back to the West of Ireland to areas where Irish is used regularly (*Gaeltacht*), you will see how the spirit and culture of the land is strongest. The days of the Irish language being forbidden, if not just ignored, in the schools, on public signs, etc, might have continued if not for the efforts of the Revivalists. Yeats and Lady Gregory had a lot to do with this. You will hear more about that when we are in Sligo. But, here, their influence in founding the National Irish Theater at the Abbey with plays offered in Irish is especially important. Literary works, as well as folklore, music, and dance from Old Ireland were reintroduced and 'given spin' as we would say today.

"To an American's understanding of two Irelands (the free Catholic South versus the Protestant-North which was part of Britain), it might be a surprise that most of the authors and playwrights, with the exception of James Joyce, were Protestant. It points out that Irish identity transcends religion as well as governance.

"And here we are approaching St. Patrick's. Again, you may be surprised that it is not a Catholic cathedral as is St. Patrick's in New York. But the guide will tell you more."

What? Not Catholic? Even though Timothy gets us a parking place along the square, it's a long walk up to the cathedral. But it's worth it. St. Patrick's Cathedral, Dublin, Ireland. Even if it's not Catholic, it is named for the saint and he is without doubt Catholic. No one can argue that. Who would have thought I would ever cross its steps? There's one for the record books. I have Trish take my picture on the threshold.

There is only one guide inside. A number of folks are down front on kneelers, but it's not a service. Trish recognizes the statue of Swift and tells me it makes her think of Capitol Hill. Lots of busts of men no longer known to the average person. She says she liked to think about that when she had to deal with some puffed up politician. She is so right, I've never even heard of Jonathan Swift. And he has nothing to do with St. Patrick. Leave it to the English.

It's a beautiful cathedral. Not as grand as St. Pat's in New York City. Others say it doesn't compare to Westminster in London or Chartres or Notre Dame in France, either. But then, it is not about the building, it is about the religion. Unfortunately, it misses the mark here, too, since it is an Anglican Church of Ireland, not the Catholic Church at all. Nonetheless, it is the house of St. Patrick, the Patron Saint of Ireland. Praise Be.

So when that sullen teenager starts in with his sarcastic mouth, I give it to him, "This is a church, you know, dedicated to St. Patrick. Watch your mouth. While it might not be Catholic, it certainly is a cathedral and a holy place of the blessed Saint. Not a museum. You could at least be respectful."

Jackson just glares at me, bold, undisciplined kid that he is.

Then, Rob, the minister of those ultra-liberals, starts to butt in and I won't stand for it. "And Rob, you don't have to come in to mediate. Young Mr. Attitude here is old enough to learn respect. And you may be a minister, but you are not MY minister, so just stay out of it. It's about time someone set this boy straight."

I probably should have kept my mouth shut, but everyone is getting on my nerves. The more lovey-dovey they all are with this sweetness and light attitude, the more cantankerous I feel. Thank God, before long, Dorrie rounds everyone up and we head out.

As Timothy navigates through traffic that makes Kenmore Square look tame, one of the men in the back starts singing *In Dublin's Fair City*, and all join in, at least on the parts they know like *Sweet Molly Malone* and *cockles and mussels, alive, alive, oh.* It certainly brings back fond childhood memories. Now this is more like the kind of trip I imagined.

Soon we're in Centre City, the literary, cultural, theatrical center of Ireland. Real commercial, too. I'm surprised at all the heavy traffic, big trucks, smog, and shipping activity as we drive right along the River Liffey from one quay to the next. I thought Boston traffic was bad.

I guess I expected Dublin to be more like Boston, but it looks more like the London of old movies and television. I should have realized it would. After all, the English have been messing with it for years and years. Timothy identifies important buildings as we pass: Parliament House, now the Bank of Ireland, and the Corinthian front of Trinity College. I can't keep track. But it sure seems like the English were trying to build another British city.

What I want to see are the Irish Georgian homes along St. Stephen's Green that are always in all the pictures. When I told Timothy how much I would like to see them, but knew I wouldn't be able to walk that far, he said he would swing the bus past there. So here we go. The bus turns onto O'Connell Street.

Then we come upon the stately statue of O'Connell himself. The O'Connell Bridge is filled with street vendors and according to my daughter, features an *Irish Times* web cam. I wave to our friends and family back home as we slowly travel through the area. Gordie points the way to Bewley's Oriental, the famous café. He suggests it's a great place for people to meet up.

Timothy drives right by Trinity Gate saying "the lady has a request to see St. Stephen's Green so we'll be goin' just a bit further and around." He takes us right around the square. It is so beautiful, the row houses with their colorful and vividly painted front doors. I've read three or four novels that involve the Green and this is exactly how I pictured it. It's a bit hoity-toity for Ireland but right just the same, kind of like Beacon Hill is upper crust Old Boston.

We end up at a side entrance to Trinity because of traffic patterns, but it isn't much of a walk. Dorrie seems to know her way around the campus.

The *Book of Kells* is the only scheduled stop within Trinity. Dorrie recommends that we walk around the campus, linger in the library, or head to the National Museum. But, I don't want to. It is amazingly quiet and spacious and with lovely grounds, a little urban oasis. Gordie stops us at an old oak tree. God love him, I think he did it so I could catch up to the group, but he makes a quiz game of it. He asks if anyone knows who founded Trinity. Of course, it is a trick question. Sure enough, he stumps us and surprises everyone by telling us it was founded by Queen Elizabeth I. He adds it also was the first university to admit women in all of Europe. But I hear Catholics weren't admitted until the mid-fifties. Doesn't seem right, but, oh well.

Dorrie stops us one more time in front of some modern sculpture that looks like a planet or UFO or some such nonsense. I guess these modern intrusions are to be expected, but I'd rather have the historic look. There's quite a line in front of the library. Once inside though, it is so beautiful, I don't even mind waiting.

"Like Hogwarts!" Nathan says to Megan, half teasing her for always having an example from movies or television. There the two of them go again, talking about that silly Harry Potter movie. My grandkids do the same thing.

But, the room is amazing. The extraordinary wooden concave high ceiling looks like the inside of a barrel and the incredibly high and beautiful stacks are magnificent. I hear the boy add, "I could stay here forever." I wouldn't go that far, but it is nice.

I notice this beautiful wooden harp, supposed to be the oldest in Ireland. It is like the one used on coins and such as the country's logo. Lily looks at it with her eyes half-closed as if she is imagining playing it. I think I hear harp music myself.

The library has other books, completed by the monks with similar calligraphy and illustration, but none as well–known as the *Book of Kells*. Scriptures start, "And in the

Beginning was the Word, and the Word was God." The monks, then, began the first letter of the first word of each chapter of the *Four Gospels* with beautiful flourish and color as well as intricate illustrations. The pages are magnificent today, even though we see color and multimedia things all the time. Think how incredible and sacred they must have seemed to people in the Dark Ages. I never paid much attention to the ins and outs of the Bible, but it was the Church that kept it alive and saw to it that these beautiful renditions were made and saved. God bless them.

The display offers a view of only one page of the illustrated manuscript at a time, obviously under special protective glass. You wait in line, single file, and walk through single file to see it. They change the page daily. It really is impressive to think this was hand done by monks on primitive stools and tables by candlelight and in the damp and cold of the drafty monastery scriptorium.

Tomorrow we visit Glendalough and hear more about St. Columba, the beloved monk and religious leader who was excommunicated and went to Iona, Scotland. I hadn't realized he was the one involved with the *Book of Kells*. My cousins' church is named for him, but I never paid him much attention. As I kid, I used to say St. Columbus and think the church was named for Christopher Columbus. No one bothered to correct me. It wasn't until I saw a printed wedding invitation that I realized the real name of the church. *The Book of Kells* brochure says a lot of the work was done in Scotland as well as Ireland. It says, though, that to protect the works from coastal raiding parties, they were brought to the monastery at Kells and somehow got named for it.

Everyone files through. Those with a plan take off as they come out of the library. Those not yet sure of their plans walk together toward the gate on O'Connell Street that we had passed en route to St. Stephen's Green.

Kevin gives Jackson permission to spend the day with Megan, as long as they restrict themselves to looking around Grafton Street, going only as far south as the Green and north to include the James Joyce statue. He goes on to tell them also to stay between the Ha' Penny Bridge and O'Connell Bridge (As if the kid would obey, but it was none of my business.) Trish agrees, but says she wants Megan to check in with her mid-day.

I am getting impatient with all the talk and round-in-a-circle planning. I tell people I am headed to Bewley's.

Trish is part of the group who wants to follow the poets' pub crawl, even though it is daytime. They are going to have a progressive lunch, so to speak, as they visit the old haunts of the literary masters. She and Megan agree to meet at the Molly Malone statue at 3 p.m. She asks me if I will be okay. What choice do I have? But I reply I will read my book and have a cup of Irish tea.

Jake plans to lead a small group to some of the buildings of historical and architectural significance like the 1796 Four Courts, the Custom House, etc., and they are going to squeeze in a tour at Guinness Brewery.

Some of the women want to shop Grafton Street. John wants to explore the Temple Bar district. All agree to meet at Bewley's before dinner, so I start off.

Bewley's Oriental is truly Irish—I don't know where the Oriental part comes in though. The leaded glass, wood paneling and classic turn-of-the-century light fixtures are exquisite. Dorrie said it reminds her of the old Schraff's in New York City. It reminds me of the old Bailey's in Boston or the old Brigham's on Brattle Street in Cambridge.

It is a three-story, mid-nineteenth century building. You can almost hear the steamers and espresso machines hiss from the doorway. The wonderful antique fixtures and all the accoutrements for a "proper tea" seem right out of Agatha Christie's Orient Express. Maybe that's the Oriental part. Then, with the coffee grinder and aroma of coffee beans, it also is the Starbuck's of an early time.

People are looking out from the second floor window when I enter. I don't want to climb the stairs, so instead I find a cozy corner on the first floor where I still can see everyone enter and leave. I start to enjoy the hustle and bustle as I watch everyday Dubliners come and go.

I figure some of the pub crawlers would be back for a good strong cup of coffee and so will the folks who went off to Guinness. Meantime, I'll read and people-watch.

On my walk here, I saw the boy and girl handing money over to a scruffy looking kid about their own age. They had wasted no time in getting over to the vendors. They looked pretty suspicious, probably buying drugs. I'm not surprised about the boy, but I am disappointed in the girl. I'll have to tell Trish and Kevin.

Trish will be terribly upset, even though I'm sure it's the boy's doing. Kevin seems such a fine man, but so sad and put upon. I hate to add to his worries, remembering what it was to bring up teenagers as a single parent. But, I would want to know. They both need to know. And he needs to give the kid a good swat. But, then again, what do you do when a boy gets that big? Thank God, I had all girls. Well, I hate to be a busybody, but I must tell whichever parent I see first. It really is my duty.

Anyway, I settle into reading after getting a hot cup of tea. It's kind of fun watching the Irish women fill the steam table for the mid-day meal. I'll give a look, but I'll probably want to move to the section with wait staff later so I don't have to carry a tray. For now, I just get a couple of scones from the bakery.

Imagine. I'm sitting here in Dublin, reading my Maeve Binchy novel, right here in Dublin. I have read *Circle of Friends* and something about under the copper beech tree—which reminds me, I want to see one of those trees and I want to ask little Nathan to look up its meaning in his ogham book. Then, for awhile it seemed all of the Binchy books I read were the same: young people leave their small country villages and head off to Dublin, girl gets pregnant, and heads home. Then Binchy came out with these Dublin-based ones. This one, *Quentins* is great.

I am just noticing that my tea is cold when in walks Peg. I hope she isn't going to go on about how our childhoods were alike, growing up with the drink. Supposedly, she was off checking out that historic Unitarian Church on St. Stephen's

Green she had bragged about. But here she is standing in front of me, looking all sorts of nervous, and refusing to sit down.

"Mary Helena, I have a note here I would like you to give Rob as soon as he arrives back here this afternoon. I hope you don't mind?"

"What on earth for? What do you mean give a note to your husband? You will be seeing him in just a few hours."

"Please . . . please, just do it." Peg says with her hand shaking. Her eyes plead, "Don't ask; don't."

"Well, I never," is all I say, but you can be sure I am thinking a lot more. They certainly are a strange couple, Co-ministers? What kind of thing is that? And they don't seem to have a very strong faith, with all their critiquing and questioning religion. But the poor thing does looks frazzled so I bite my tongue.

"Thank you. It means a lot to me," she says and she goes out the door before I can say another word.

Hmmpf. It's easy enough to do, but what in the world is she up to? The note is in an envelope like a birthday card and is sealed. If it were a birthday card, there would have been no reason to come in here to leave it. I try to go through all the Hallmark card themes and other possible explanations. None fit. So, finally, I just tuck it in my book and go back to reading.

John comes in just as I am going to have my mid-day meal. "Good," I say. "Will you hold the table until I get some food? This way I won't have to move to the area where they serve you and where I'd have to tip." Gentleman that he is, he offers to get my plate for me, but I want to look over the choices myself. Then he can come carry the tray over for me.

We have a nice chat as he gobbles down some of their delicious looking tarts with their rich, dark coffee. I have creamed cod on toast and a side order of champ. My grandmother used to make it when I was a girl. I still have one of the little grooved-top wooden boxes the salted cod came in. I wondered what people in Bewley's thought of this 60ish white woman sitting with this handsome 30-something African-American? But these are modern times and this is a cosmopolitan city. I just enjoy the company. We talk about a lot of things, including Melanie's attempts to get pregnant. I tell him about Croagh Patrick and the pilgrimages women take there in supplication when they want to get pregnant. All of a sudden, he says he has to leave. He mumbles that he forgot to do something and he is off.

Men. I have no idea what is going on with him. So with a shrug, I go back to Maeve Binchy for the remainder of the afternoon. *Quentins* is about present day Dublin and trendy, urban folks. It's fun to imagine that some of the folks coming in and out of Bewley's are characters in the book who work at or frequent Quentins restaurant. I wonder, is there really a Quentins? Probably not.

At one point, I stop to do some journaling and begin glancing through Dorrie's handouts. At my age, I don't see myself transforming anything about my life so what's the point in a lot of reflection and introspection. Instead, I give a prayer to St. Patrick and to St. Brigid for my health and go back to my story. If the Mary-of-the-Gael wants me to change, she will change me. After all, I have taken her other Irish name.

Eventually, people stroll in one at a time and in the little groups that had ventured off together. People start talking about dinner options. Trish tells me she thinks it is too far for me to walk to the Abbey. She suggests some places for dinner that are near the Abbey. That way I will only need one cab. Sounds good to me. We wait for the men who went to the brewery before deciding which one.

It is then that I tell her about seeing Megan and Jackson on the street buying drugs. Megan is standing right there, but there is no choice but to put it out there. Trish is shocked. Megan turns beet red.

"Mom, it's not what it looked like . . .. I swear."

"So what were you doing? And what was the big secret?" Trish asks in a steady but intense tone.

"Mom, you know me. Like, I was not buying drugs. I am not responsible for what Jackson did after I left him at Temple Bar and joined you, but while we were together there were no drugs. I promise." Then in a lower voice, she pleads, "Do we have to discuss this in front of everyone?"

"Yes," is Trish's simple, yet stern, reply.

"We were buying lapel pins," Megan sighs.

I jump in, "You expect us to believe that the clandestine little money exchange I saw was just you two buying souvenir pins? Try again, little lady."

"Actually, they were kinda embarrassing and I didn't want to show them to anyone. I agreed with Jackson that our friends would get a kick out of them but, in front of adults . . . .."

"What are you trying to say, Megan? Get on with it," says an exasperated Trish.

"See the pins are in Gaelic and the guy said one says, 'Shit Happens' and the other says, 'Feckin' Eejit.'"

There is parental silence from the entire group. Then Trish bursts out laughing with explosive relief.

I break in, "Well, then, that explains it. We will just pray that Jackson didn't go on to do something else." Turning to Trish, I add, "I will leave it to you to fill Kevin in on his son's activities."

What we did not know is that an hour after parting from Megan at the Temple Bar, Jackson was hanging out with a questionable group of boys along the quay. Good thing for him that the *Irish Times* webcam was at O' Connell Bridge not Ha' Penny. Later, we discover the little eejit went off in search of the Glasnevin Cemetery featured in *Ulysses*. He'll have to keep one of those pins for himself. But I say no more.

SIDE TRIPS

THREE OF OUR MEN
AT THE STAG OF SEVEN TINES

"Thanks, guys, for stopping here with me. You know my fascination with Irish pubs and with a name like Stag of the Seven Tines, I just gotta stop."

"We get it. What could be more Celtic, eh?" Peter interrupts. "Not that we need more beer after the Guinness tour, but it will be fun. Let's go in."

"This is too much," Jake says, taking in the old oak bar, all the colorful bottles reflected in the mirror, and a dart board on the wall. "I have a jigsaw puzzle at home that has a picture just like this. Talk about atmosphere."

"Oh, look! We even have the Green Man staring back at us. Rob, you do know how to pick them, eh?" comments Peter.

"This is exactly what I pictured. Wow. Drinks on me, guys. Stouts?" Rob asks as he summons the bartender.

"We're only missing the white hind," quips Peter.

"You're right. We have found us a totally manly-man place," laughs Rob.

"It's nice to be off on our own, isn't it? I'm feeling up to my eyeballs in female hormones, spirituality, and goddess stuff. I'm a businessman. This is my world," Jake says, gesturing out to the street. "City, commerce, hustle-bustle, concrete facts, and commodities."

"To Jake, to commerce, and to the company of good men," offers Peter as they lift their glasses and chuckle.

They joke and kid around a bit more and then Peter gets more serious. "Did anyone notice the display in that book store we just passed? That guy, Korten, you know, who wrote *The Great Turning*, is coming to town. I wish it were tonight; I would rather hear him than go to this play Dorrie has planned. He's become quite the international spokesperson for environmental and economic change. You Yanks have a good man, there. He's very progressive, very Canadian in his thinking."

"I admit to it, you Canadians are a lot more liberal. But who's this guy? How come I've never heard of him. Rob, have you?" asks Jake.

"Yeah, the social justice folks in my congregation are really into him." Rob replies. "I've heard him speak a couple of times, too. But keep talking, Peter. I would love to hear what you think of him."

"OK, well to fill you in Jake, Korten does a take on this ancient goddess culture and the way things were done before empire-building and says we need to return to a respect for the earth, sustainability, and all that," Peter explains.

"So, he trashes capitalism, then?" asks Jake.

"Not exactly, but he talks about the assumption of privilege, etc. A precursor to the ninety-nine vs the one percent talk in a way," Rob adds.

"Damn, this mandate for change stuff, can't get away from it, can we?" Jake laments, only half-jokingly.

"So here we are with Korten's call for Earth Community summoning us the way the Summerland must have called Arthur and the Knights of the Round Table. Let's lift our glass once more . . . to noble causes."

After a moment or two, he adds "Now, we best get back to our women."

They arrive at Bewley's as people are trying to decide about dinner.

"Where's Peg?" Rob asks.

"Don't know what got into her, but she came in early this afternoon with this note for me to give you. No explanation, nothing," offers Mary Helena.

"Really? That's odd. Let me see," he says as he takes the note and walks toward the stairs and up to the second floor.

"Does anyone know what that's all about?" asks Mary Helena, demandingly.

Murmurs, but no real response from anyone.

"Let's mind our own business and decide about dinner," Jake suggests.

The group weighs in on options and, as they choose, Rob returns. He simply says "Peg wants some alone time. She won't be joining us. But, don't worry about it. Where are we going for dinner, anyway?"

DORRIE and GORDIE
AT PHOENIX PARK

Dorrie and Gordie decided they might as well do something light and fun since people would be scattering in every direction anyway, so they planned a day at Phoenix Park, the largest city park in Europe. On the way to the bus stop, they stop at the statue of O'Connell. Gordie suggests they pause. "You know," he says to Dorrie, "here stands Daniel O'Connell asking me to take on the struggle for Ireland. Yet, if I go up another few blocks, there stands James Joyce with his quirky stance, saying quite a different thing. The question is, do I take on the struggle within or do I take on the outward struggle for justice? Both men are stalking me, aren't they?"

Dorrie laughs. "And they will keep it up until you get beyond the thought of duality, my love." With that, they take off on a brisk walk to get the bus. They enjoy mixing in with locals, seeing how diverse a city Dublin had become and even reading the ads on the bus walls and shop windows they pass. With fresh eyes, the routines of others always seem exciting.

They stroll through a good bit of the park, picnic, watch the deer, and then stroll the zoological gardens. They eat dinner at an intimate little French café and then get to the Abbey Theatre to arrange tickets and seating for the group.

Dorrie senses something amiss, "I'm concerned, about Jackson and about Mary Helena, too."

"Give it up, Dorrie. Chill. You make too much of things."

"I know you'll keep an eye on and deal with Jackson. And something is coming. That is all I am saying. But, this negative energy from Mary Helena is really throwing me off balance. I don't want it to adversely influence the readings I choose and how I write the rituals."

"Look, you are the first to say that Celtic spirituality is not owned by any one religion but embodies so many different world views. Stay with your principles and stick with your gut."

"But . . ."

"Look, it is not like you brought the Rosary Society from Father David's parish over here. These are people attracted to your vision and your message. You don't lean into all the Druid stuff because Nathan came for Harry Potter. So don't cater to Mary Helena either."

"Expectations about covering more Catholicism in Catholic Ireland is a little different from those of the Wizardly World of Harry Potter."

"Just don't obsess so much."

"How come when you are all caught up in details and such, you are just being thorough, but when I get caught up in something, I am obsessing?"

"Where everyone sleeps is more important and more real. You see that, don't you?"

"Let's just drop it. I don't want to argue. We have so little time off like this and it is so beautiful here."

"I'm not arguing, I simply am saying you should let things go, lighten up. I hate to see you get worked up. Besides, this is supposed to be our time off."

"Okay . . . okay."

TIMOTHY and KATE
OFF SAILING

The traffic, the smog and the noise of Dublin had gotten fierce. Timothy figured he could leave Dublin, go out to Howth to sail with some friends, and drive back in plenty of time to meet the group coming out of the play. Now, he wonders about the time, but he still thinks he can make it. When he presented Gordie with the idea, Gordie was fine with it. Now, he just needs to make good on his promise to be back in time.

On a whim, Timothy had decided to ask Kate to join him. And, lo and behold, she agreed. He called his friends to forewarn them he was bringing a lady with him. So off they go after leaving everyone at Trinity. He puts aside his worry about the time, but keeps mindful of it as well.

The day is glorious, and the little town known for its sail boat races is buzzing with activity. Since it is a weekday, it is easy enough to find the right dock. His banking friend Eamon and wife Maureen had already rigged the *Frolic* and are ready to sail.

The four of them have a grand time. Kate had done just enough sailing to be relaxed but still find it a real treat. They share some good wine and some good stories and then just soak in the sea air and the sound of the gulls. Actually, by the time they return to Dublin, the traffic has quieted down so they are in plenty of time to meet the group. Kate rather wonders if anyone will ask where she has been, but no one asks. Just as well.

THE PLAY AT THE ABBEY

The original Abbey burned down in the early 1950's. Those looking for a historic building are disappointed. All that remains is a display of pictures of the original building. The new theatre is still known as the Irish National Theatre, the first theater in the English-speaking world to be subsidized by the state. Those who come early have a tour of the facilities.

Mary Helena, of course, is none too happy with the walk from the restaurant, but glad of the cab from Bewley's. Rob is distracted. Kevin is even more so, as he waits for Jackson. Megan and Trish are concerned about Jackson, too. John also is quiet and distant. But, everyone else, including Lily, seems to have that Broadway-electric-opening night feel about them.

Dorrie and Gordie wonder to themselves if anyone will miss Kate and Timothy, and are unsettled about both Peg and Jackson. Dorrie wonders if everything is coming unraveled. But, "the show must go on" as Mae West or Kate Smith or somebody once said. They get a refund for Peg's ticket. Gordie goes out to the marquee with two tickets for Kevin, encouraging him to come in and leave Jackson's ticket at the box office, if need be. He truly believes Jackson will show up at the last minute and tells Kevin that. Then, he catches up with

Dorrie and they enter the darkening theatre holding hands, ready to be swept away into another time.

The play is Brian Friel's *Dancing at Lughnasa*. Some of the group have seen it on Broadway or in Toronto, and there has been a movie version, as Megan reminds them. Nonetheless, it is a wonderful choice and the actors are outstanding.

The setting is a rural home in the West of Ireland where three sisters bring up a small boy, the fruit of a short love affair. The bleakness of poor Irish families has already entered the sensibilities of the group. The continued imprint of early Celtic gods and goddesses on the modern Irish culture is also something added to the consciousness of many in the last few days. This story of a twentieth century family getting ready to celebrate the remnant of an ancient rite, named after the Celtic God of the Sun, fits perfectly with the theme of the tour.

More importantly, it is great theatre. Plus the theme is so apropos—talk about paths and journeys and choices we make or avoid making. In this instance, the harvest was bleak for those who had lived "lives of quiet desperation." And yet they danced.

It is powerful and thought-provoking.

DORRIE

The play is riveting, even though I have seen it three times. Seeing it here in Ireland is special. This time I became really focused on these women living their daily lives without male relationships. I can't help but think of Gordie and me. We have had a delightful day. And the trip is going well. But what about our relationship? I promised to let go, but monkey-mind creeps back.

Is testing a relationship ever a good idea? I have asked myself that before. Aren't relationships fragile enough? And why put something under a microscope and dissect it? Love? I make more and more space in my life for Spirit; he has to be actively engaged in doing something every moment. I know I bring him spiritual optimism and lightness—the pure joy and fun we have are as powerful and seductive as the physical chemistry between us. But when all is said and done, does he even believe he deserves more than a few moments of bliss? Or will he retreat into his work?

I've always seen him as driven to help people, to fight for justice, and try to make a difference. He lets himself be defined by his deeds and actions and seems to have no identity beyond his work. He has become impatient with me for wanting more lightness, more open space, and more suspension of time, saying it is unreal and childlike.

But, this week, he has been more laid back. I was beginning to think Ireland was working its magic on him. Then, today, I wanted to get serious for a bit about my work and he chastised me. I don't get it.

GORDIE

It is so much fun to watch her do her thing, her passion is so real, her spiritual depth is astounding. This trip has given me a better appreciation of her as a strong leader. In our relationship, she's the flexible one. I see though, that when she has reason to do so, she can stand firm. And she can focus. Sometimes I don't give her enough credit.

Sometimes I confuse organization and control with strength. She never does, she has the strength of water. In point of fact, all this work she does with the elements, she gets her strength and direction there. I am trying not to get so impatient with that "being" time, as she calls it.

We are good together, but are we good enough? Is there someone out there who would make a better partner? Better wife? And do I want to commit? There are a couple of older guys on the trip who seem very happily married. The idea of having someone in old age sure is appealing, but now?

The main thing is this spiritual development stuff. I feel like I get it more than ever before. But, I also know I will never catch up with her. It makes me feel like the little kid on the block, tagging along with the older neighborhood kids. I am always out of my comfort zone when she is most in hers. Is it just male ego? And even if it is, does it matter? I don't want to be the kind of man who is threatened by his wife's growth. Is that what this is?

I think of my grandfather always saying, "Send me a message, God." He said that all the time. Well, I need a message. I know that not to decide is itself a decision, but I feel paralyzed to move the relationship forward.

ROB

Peg would have loved this play. Although, in the state she is in, it might have been too much. Seeing *Da* in Limerick really threw her, but she would have liked the strength of these women. Steeliness, practicality, and joy. Plus, these Irish women know how to start each day anew, and so does Peg.

I know in my mind that she is safe and will be okay, yet I keep wondering where she went. What will she do? What does she need? I know that it has to do with deep family issues. I know she resents the injunctions of Irish Catholic immigrant culture and the Church for perpetuating ideas and practices that she deems unhealthy. But why couldn't she talk to me? Why did she need to leave?

There must be more to it. Early abuse of her or her sisters by one of the alcoholic uncles, I suspect. But I know enough to wait for her to tell me, not try to guess. Whatever it is, she will now deal with it. That's her message. I trust her ability and determination, I trust our relationship. I can wait.

She will be back . . . soon. I keep repeating these things to myself as I reread the note during intermission.

> My dearest Rob,
>
> I had to get away–lots of stuff from childhood needs processing and I need to do it alone and I need to do it now.
>
> Trust me, love, and do have a good time until I join you on the tour. Not sure when. Just pack me up and tell the others I will be back— don't worry.
>
> Love, Peg
> p.s. I have my credit card.

"Have a good time."

Sure, but easier said than done, dear.

JOHN

Women! Maybe there is a reason the guy in the play takes off—too many women. I would never walk, but I sure do feel like it at this moment. How could she deceive me like this? I truly thought we were giving "the baby thing" a rest. I had been enjoying the trip. Today, I was really feeling relaxed and just staying loose as I wandered around soaking in the sounds and energy of the city. I hung out on my own while the women went shopping on Grafton Street. If I hadn't gone over to Bewley's because I was dying for a good, strong cup of coffee, I still would not know I am being played. These Irish make their tea strong, but not their coffee. Besides, I wanted to indulge in a couple of those strawberry tarts I see in every bakery window and the treacle ones that are like Georgia pecan pie without the pecans.

But, good ol' Mary Helena and her mouth. Talks a blue streak. I was only politely half-listening until she started talking about our fertility problem. Good God, did Melanie talk about it everywhere? To everyone? And this notion of a miracle pilgrimage to some mountain so St. Patrick will bring us a baby? We are not even Catholic. Girl, what are you thinking???

The worst is she never told me. Sounds to me like she knew about the pilgrimage part from the beginning. Mary Helena was talking about the Croagh Patrick listing on the brochure. Damn. I was such a dope. "Let's just get away, dear," Melanie said. Bull.

My heart aches for my wife and I feel sad and inadequate. But this . . . how can I support her with this nonsense about miracles? I know we would make good parents, I am sure of it, and it is time. My dad was old when I was born. He missed all the things a younger dad might have done with his son and he died before I really got to know him. I want to do stuff with my son—or my daughter. A girl would be okay, too.

We tried everything, went to every doctor, spent a fortune. As far as the docs know, there is no scientific reason for us not to have a kid by now. But, the rabbit lives, as they say. I personally think we are just too uptight about it. We schedule sex and then go at it mechanically trying all these old wives tales until it has lost the magic. Of course, when we had the magic, we were hoping against hope not to get pregnant and using two kinds of birth control to make sure there was no baby until we had a house and some money set aside. Damn, go figure.

I was the one who had been adamant that there be no baby until we were financially secure. It had been all my family could do to give me some spending money for college. Loans and the sense of obligation I felt toward my younger brother, who probably wouldn't get scholarships, had weighed on me. Was I wrong to have insisted we wait?

As I walked across the bridge to Bewley's this afternoon, I thought how lucky we were to be away like this, traveling around Europe. I had prayed at that well for us to be happy, happy with whatever came our way, baby, no baby. We need to remember we could continue to have a good life. We can adopt. We can be foster parents. I just need to get Melanie to let go of what is becoming an obsession.

Of course, she is right that it isn't fair. Plus, it's got to be much harder for her working in a school, seeing all these teenagers dropping out because they are pregnant or coming back after summer vacation with big bellies and no plans and no husbands. As assistant principal, she has worked hard to get funding for teen pregnancy programs and provide parenting resources. She sees what is going to happen in seven out of ten cases. None of it is good. She comes home some nights in tears.

As an economic developer, working with primarily high end, tech companies, I don't see kids and families much. It's just when we go to my brother's or Melanie's sisters' that I feel it. The nieces and nephews are so great and so much fun to be around.

That Mary Helena sure knows how to snap one out of a good place. There she was with that shrill voice calling me over . . . So I asked if I could get her something, and she got in line. Then I got myself some tarts and coffee; we chatted, and she complained about all the walking. Yaketty, yak.

Then all of a sudden, she was talking about Melanie and me. How in the world? No matter how many times I try, I can't move beyond it. Her telling ME about Melanie's plans. She told me that she and Mel had a great talk at the Well about St. Brigit and how to pray directly to her for something–or–other. I didn't know the term. Then, she added that I should start praying to St. Patrick, as well. Good God! That was a new one to me. So, I contained myself and calmly asked what she meant. She replied that she was talking about Melanie climbing Croagh Patrick in County Mayo. It is a known fact, she said, that the pilgrimage to Croagh Patrick will bring a child if nothing else will.

Whoa. This whole Croagh Patrick stuff was news to me, but I controlled my emotions, thinking, I will be damned if

I let on to her that Melanie has not clued me in to this. I get angrier and angrier. How long has Mel had this planned? Why didn't she tell me? Has this whole trip been about this pilgrimage? Have I been wearing a dunce cap that everyone can see but me? As soon as I possibly could, I said my goodbyes, and got out of there.

So I walked across and along the Liffey and walked and walked some more.

By the time I came back to meet for dinner, I still had not worked through the anger. I joined Melanie and the others long enough to say I would meet them at the theatre and took off to a bar for a few shots of Jameson Best. Normally, my drink was Scotch and only two, but you know what they say about when you are in somebody's country. It did go down smoothly, more smoothly than Melanie's little plan, that's for sure. Now, I sit through this play about the women and a child they are bringing up with no daddy. How am I supposed to keep from exploding?

KEVIN

Lots of the folks on the tour know I lost my wife to cancer and that I like Yeats, but not much more. I am not intentionally secretive. The occasion to talk much about myself just hasn't come up.

I was so excited to go do all-things-Yeats today, here in Dublin.

As an English major at the University of Delaware in Newark, I was thinking of going on to graduate school, specializing in the literary works of W.B. himself. Then I met Jane. We fell madly in love, as trite as that sounds. We got married right after graduation and got pregnant sooner than the graduate school plan could accommodate. So, I dropped out. I got an administrative job at the Delaware Department of Motor

Vehicles and have been there ever since. Now, I'm a deputy commissioner, known as the policy wonk of the department.

I like keeping a low and non-controversial profile. I seem to know every Democrat in the state and at least half of the Republicans. But, when asked to run for the legislature, I declined. Janie had just gotten the cancer diagnosis. But I probably wouldn't have run anyway. Unlike Joe Biden, our extroverted Vice President, I would rather curl up with a book or attend a poetry reading if I have any extra time. Janie was the social one and the community-organizer of the family.

She died three years ago. I still am totally devastated. Yet, most worrisome is the struggle of relating to KJ, Jackson as he wants to be called now that he thinks he is grown up. Until the last stages of Janie's illness, we had a good relationship. KJ was closer to his mother, but that was okay and understandable at that age. She taught her boy to share his feelings and to deal with them up until the day she died. I actually was surprised when KJ shut down.

I know he blames me for not being able to rescue Janie, for being weak, and giving in to the sorrow of her death. But, what can I do if he won't talk to me? I wish he would engage me–even if in anger. I read all the Iron Man stuff and went to a grief support group, but KJ wanted no part of it. It seems the harder I try, the less KJ wants to be around me.

I thought this trip would be good. Janie always talked about Ireland. We came here on our honeymoon. In fact, KJ was conceived quite by accident in a romantic Ring of Kerry hotel under a down quilt one starry evening. Janie had the most angelic, goddess-like look that night in the thinnest of white lingerie with the moon shining in the window and straight through her gown. There was a sweetness and urgency to our love-making that night that had more intensity than anything I had ever experienced. God I loved that woman. Twin flames, as they say.

If only she were still here, not just for me–although I miss her to the very root of my being—but for the boy; the child we conceived that night, the child of our intimacy, who has always had her vulnerability and deep sensitivity, whose heart has been closed by her loss.

I fear I am losing the boy, as well. I get why he is so despondent. KJ lost a wonderfully nurturing mom, the comic and cheerleader and best friend a boy or a husband could ever want. Why can't I get through to him? I had such high hopes for the trip.

That was my wish at Brigid's Well—that my son finds his way, finds joy again.

I had so looked forward to Dublin, to actually get to visit the National Library and the Yeats Collection. Wow. What an indulgence. Yet, I knew KJ would not want to come with me. I hope I did the right thing trusting him to go off on his own with Megan.

I was distracted at the library and had a hard time focusing. But, I did get pretty fired up at the Old Post Office, the site of the Easter Rebellion. I had done my senior thesis on this poem by Yeats, especially discussing the ambivalence, then futility of war. The line "Romantic Ireland's dead and gone" keeps coming back to me. Maybe it's a message about my own need to let go of the past. There is a certain futility in holding on. I guess that's the message of this play, too.

When I got to Bewley's, KJ was nowhere to be found. Megan explained that they had agreed to split up and she had gone to meet her mom. She wasn't certain if he would come to Bewley's or go right to the theater. In reality, he probably had blown her off when she asked him. I told them all to go on to dinner. I would eat something at Bewley's and wait for him. The more I thought about him reading *Ulysses*, the more I thought he might be enacting the day it describes. That is a cool thing, actually, but outside the perimeter we drew. I just hope those neighborhoods are safe these days.

Finally, I came over here to the theatre, hoping he would be here.

Yeats led the Irish theatre revival and KJ knows how much I wanted him to see the Abbey. More importantly, he should realize how worried I am. I keep thinking he will show.

Reluctantly, I enter the theatre just before the curtain goes up. If he isn't here to meet the bus, I'll start backwards tracing the path of the day's activities in *Ulysses*. No way I can concentrate on the play, but where else would I wait? As soon as the curtain goes down, I start pacing in front of the theatre. I barely notice that I am standing where my heroes had stood, where literary history had been made.

Then, I see him trying to quietly slide into the queue for the bus. Timothy takes the lead. In his most charming Irish accent, Timothy loudly says, "So, Jackson, would it be that you finally decided to join us? Were you thinking you could just slip onto me bus, with nary an explanation or apology? Were you thinking no one had noticed or worried about you in your absence? You are part of us, lad. So you better act like it. Now, I will give you that you are not holding us up from returning to the Conference Center. But, the worry you caused your poor da. What could have been so much fun that it was worth all of that?" Timothy continues sternly talking as Jackson slinks into a seat toward the back of the bus.

He takes a window seat. I board right behind him, giving Timothy a grateful nod. Timothy responds with a look that says he's been there as a parent. I slide in the aisle seat next to my son. "Are you all right?" I inquire. The boy nods. "I see," is all I can get out of my throat, it's so tight. We sit in silence, stone silence, all the way back to the center. I have no words. There is nothing to be said. All the words are gone; and the trust. There is still love, of course, but, at this point, I truly feel at a loss.

So much for my prayers to St. Brigid.

PEG

By now, they will have finished the play and gone back to the Conference Center. For some reason, I keep thinking of what Daniel Patrick Moynihan wrote after John Kennedy's assassination:

To be Irish is to know in the end
the world will break your heart.

I woke this morning feeling overwhelmed. It got worse, not better. Even though I knew the ride to Dublin wasn't that long, I couldn't bear having to sit with Mary Helena and listen to her negativity this morning. I was feeling too fragile. The young boy, Nathan, was already on the bus and I asked him if I could join him. He was fooling around with his set of Druid animal cards. My mind wandered to a memory of my own children when they were his age. We often enjoyed reading the Sims Native American animal cards together. It was one of the few rituals that they liked and they found the cards far more engaging to them than the readings Rob and I were into. But, so what? The concepts and lessons were just as powerful and thought-provoking as more traditional meditation readings would have been. And here this little fellow had the benefit of visiting the land and culture whose mythology he was learning. It brought a smile to my heart. The only smile of my day.

On a lark, I asked Nathan if I could draw a card. I did, and it was the Wolf. Interesting, I had just recently read that the last wolf in Ireland was seen in the 1700's. Did those Druids use too many wolf skins? I thought of the Save the Wolves poster in one of the religious ed classrooms back home. Then, I also remembered that the meaning of wolf in the Native American set was teacher/leader. No surprise. What struck me in this reading was the notion of the she-wolf. "Distorted from matriarchal times to a misogynous legend akin to the evil hag."

The she-wolf . . .. This interpretation accepted the Middle Ages' assumptions that denigrated the female. I started thinking about how I was drawn into feminist spirituality and its meaning. It had been a long, gradual path, one that seemed to involve continually "unplugging from the tribe" as Carolyn Myss called it. Now here I am back at my tribal roots.

Step one was entering the convent. As a teenager, it seemed there were only two paths out of poverty, marriage or college. I wasn't ready for marriage, fearing I wouldn't be able to shake the syndrome of family abuse I experienced, at least not with anyone from my neighborhood. Yet, I couldn't afford college. Then I discovered a path to college through joining a convent. The order to which one of my teachers, Sister Agnes, belonged was very encouraging of higher education and so was Sister. Even my ma, who seldom thought anything I did was right, favored the move.

Celibacy did not seem so bad; after all, I had no idea what I might be missing. And to be honest, it was the only way I saw to get away from the drama of my family and get a chance to go to college. I was a little worried about whether or not I was a good enough Catholic. But in this Order, I could focus my devotion on Mary, Queen of Heaven, and on Jesus as a Teacher; that I was happy doing.

It was the beginning of my understanding that spirituality was the experience of heart and soul while religion was the holding of beliefs and constructs about Spirit/God. With the incredibly spiritual women of the Order, I embraced Christian mysticism. I was especially drawn to learning about and honoring Sophia–wisdom. Those nuns were so ahead of their time!

It was that meditative life of my young adulthood that was evoked as I walked through the Celtic crosses at Clonmacnoise. I was taken back to that time of deep, unwavering devotion.

But then there had been step two. Even within the confines of my meditative life, I still experienced inequality and injustice. I sometimes was overwhelmed by the patriarchy of the Church, the decisions made in the name of God that glorified ego and power over love and light, and the improper practices of some of the priests who were protected by their collars. The anger I had felt toward abuse in my own family became anger at the Church. I prayed and prayed to see things differently, to let go of the anger, but I couldn't, not while I was still seeing these things happen right in front of me.

I started attending courses on liberation theology and then feminist theology over at Boston College. God love those Jesuits. They gave me a framework for addressing my concerns and channeling my anger. I joined an interfaith women's group over in Cambridge that was exploring the Divine Feminine and found my own voice. I met Rob in those classes. Roberto—earnest, handsome, and serious, but a light-hearted, passionate Spaniard who worked as a community organizer.

And so began step three. I left the Order, left the Church, and married Rob.

Rob was working with a Unitarian Universalist Service Committee project on advocacy for marginalized immigrant groups when we began to date. I got a job coordinating a Central Square neighborhood Meals-On-Wheels project, thanks to a former nun who ran the Office of Aging. It wasn't until we were looking for a place to get married that we took Unitarian Universalism seriously. It became our spiritual home. So much so that we both went back to seminary and became Unitarian Universalist ministers, taking turns as we started our family; thus steps four, five, and six.

The stop at St. Patrick's Cathedral jarred me back into the present and then back again to childhood. There I was again, on my knees, more out of a sense of instability from weakness in these old knees than from reverence.

All the images of the trip thus far swirled in my head—the poverty of Limerick, recalling *Angela's Ashes* and thinking of the play we had seen, then of my own da. I thought again about all the lost souls of the famine—whole families dead without anyone with the strength to keen and bury them, families spread all over the globe, or families trying to hold on in the bleakness and damp of the Burren. I prayed for them all, between my sobs. Then, I prayed for myself, asking for support and guidance to work through whatever was causing this deep sadness and this rawness within me. What were the lessons? Why was this disorientation, this dizzy yet heavy feeling, overcoming me?

Rob had come up to me, and just held me. He knew better than to ask. In spite of my outgoing nature, he knew that

I like and need to process things alone. In that way, I've always been extremely private. So we all got on the bus. The next thing I realized we were at Trinity. I had always wanted to see the *Book of Kells*, but now I was in a fog. I vaguely realized that Dorrie was naming many famous people who had attended Trinity. I also heard her remind us that few of those she named were Catholics, since enrollment policies finally were worked out so Catholics could attend.

Where did that tidbit fit with what I was feeling? I didn't really know. I just followed the group, in a bit of a daze. We stopped in a quiet and picturesque place on campus, near a fountain for a short meditation. Again, I couldn't focus. Dorrie was cautioning us to enter back to the challenge of worldliness and city life gradually and gently. She reminded us that, to date, we had seen sacred sites isolated in space and time. Today, we were merging back into everyday life. She talked on about how to remain mindful of the balance of doing and being. Good advice, but it was lost on me today.

I heard the words, but I was drawing further into myself, thinking I can't be with these people, I cannot pretend all is well. I must work through whatever is going on inside of me. If I pretend everything is okay and start functioning in my all-together, professional mode, I might never do this internal emotional work that is finally bubbling up within me. I knew I needed to allow myself to fall apart. But, how could I do that here in Dublin?

I stayed with the group, through a gorgeous library and into the special line to walk single file past the *Book of Kells*. The calligraphy really was amazing. The letters were beautiful, each and every one. Oh, for that simpler time when Celtic spirituality was "pure."

Somehow, we were back out at O'Connell Street. There was a conversation about who was going where. I knew I needed to think. I did not even want to be with Rob, but he was going off with the men so that wasn't a problem. I knew if I talked to him, I would just dissolve into a puddle and allow him to soothe me into complacency. I had to work through this, and I had to do it alone, and I had to do it now.

People were talking about a rendezvous at Bewley's, where Mary Helena would be spending the afternoon. I mumbled something about meeting folks then and took off, headed toward St. Stephen's Green and the Unitarian Church I had read was somewhere on the Green.

I stopped myself and decided I needed a plan first. I sat on a bench and thought. First, I figured I could easily buy a toothbrush and such, a cheap nightie, and an extra set of clothes that could be carried right in the bag I already had with me. I had my medicines and contact lens case and my credit card. Rob could pack up my things and cart them on to the next place. I had the itinerary so could catch up with them by bus. With the credit card, I could even rent a car if I needed it.

Yes, that was it. I would leave Rob a note and just go off by myself for a few days. So I stopped at a card shop and bought one of those cards that are blank inside. I wrote out the note, found Mary Helena in Bewley's, left the note and got out of there as quickly as possible.

I checked into a lovely, posh, old-fashioned, and safe Irish Georgian hotel along the Green, planning to stay inside until I knew the group had gone to the play at the Abbey. I had picked up a copy of Joyce's *Dubliners*. If I couldn't fall asleep, the book would be just the thing.

I wasn't sure whether I just needed quiet time, or whether I needed to travel back to my family's place of origin, or perhaps go to the Famine Museum, or something else. I had to trust that the way would come clear to me. I would find a way to address and move through the feelings that had been stuffed down for so long.

And so this night, a dark starless night in Ireland, in a quaint hotel on the Green, I allowed myself to confront my past. Ever since my conversation with Mary Helena at the mansion, I have been on the edges of acknowledging a deep, dark secret kept hidden all these years. I had not even told Rob the extent that my family had been ruined by alcohol.

Thinking about abuse of any kind always brought a knot to my stomach, but here in this place, ever since the conversation with Mary Helena, the knot had crept up into my chest and now was at my throat. I couldn't breathe, I couldn't swallow. I tried to do my breathing exercises. I tried Dorrie's sound meditation. I was too blocked. When I tried to meditate, my whole body resisted. I had been told by a dance therapist that I didn't use the space around and behind myself. I had been told by a masseuse that my energy was blocked. I now understood what they meant.

What would happen if I couldn't get unblocked? Stroke? Heart attack? Cancer? Depression? I have seen so many suffer. I have seen the impact of stifling strong emotion. I will not go further down that path. Now that awareness has surfaced, I will find release. But then, I was also afraid of the opposite. What if unblocking the emotion floods me? What if the scenes are not bearable? What if the pain is overwhelming? What if it is like a pinprick of light getting into a camera. Once the least bit of light comes in, the film is exposed and once exposed, cannot be changed back to the previous picture? That was just as scary.

At first the pain did seep in slowly, like water finding a weak spot in the cellar stonework, and then a steady stream of water, strong and unflinching; finally, a flood. Tears, sobs, shaking. Then an image of Uncle Charlie, becoming more and more vivid. I struggled to erase it from my mind, but then told myself not to fight it. I had to face it. I had to confront Uncle Charlie.

I thought of Rob, the opposite of Charlie. Rob had helped me trust men again. And now, how hurt he would be that I didn't come to him, to let him share the pain, help dissipate it. I also knew he would understand. He would understand why I took off today and why I had not shared the secret during all these years. In fact, he probably wouldn't be surprised.

The child in me still wanted to believe that experiences are not completely true if no one knows about them. But, I knew better. I also knew as an adult I had the resources within me, the wellspring of strength, the love of the Mother, the healing energies of the elements to deal with the past. So, finally, I released the pain, I acknowledged the abuse, I named the culprit and the act of molestation by the man everyone loved and trusted. . . when he was sober, that is. Uncle Charlie.

Then, I cried and cried some more. I cried for the innocence of that little girl I had been, I cried for my family and its secrets, I cried for the young woman who had found the strength to move on, I cried for the woman I had become who had held the pain too long. And, then and only then, I cried myself to sleep, wrapped up in the traditional down coverlet of this posh, old Irish hotel.

I woke the next morning, had a hearty Irish breakfast and visited the Unitarian Church on the Square. My free faith, my chosen faith, my non-creedal religion had allowed the Spirit of the Mother to move within me. I knew now that I had faced the dragon and would heal. I just have some more stops to make along the journey.

DAY SIX

GLENDALOUGH

We will motor down to the beautiful Wicklow Mountains today.
Our entire day will be spent at the enchanting Glendalough.
The monastery of St. Kevin, its round tower and beautiful vistas have
inspired poets and writers as well as spiritual leaders
and seekers for centuries.
There is a magnificent hotel and restaurant on the grounds as well as
lighter fare at the Visitors Centre so people may spend a comfortable and
leisurely day as they choose.

MELANIE

John is right. I should have told him about Croagh Patrick. He is still steaming. The fact that he heard about it from Mary Helena put him over the top. I feel terrible, terrible that he feels so betrayed.

It is just so hard, we both want a child so much. Dorrie says there are wonderful hiking paths throughout Glendalough. Hopefully, he can walk off some of his anger

153

while I try to get back the positive spirit and sense of wonder I've been experiencing. If his anger ruins that, then this trip will be a disaster and we might never forgive each other.

It's misty this morning, but the view is still spectacular. We are now coming into the valley between the two lakes. I had never heard of St. Kevin or the history of this monastery, but I do remember Glendalough from a course on English poets. Now I can sure see why this glen between the lakes was such a draw. It is heaven. No wonder it's been a favorite of poets and contemplative souls down through the ages.

Wordsworth's *To a Skylark* comes to mind as I watch a singular bird soar through the trees against all these muted blues and greens and purples. My, but it is beautiful. If this place can't set me, us, right again, what will?

The sun's rays poke forcefully through the distant mist as Dorrie asks Timothy if he would first drive us to the Deer Stone before dropping us at the main entrance. On the way, she tells us about St. Kevin's way with animals and the Deer Stone legend.

"The story goes that when a woman died in childbirth, Kevin prayed at this site and a doe came daily to place its milk in this natural basin-like indentation of stone so the baby would have milk and live. The child grew up to be a disciple of St. Kevin."

Not sure what kind of message I am meant to get from that, but maybe later it will mean something to me. They say every experience has a message. One just needs to know how to process it, so I think about it while she has us get out of the bus at the site and stand around the stone.

"I would like to share a Yeats reading with you to begin our day here at Glendalough," she says.

Glendalough

Through intricate motions ran
Stream and gliding sun

And all my heart seemed gay:
Some stupid thing that I had done
Made my attention stray.

Repentance keeps my heart impure;
But what am I that dare
Fancy that I can
Better conduct myself or have more
Sense than a common man?

What motion of the sun or stream
Or eyelid shot the gleam
That pierced my body through?
What made me live like these that seem
Self-born, born anew?

My, always something to stir me. I look at John for affirmation, and forgiveness. His face is as hard-set as the Deer Stone itself. St. Kevin, whoever you are, help my husband back to the gentleness of his soul.

By now, we are back at the main gate. Gordie gets our tickets and gets us oriented to where we will meet to return and goes over other logistics. There is a wonderful hotel and restaurant on the grounds and a snack bar so people can individually pick and choose. John mumbles that he will see me later and heads off up the hill. Sandra and Jake talk about a 'just-the-two-of-them' lunch there after the tour. Will John and I make it to their age as a couple? How quickly negativity can set in. So I consciously shift to taking in the beauty of this place and focus on my gratitude for God's blessings.

The setting is so different from Clonmacnoise where it was all about the past. There, remnants of the buildings told a story of industry, prestige, and the religiosity of medieval Ireland. Here, the glory goes to the God of Nature and Beauty. I have a sense that, though beautiful, these wonderful rustic stone edifices were simply built to provide shelter.

Dorrie encourages us all to take the guided tour. She offers that she will then be doing a short ritual at the ruins of a women's chapel and a goddess site for those who would like to join her. It sounds wonderful. She adds that there still should be time for those in really good shape to walk up to Kevin's Bed—the cave where he withdrew for contemplation. Folks chuckle at the idea that this bucolic place was not isolated enough for contemplation, but then again, we are hardly hermits. I grimace because I know John has already high-tailed it up and away from me. I just pray his withdrawal is temporary.

The guide could have come from central casting; he is so perfect for the role. He has a worn tweed jacket, an Irish cap and a line of blarney that, while not irreverent, is more suited for a vaudeville show. You can tell he loves his work and takes great pride in sharing facts and figures as well as stories about the monastery. From the way he drops the "H" sound in his "THs," much more than Timothy, I guess he is from the West of Ireland. Whether it is real or for effect, it is cute on the old fella.

"The valley so you see is called by a name whose meanin' is the valley of the two lakes and the place was also known as the valley of the seven churches. T'ere actually are ruins of eight shrines on the site. 'T'ere was an earlier site at the upper lake, but 'tis here 'twas the gateway to the monastic city."

We first go to the round tower, reputed to be the best specimen of such towers in all of Ireland and the scene I have seen in numerous books. I catch a look in Timothy's eye. It may just be the school administrator in me that has an eye for mischief, but I imagine him restraining his desire to add his famous line "sure, you have nothing like this in America" in deference to the elderly man. The man surely enjoys being the center of attention.

" 'Twas built now originally in the nint' or tent' century and no, 'twas not built by the Danes, t'ank ye very much, but it was built to keep out the Danes and all who tried to raid and steal from the monasteries. Gold and silver relics were valuable even to the non-religious and so t'ere was always a t'reat. T'is here particular tower is seven stories high. 'Twas rebuilt in the 1800's using all the original mica-slate and granite."

He points out the Wicklow Way, a walking route opened about 1980. It's a trail that follows the high spine of the mountain that I would love to take. From the top, on a clear day, he says you can see Wales. The mist has lifted and the sun is shining brightly now. The valley is even more beautiful in the sunlight.

Mentioning Wales leads the fellow into a discussion of how St. Columba was here until he was excommunicated and fled to Iona, across the Irish Sea in Scotland. Iona is only twenty miles or so from Ireland; in fact, the Giants Causeway was said to have extended to Strata, the island next to Iona. It was already a place of sacred sites and enchantments, but Columba set up a ministry there.

"And have ye heard of the *Book of Kells*?" he asks toward the end.

"We saw it yesterday in Dublin."

"Ach, well t'en, t'ere ye have it. Ye have heard the story. Let me tell ye another just to give ye a boost on t'is cloudy morning. T'ere is a favorite story about Columba that Yeats tells in one of his books.

"Seems an old lady is feeling mighty sorry for herself. The priest comes to visit each day, but 'tis nary enough. Each day as he leaves her he says, 'have a good day' and she replies, 'sure it will be terrible day, no doubt about it, Father, but I t'ank you for comin.'

"T'is happens many a day and the priest gives in to her for a bit. T'en he tries sometin' else. For t'ree days as he leaves he says, 'Mind you make it t'rough yer terrible day, now, since it seems to be all ya know,' and he leaves with a nod and a smile. Finally on the t'ird day of his wee experiment when he is about to leave, she preempts him with a 'Good day, Father, aye, a good day to ya'!' He nods and smiles as he says cheerio.

"T'anks be to all the saints, I say."

As the Buddhists say "when the student is ready, the teacher will appear." I hope that this guide and his story is a lesson being grasped by our dear Mary Helena. What a blessing that would be.

"But back to our monks, now. Monks were about t'ree t'ings: prayer, work, and readin'. St. Kevin's love of animals was seen as an acceptable indulgence. Nonetheless, he placed himself in solitude at the old hermitage along Upper Lake, and ye might want to visit Kevin's cell and cave if ye have the time."

He then draws our attention back to St. Mary's, or Our Lady's Church. Then he points out the Cross of St. Kevin, explaining that Kevin is actually buried in this area, not in the chapel bearing his name. He then reminds everyone to hug the cross and make a wish. It is legend and tradition and he guarantees success. This is said a bit tongue-in-cheek but you sense he really believes it, he just isn't sure group members will.

Kevin's chapel or "Kevin's Kitchen" is the name given to the sweet smaller chapel which seems a favorite of the group, if picture taking is any indication. People then walk by or into the rest of the churches, the newest being St. Savior's Priory.

Going from building to building, the guide explains that the place experienced a new peak in interest in the 1800's. Its beauty combined with its proximity to Dublin brought many English gentry to have a look, including Sir Walter Scott, Wordsworth, and the like. This is the part I am familiar with and that most interests me. Thomas Moore wrote a song and another writer joined him in versions of a legend where Kevin rejects the advances of Kathleen, a maiden smitten with him. Some versions say he threw her off the cliff or into the lake for approaching his bed and trying to kiss him. Unlikely, we think, for a man known for his gentle ways, but the stories bring life to these ruins.

Folks are getting restless, me included. Gordie finds an opening, and he takes it. He thanks the man for all his time with us, handing him a tip. Some others pull out their money, too. But I don't want to lose Dorrie, so I take off after her. She is leading us away to the lower end of the grounds where the oldest ruins are. A number of people take off up the hill behind us. I am too focused on our new adventure to notice or care how people divide up; except, of course, wondering what's up with John. But I try to put that aside.

The grove leading down toward the creek is a woods of tall, straight pine trees planted in rows far enough apart to mature regally, encircled by a carpet of velvety green shamrocks. It is magical. A true fantasy land. I could stay and roll in this luxurious rug of nature for eternity.

But the cinder path calls us to continue. Besides, it seems sacrilegious to veer off or step on the fragile little plants.

We are now out of sight of the site, so to speak. The buildings which had contained and made the energy of place powerful back at the round tower are opposite here. This new energy is just as strong, if not stronger, but it is encompassing, yet expansive and light. I love it.

There really is a babbling brook. Story Land, for sure. In fact, the sounds of the creek are a perfect augmentation to the scene of big oaks, holly, hazel and ash lining its bank. Wildflowers in blues and purples, butterscotch, and poppy-orange blaze amid the rocky ruins of the oldest of the dwellings on the site.

We stop and say a short prayer at the ruins of both the chapel and the pagan site that preceded Christianity. I feel the presence of the Divine Feminine. I feel the grandmothers. I feel my own grandmother and a sense of safety that brings me to tears.

Dorrie then moves us over a few yards, telling us about the fairy circle, saying it stands ready for the group. I see a faintly raised earthen ring in the grass field to the right of me, but fairy circle? That's a stretch for me. But, some of the others sense or report seeing it. Lily is skipping with joy and delight. She tells us we are being welcomed by the Royal Court of the Other World. Rose is nodding in agreement. Peter whispers something to Penny and she looks in the direction he indicates. I try to suspend judgment. In my classification of things, fairies and sprites are the creation of imaginative writers, a tool of fancy, if you will.

Dorrie silently gestures for us to form a circle and we do, maintaining a respectful silence, yet clearly, she herself is bubbling with anticipation. This time I can hear Peter whisper to Penny that he feels the stirrings of the Green Man. Rose is looking transported.

Thankfully, Dorrie speaks because I am not sure what is going on.

"We are gathered in this place of sacred enchantment: this place where people have gathered for century upon century; this place where all sentient beings are welcomed and loved; this place where love and light are honored and magic is created by the interconnections we make.

We humans have been blessed to have the capacity to co-create our journey. We know that our health, our well-being and our happiness depend on so many other beings. We would have no food, we would have no flowers, we would have no wind or water or fire without the elemental beings who attend to such things with love and dedication. And yet, we forget to be grateful. We forget to cherish, we forget that we are partners in this earth community.

We are here, today, to rededicate ourselves to partnership with all beings for the Highest Good of all and for the healing of our planet, our earth home, the mother of us all. Amen. Blessed be. May it be so."

And then Lily plays her harp, playing even more spectacularly than she has played before. It's like she is joined by the wind, the birds' song, and the rustling of the trees. Her music lifts my heart, her song penetrates my bones, and her rhythms stir my soul. I can tell I am not alone in this reaction.

"Go your way now. Consider the meaning your presence in this sacred place called Glendalough has for your own life. Decide how you will help heal the world."

With that, Dorrie steps away and the circle is broken. People go off silently in all directions. Good thing, too. I need quiet time to contemplate what is going on. I know I feel moved. This whole area has such wonderful energy. Yet, I also know I don't believe in fairies.

I see Leslie has found herself a wonderful place under an oak at the creek side. Rose is behind an even bigger oak tree to the south. I need to give them privacy and hopefully find a place equally alluring.

I find my own little spot upstream and snuggle into a nook between two bushes. Bet Nathan can tell me what magical wood they are. Rowan, maybe? That certainly fits the story of my day as it is unfolding. Without the slightest preparation, my mind is flooded with my teenage fantasies of being at the shore of a lake. I am looking across the moor, seeing the shimmering water reflect the purple mountains, shadowing the lily pads. Then, I fly, like Wordsworth's skylark; I soar above the lake and take in all that is around me.

A noise brings me back. Awareness of my body and the ground I sit upon returns. I am stunned. I have no specific revelations. Nor do I have words to express any of it. I try to journal but only fragments come . . .soaring . . .flight . . .high above . . . Free to see it all . . . beauty all around me . . . the Big Picture.

As I look up from writing, Kate is sitting quietly and respectfully to my left. Oh good. She is probably the only person I want to see or talk to at this moment. I so admire her equanimity and wisdom.

After a bit, she says simply, "You looked very far away."

"It was like a guided visualization, but without the guide. Amazing. I envisioned myself soaring, like a skylark across a beautiful blue lake."

"I sensed I was crossing a lake, too. I was going to Avalon, at least what I have always imagined Avalon to be."

"I probably should know about Avalon, but don't really. Say more, please."

"In the Arthurian legend, Avalon is a magical island that can disappear into the mist. It is considered the home of The Lady of the Lake and represents the Goddess culture which fades as Christianity comes to The British Isles. We mostly hear about it in association with Merlin, Morgan La Fey, and Arthur's sword, Excalibur."

"Of course, that's why it sounds familiar."

"But a series of books starting with *The Mists of Avalon* developed the legends from a feminist perspective and became really popular with my generation of women. I think you would like them," suggests Kate.

As I nod in agreement, Dorrie approaches, "Am I interrupting?" she asks.

"Not at all," we both say with Kate adding, "We were just talking about Avalon. We both had visualizations of lakes, mine specifically being Avalon."

"This place will certainly evoke those energies," Dorrie chuckles. "Any message?"

"Joan Borysenko taught me to immediately give a title to a dream or visualization to help remember it and get to its essence. I labeled this Revisiting Avalon. Sort of have the impression I was going back to make certain it was still there and will always be, but also to realize it is no longer where I belong."

"That is a cool technique," I'm thinking, then realize I have said it out loud. "Kind of a right brain thing that short-circuits logic and analysis. I like it. I guess my title would be Flying Higher, but I'm not sure what it means. And, Dorrie, what about you and your meditation?"

"Thanks for asking. Mine, too, related to Avalon, in a way. I found myself sitting around what felt like a futuristic Round Table with a host of different beings, all seeming to be leaders. We were all touching a huge crystal and meditating. We were sending healing energy around the world. I could feel it and it was beautiful."

We all sit in silence together for a bit. Finally, I say, "I know I could talk to the two of you for hours about the books and ideas that this place stirs up. But it's so nice to just sit."

"Yes, I kind of feel that this trip is about my deepening my heart's understanding of all my intellect has learned," Kate notes.

"That reminds me of that Joseph Campbell line you read yesterday. What was it exactly?"

*Your sacred place is where you find yourself
again and again.*

"Yes, that is so beautiful."

We are silent, again, until Kate softly shares, "I may be staying longer in Ireland than I originally planned. Not sure when I am heading home."

"You mean you and Timothy?" Dorrie asks gently. I am so glad she responded first, because I was about to blurt out "What?!"

"Yes," Kate says and then is silent.

". . . didn't mean to pry."

"No. No. It's okay. I don't talk much about my private life, but I would welcome talking a bit about it to you. Thanks for asking so gently." She looks to us both, but I sense she is really talking to Dorrie and I sit back a bit and just listen.

She continues on, "At Brigid's Well, I asked to grow old with grace and wisdom and to find my Higher Purpose for this last period of productivity. The message I got and keep getting is to pursue writing and use my university contacts to create something along the lines of what we have been discussing. Yet, I have never felt more at ease with myself than here with Timothy. His gentle wit and common sense, his loving way."

She trails off a bit. We just wait silently. Then she continues, more animated now, "He talks of opening a pub while running the bus service in tandem with his daughter and son-in-law. It first came up around a table at the pub in County Clare when we talked about an old Guinness contest to win a pub, but he keeps talking about it. We talk as if we are going to do it together. Then I asked myself where the game is going? Where could it go?

"Did you know yesterday I went sailing with him? The boat belonged to old friends whom he and his wife had known since their University days. They were very welcoming and it was amazingly comfortable and fun. It was clear, although they downplayed it, that they had never seen him with another woman.

"Then, driving back into the city, he spoke about this big family party, a *céilí* actually, that his daughter has planned for the Saturday after the trip ends. He said how great it would be if I was still here to meet a real Irish clan and to experience a real Irish céilí.. I think he was testing out whether I would stay to attend, but it could have just been conversational and hypothetical."

Feeling totally engaged since I love a good love story, I ask, "What does your intuition tell you? What does your heart say?"

"When we were at the fairy ring, I saw myself at a big Irish party, then in a pub helping him at the bar, lots of people around having fun and clapping to Irish music."

"And?" This time Dorrie does the asking.

"I feel like a school girl on a first date, all nervous but excited. I'm thinking of calling the airline to upgrade to an open ticket. But, if I do change the ticket, I won't tell him about it; at least, not yet. If I change it now, the option is there. I can always just go off on my own for a few days if going back to his party doesn't feel right. Does that sound foolish?"

"Not at all, girl. I say, go for it. Dorrie, didn't you say that opening to what is meant to be is a key principle of transformation?"

Dorrie nods and Kate smiles pensively, a look full of possibility and trepidation.

I go on, "You know, you don't have to choose between Timothy and your life as a professional woman. You know you can do both. Live in Ireland, grow old gracefully with Timothy and still pursue the call of your work. You can work electronically on connecting with university colleagues, and come home as needed to see family and friends and do on-site work. The world is a smaller place than ever before."

"Anything is possible when you think creatively," adds Dorrie.

Kate pauses. "Whew! I am overwhelmed! This conversation, verbalizing all that has been happening and all that I've been thinking, has overwhelmed me. I need to take a walk through the grove before it is time for the bus to leave. Thanks; you are such dears," she says, giving us quick hugs and walking away.

Dorrie and I sit for a moment in silence. Dorrie indicates that she wants a few more minutes of contemplation at the stream. I start back along a path through the magical woods, offering a prayer to the power of this place. I ask that I may someday have the wisdom of these two amazing women.

I catch a bite to eat and wander around until it is time to go. No sign of John and it gets harder and harder to maintain the inner peace the afternoon brought to me. The early evening shadows make wonderful patterns on the hills and the crosses on the grounds make circles and lines. Seems to me the place takes on a whole different feel and meaning now, richer and deeper. I board, silently hoping that John will appear. He does and we are soon off.

The ride back through the valley and over the mountain ridge is spectacular. I am beginning to understand what the Irish mean by the phrase the 'mountain behind the mountain.' Not that I have developed second sight or even a belief in the Other World, but I think I get it. Timothy puts on a ballad sung in Gaelic. It's just the right music as we remain lost in our own thoughts. It doesn't move John and me closer, but it is soothing. Then, in English, we hear "Go Lifted Up," another perfect choice. But, in spite of, or maybe because of, all the wonderful conversation, the magical play of light, and the energy of the day, the tears roll down my face. I can't get lifted up until things are right between John and me again.

Thankfully, Timothy distracts me from getting emotional and fearful as he pipes up with that wonderful Irish accent of his. "Now that we are on the carriageway, I will be after telling you of a custom of church groups and the like here in Ireland. It is the taking of mystery tours, where the destination is known only to the planner and driver. Gordie and I have a mystery planned for you now. We will not be taking your questions nor will be giving any clues. Mum's the word until we arrive at our place."

After trying to tease more information out of the guys, folks give up, nap or chat for a bit until Timothy pulls off the highway and down a country road. We end up in a picturesque hamlet, much like the street scene in Ballykissangel, only a bit more modernized as becomes a place so near Dublin. He pulls up and parks in front of a pub named Rory's with big Guinness and Harp signs in the windows. Antique-looking lights and a display of old glass bottles give it old world charm.

"Here's the place. Come in, if you please. Me old school mate, Rory, wants to meet you all and show you our legendary Irish hospitality." As everyone enters, Timothy introduces Rory, lingering a bit when he gets to Kate, as if to signal Rory that this is the one the party is really planned to impress. I wonder if I would have noticed had Kate not shared what was going on between them.

Rory is charming and sees to it that we have a grand tour of the place and find a comfortable place to sit. "The ale and stout are on the house. Enjoy yourselves, now, whilst I assist me wife in the kitchen; you see we are not used to so high a number of diners on a weeknight. If you will excuse me for a wee bit, Timothy here will take to the tending of the bar. Gordie will take a count on chicken and chips or fish and chips. Or we can make omelets for those of you who are vegetarian. We will also be serving a bowl of salad and a bowl of fruit family style at each table to go with the plates. Make yourselves at home."

Timothy relishes the role of bartender. He quickly fills pitchers of draught for Gordie to take to the tables. He asks those with special orders to write them down. He'll fill them and then get payment later. Before long, a nice buzzing sound fills the main room.

Dorrie puts out a small glass of beer at each table for the leprechauns. She and Rose are talking about elementals and the fairy kingdom and why it has stayed so alive here in Ireland. Jake buys beer nuts and potato chips for each table. Gordie gets a game of darts going with Kevin, Jackson, Nathan, and Peter.

To this point, I have just been taking it all in, trying to be okay with John's silence. Then, John disappears into the men's room, coming back out to the bar and downing a shot of Jameson without even looking over at me. After shot number two, he comes over and suggests we take a walk before dinner. We have never had this much cold space between us for this long before, and I have no idea what to say or how to handle this. We walk around the little town, trying to distract ourselves by observing the quirks like a sign "sports bar with free telly." Finally, John and I both murmur "I'm sorry, so sorry," almost simultaneously and it's over, kind of. We walk hand-in-hand around the square and back to the pub. I wonder if I should say more, but decide to just breathe deep and pray that the magic of the day will keep doing its work.

We walk back into a pub abuzz with talk and laughter. As we try to blend back in without attracting questions, I hone in on a conversation Leslie is having and John heads back to the bar. Leslie is sharing something of her meditation experience with Sandra and Jake and Rebecca. I am really curious to hear how it compares to Kate's, Dorrie's, and mine.

"I am still dumbfounded. I do yoga and, you know, take time to reflect and go deep, but not like this. I had this sense of knowing, a persistent knowing that I never experienced before. It was both calming and unsettling at the same time."

"I think it's called clairsentience. You get things by inner knowing, not by sound or sight," offers Sandra.

"Okay, well, whatever, I got this sense that I was being called to become a major, not just a minor, but a major change agent for sustainability. Like, I am to drop everything and focus on environmental work. And the strangest part was it felt right and I felt no resistance."

"Wow," Sandra says. Jake just nods.

"When I finally gave myself permission to move from my creek-side oracle, I was in a mental fog. I started back through the ancient grove of wisdom trees and the bed of shamrocks lying like a blanket between the rows. You know the place I mean, right?"

They nod.

"Only this time, I stumbled upon an empty liter plastic soda bottle, some beer cans, and a plastic bag, trashing this sacred grove. Now, there is a sign, I thought. If people can trash this sacred spot, we are in deep trouble. I snapped a picture to record the moment and continued to walk back toward the center. In fact, I've got the picture here on my digital camera."

Sandra giggles. "Excuse me; I just got this crazy picture of us all in orange vests, like the road gangs back home, picking up trash. Don't even know why I think it's so funny. Please go on."

"Yeah, it's not like we haven't pitched in ourselves on Earth Day and the like. Do you think the Little People are tickling you or something, dear? But, speaking of pictures, I wish we had a picture of you picking the trash up, Les. What a powerful visual that would be, that even here in the Emerald Isle, the environment is being trashed. Too bad no one was there to get your picture," adds Jake.

Leslie turns bright red. "Oh, oh my . . . I don't believe it. I am sssssoooo embarrassed. Oh my . . ."

"What on earth did I say? How did I upset you?" asks Jake, totally baffled.

"I never picked that trash up. I saw it. I thought how awful it was. I took a picture of it. But, I never picked it up," laments Leslie.

"I didn't mean to embarrass you, I just assumed . . ."

"I know, of course. But, I was so caught up in myself. I never picked it up," Leslie says, while shaking her body in a way that suggested she wants to shake the thought off, like a cat that just got sprayed with water.

"Well, now, doesn't that just point out what needs to be done? This whole environmental thing has so many facets."

Jake scrambles to normalize the conversation and give Leslie a chance to regain her composure.

The food arrives. I dive in. It's good, too. Rory and his wife Nuala, hop from table to table to check on us while Timothy eats standing at the bar. After a bit, Rob and Kate join him and talk pubs—what it takes to open one and be successful here in Ireland. Rory, of course, is pulled in for his expertise. I wonder what is going on with Rob. He seems so calm about Peg's absence. When I compare my spat with John to Peg's disappearing for two days now, well, I just wonder.

Finally, it is time to help clear the tables and head back to the Conference Center. We fill Nuala's cart and she wheels it into the kitchen. She's back in a flash saying she prefers to enjoy us Yanks now and do the clean up later. Some of the women get caught up in "how do you do this in Ireland, we do that in America" chatter. I never read *Good Housekeeping* at home and am too tired to listen to the international version tonight.

Leave-taking is a series of thank you, cheers, and hugs. All the gestures are very genuine. I wouldn't doubt that our goodbyes and cheerios are heard throughout the village as we wave and shout out from the bus to our new-found Irish friends. And best of all, John takes my hand as we board the bus. He guides me to a seat at the very back of the bus.

JACKSON

Last night, people left me alone, even Dad. Today's a different story.

Gordie starts with the stuff about breaking trust and walking too close to the edge. Blah, blah, blah. Says he figured that I would be there at the very last minute, but thought that would be before the play. He said even he was anxious when I still had not arrived by curtain time or at intermission. Shit. I stay quiet. I do not say a thing.

He said that I might be acting out against my dad but I was affecting the whole group and that he and Dorrie would not let that continue. He told me that the parents of minors had signed agreements that allowed him (Gordie) to terminate their participation at any time the safety or wellbeing of the group or issues of liability were in question. F—K. He said that meant leave the group and no refund. As the legal representative of the group, he was giving me a warning and would give the same to my dad. Details, more blah, blah, blah.

I think he was laying it on a bit thick but still…shit.

Then he proceeded to give me his emergency number— he said to call it if I ever needed to, that he cared about me, and he knew I was trying to work through a lot of stuff and he would help if I asked. Then he nods and goes, "Let's not have this talk again," and headed off to breakfast.

Megan and her mother avoided me at breakfast, or maybe I avoided them. I know I got as far away from that Mary Helena as I could. I knew she would start in on me for sure.

Dorrie got me after breakfast. It started with a gentle lob, "I see you are taken with Joyce."

"Yeah, I am Stephen Dedalus."

"And you, too, would like to fly away?"

"Yeah."

"Does getting high do it?"

"I don't know what you mean."

"Jackson, I am not that ancient, I am not that dumb."

I said nothing. She went on, anyway. "You may think you are living a story you can control, but just remember that each choice you make can have life consequences. You can choose where it goes. I think it is time you asked yourself if this is the story you want to live."

I still said nothing.

"I didn't know your mom, Jackson. But I am so sorry that she died and that you and your dad had to experience the loss of someone you love so much."

She was silent a long time. Then she continued, "I'm not a mother myself, but I know as truly as I know we are standing here, that your mom's most fervent prayer would be that you and your father be well, especially you, Jackson, the light and love of her life. Keep her memory and legacy alive by living the life you were meant to live. Do not let her death change what she most loved."

Shit. That about did me in. I wanted to react in sarcasm, my standard shield against all this kind of talk, but I couldn't. She had zeroed in, and I knew she was speaking the truth. The tears came, but I said nothing.

"Sometimes we can use a little help developing the story we truly want to live, Jackson. Call on me if you want to talk. You are going to be okay; just remember that you are loved, you are watched over, by your mother and the Divine, and you have much to give."

With that, she gave me a hug and was off. It was a long hug, and it felt like she had pushed warm energy into my heart, a cold and hurting place.

The ride to Glendalough was boring except for a weird thing with Lily. She came to the back of the bus where I was sitting and joined me, at least I thought she was going to. She did sit for a sec. Kind of like a bug landing on you out of nowhere. Then she turned to me, looked at me with her piercing eyes, and poked me in the chest with her finger, saying, "lighten up, boy, lighten up." Then she just jumped up and left. She took a different seat across the aisle and toward the front. Weird. It sent a chill right through me.

Then there was Dad. He was so quiet and distant. If he had started in on me, I probably would have just gotten really pissed and gone into that do-not-touch me place. But he was just silent, from last night on the bus right on through this morning. He has never done that before.

Shit, man, all these people coming at me. All this beautiful scenery and talk of love and light. I would like to think I know what to do with it, but I don't.

I know the "self-righteous, poor me, no one understands" game I play. I also know it's the easy way out, just not sure out of what. I've dealt with all that shit with my school grief counselor. Blah, blah, blah.

They want me "to let go of it." They want me "to let them in." They want me to pick up my life again as if everything is and will be okay. But it isn't and it won't. It will never be.

We arrived at Glendalough and first went to this Deer Stone place. The legend about the mom dying and the baby living because of the deer milk really got to me. Like my dad raising me without Mom. And, shit man, his name being Kevin and all. I suppose I should be grateful I had her for as long as I did. Twelve years. Too bad I didn't know it would only be twelve. But, I have all the memories, and Dorrie may be right that I could use those memories to feel close to my mom anytime. I did it once, but it hurt so much to think she was not here, I never tried again.

I wish I listened more to the words of a poem that Dorrie read. Something about being "born anew." I felt like she had chosen it just for me, as a follow up to what she said about how I could choose how my story would go. But it went fuzzy right after she read it. Maybe I'll ask her to let me have a copy.

We were back up at the gate, a truly awesome old entryway that seemed magical to me, more so than back at the dolmen. That place made me feel naked, out in the middle of nowhere like it was. This place feels sheltered and cozy-like, even safe. And the old Irish guide had an awesome accent, even though I really didn't listen to his spiel. All the talk of Kevin was freaky. When we got to the Cross of St. Kevin and heard the legend that your wish will be granted when you hug it, a couple people asked me and Dad to go first. We both said no quickly. I really wanted to do it, but I would find a time when the others weren't around.

I think that was the first time I noticed Dad and me are on the same level, in the same circumstance. When Mom was sick, I kept begging him to do something. All I remember are the words, "I can't, son. I wish I could, but I can't." I was so mad at him. Why her? Why not him?

After she died, I was angry. He seemed to be even more of a wimp than when she was sick. I had never seen him like that. It made me really uncomfortable. And he kept asking me to talk about my feelings. That was what Mom did, and I was not going to let him take it from her. He had never talked to me like that before, what gave him the right to do it now? I just wanted him to leave me the hell alone and I still do.

The guide was talking about Kevin's bed on the shore of the lake, the cave where he went and often slept. I had to go there, to be alone. So I asked Gordie if I could skip the rest of the talk and go up there. I promised him I would be okay and would be back on time. He said we needed to check with Dad and Dorrie, too. They gave the go-ahead. I slipped away from the group and headed up the hill.

I had thought I would want to go into the cave and just hibernate. But, the sun started to appear between the clouds and it was so warm. And the view was amazing. I ended up behind some rocks for privacy, but completely in the sunshine. I spread out there.

Mom used to say "let's go lie in the bowl of heaven." That meant lie flat on our backs looking up at both the sun and the moon together. It only happened at certain times on certain days that they both were in the sky together, but she knew when and we always tried to find time to do it on those days. She said it was a sign of "total surrender." She said one of the great mysteries of life is to learn the joy of surrender.

I couldn't see the moon today, but it felt right to lie here. I prefer dark places but today was different. Megan had told me she was reading this mystic guy who talked about people having a dark night of the soul and about how you have to hit bottom before you come back. And maybe coming back doesn't mean all cheery and light, maybe it can mean just more real.

She said she thought I was going through my dark night of the soul. She had not had hers yet, most people get it when they are older or when a tragedy strikes. Yet, she felt certain that it was a good thing because you went deep into yourself. Why was that so good? She thinks it's because you find yourself and know you can always trust yourself to make it from there on out.

She said she listened to her "inner voice," but she knew she had never really been tested; sometimes she was scared that she wouldn't pass the test, but hoped she could. She then gave me a soft kiss on my cheek and told me to be brave. It was corny, but also kind of nice at the same time. Sisterly, I guess, though I never had a sister.

So I lay there wondering if I was coming out of a tunnel; wondering if my dark night was ending.

I started thinking about Dorrie. She has a list of things for transforming stuff within you. I didn't remember it all or in order, but I knew that letting go and surrendering were biggies. I took deep breaths and I let the earth soak up all the crap that poured out of me like sweat after a ball game. It seemed I did that for a very long time.

The sun's rays pierced me in a different way than before. I started trying to remember more of Dorrie's list. It was to ask somebody, God or a goddess or something like that. What came to mind next was what she had said this morning about my mom always being there for me. James Taylor has a song that Dad played; I could hear James sing *"just call out my name...I'll be there."* Tears came. The sun went behind the clouds. I felt all alone, still. This time I held my position. I did not retreat. I lay there and let myself be in touch with my feelings like the yoga instructors said. Then, the sun's rays came back, stronger than before. I heard St. Kevin's birds, as if they were singing a song to me. The sky went on forever. I felt warm; I could hear my heart and my blood inside me, the numbness fading a bit for the first time in a long time. It felt like the tight, dark knot in my gut was smaller.

Then I felt my mom. I smelled her perfume. For the first time since she died, I had a true sense that she would always be with me. I couldn't see her or hear her; I just felt her in the air and in the sunlight that was getting stronger. Nothing more happened. I just lay there for a long time.

Finally, I saw Gordie trudging up the hill. I knew he was checking on me; it made me grin. I kinda knew they had all been worried about me going off alone, but they were cool in the end.

I wasn't ready to talk. I gestured to Gordie so he would know where I was, and he came over. He could sense that I was good on my own and that was all he needed to know. He gave me a thumbs up and said he would see me at the bus. He gave me a couple of energy bars and water in case I didn't want to join the group quite yet. He suggested a hike along the lake might be the grounding I needed before I returned. Then another thumbs up, a grin, and he was gone.

The last thing I did before going to the bus was hug the cross of St. Kevin. No one was there. No one but my mom.

DAY SEVEN

NEWGRANGE & TARA

Today we visit the amazing Neolithic site of Newgrange, built 1,000 years before Stonehenge and designed so that a beam of sunlight enters its cavernous chamber and illuminates a specific stone within.
We have received special permission to hold a short meditation within its inner chamber.
In the afternoon, we visit the legendary Tara, home to Celtic kings.
A storyteller is coming for our evening entertainment.

TIMOTHY

Running a wee bit late, I join a table that is about to begin gratitude go-round. Everyone at each table goes round and says what they are grateful for on that day. Someone promoted the idea a few days ago. The idea hopped from table to table until everyone now is participating. Herself calls it the "serendipitous start of a new spiritual practice." I call it a nice wee start to our day.

"I just wish I could hear everybody, every time. I get so much from listening to everyone's story. I just hate to miss anything." Melanie says as I slide into me chair.

" 'Tis true enough," I nod. "But, to my way of thinking, we hear what we need to hear and miss very little.

"There certainly is richness here," adds Rob. "Now that we have a full table, Timothy, would you like to begin?"

Seeing nods of agreement, I say, "Me gratitude today is for this glorious day with not a cloud in the sky and for me ancestors who knew to praise the Sun, the Moon, and the Stars, as we all will be seein' today…and for rainbows."

Rob is to me right hand and he goes next. "I am grateful for my wife, my partner, my love and for the trust I have in her," says he.

Jackson usually grunts something about the food or weather. But today he is chipper, "I am grateful to be seeing all these incredible sacred places."

John adds, "I, too, am grateful to my wife, who means the world to me."

None of us ask about Peg, after asking so many times in the last two days. Would be stupid, that.

Herself is afire this morning. She begins her morning talk gentle-like with the plan of the day, but quickly gathers a head of steam like a young filly.

"We don't have far to travel today, but we do need to keep to a tight schedule. Gordie was able to get us a block of tickets and special permission to enter the Newgrange passage chamber as a group. The guide has to come with us, but I am being granted permission to lead us in a short invocation of peace and healing. This is a rare privilege and, I hope, something that you will find as meaningful as I do. After the tour, you are free to look around the outside at the kerb stones and the nearby standing stones and all for as long as you want.

"We'll eat lunch right at the Visitors Centre at the time of your own choosing so you can see exhibits, go to the gift shop, and all at your own pace. Then at 2:30 p.m., we will head to Tara.

"Tara is a much freer and more open space where you will be called on to use your imagination to see what once was there. But it, too, is magical. There is lots of walking on rough ground at Tara, but Timothy promises to stay with the bus. For those who don't want to walk a lot, I suggest you bring a book. And, we have a storyteller coming this evening, followed by more music, thanks to another group staying here. So it will be a full day and a memorable one.

"Let me say some things about Newgrange to prepare your way. Guides and exhibits will fill you in with more detail, but we can start the process. There also is a page in your packet with more information. I personally found it took a long time for me to take it all in to a point where I could start to use my own intuition and critical thinking regarding its purpose and context. So be patient with yourself as you attempt to get hold of it.

"It is only recently that this time in history has even been studied. In fact, most North Americans who come to visit first saw pictures from the background scenery of *Riverdance* and Celtic Woman concerts.

"Newgrange is a Neolithic site. We now know it predates the Egyptian pyramids, Mycenae (pre-Greek archeological sites), and even Stonehenge. The circular mound takes up almost an acre of ground, with the outside borders surrounded by large kerb stones. From a distance, the white sides of white quartz stone and the green top of grass give an almost neo-modern look. When you get up close, you can see the ancient markings and amazing ornamentation on the kerb stones—spirals, lozenges (diamonds), and other geometrical patterns now recognized throughout the world as belonging to this place; yet, universal, too.

"The long passageway into the chamber has about twenty huge standing stones on each side of the narrow corridor. When in the chamber, you will see just how high the ceiling rises. The roof is corbelled, i.e., flat slabs of stone, stepped one upon another and narrowing in as they rise; creating a high, secure, and tightly sealed ceiling/roof that has lasted 5,000 years.

"There are three recesses—carefully shaped stone basins and more spiral ornamentation indicated rituals were performed here. It is here that the light shines in on winter solstice; it is here that we will say our invocation of peace and healing.

"It's probably hard to picture, but I want you to at least have a feel of what you are walking into. Plus, we won't have that much time inside. They move the groups in and out quickly because of the lines.

"I know you all realize that the lenses through which we see the world differ and are powerful. Historiography is the study of what was going on in the minds and culture of the historian. Women's studies and minority studies programs of the last fifty years have brought this to the consciousness of most of us. Here at Newgrange, I challenge you to identify the different lenses that have been used to interpret the site and its history. Here are some questions from this tourist booklet I bought last time I visited. Describing the magnificent location and architecture, it is said it 'is indeed a burial place fit for kings.' Yet, on the same page we learn that it was built before Mycenae or the Egyptian tombs or Stonehenge. There were no kings as such in those days. In the same pamphlet, it says it is clear the people were a settled farming community. Also, the insistence that the site be considered primarily a burial tomb is easily challenged. Scholars acknowledge that only the remains of only a very few people were found. Rather puzzling for a place primarily about burial, don't you think?

"We read that at one point the British assumed any antiquity in Ireland of any significance was Danish—including the round towers built to protect the monks from the marauders (Vikings, the very people the British preferred to credit with building them). Early historians also assumed the ogham alphabet was Danish, but we now know it to be an ancient system that predates Danish runes.

"We also read that even a professor at Trinity College in the eighteenth century called the wonderful ornamentation of spirals, lozenges, etc. 'a barbarous kind of carving, showing not the least footstep of writings.'

"It was 1967 before researchers determined that this magnificent site was built to bring light into the basin in the farthest recess of the inner chamber recess, a miracle indeed. But isn't it amazing that despite the 'local rumors' of a 'fanciful myth' connection to the light, the whole concept had been dismissed? Since the entrance was not situated to allow light in at summer solstice like Stonehenge, the concept of a different alignment to the Sun or stars was not considered.

"It is true that the roof-box had been displaced. Nonetheless, researchers were so removed from thinking of the sun and moon and stars and so bent on assuming it was a burial chamber that the idea of spirit and ritual and a religion connected to nature was not in their consciousness as even a possibility or even an afterthought.

"Why this 'fanciful myth' is treated more lightly than the myths of kings brought from Tara to here for burial is part and parcel of the dismissive attitude scholars held for the pre-Christian world.

"Also note this booklet even says outright that 'any Christian similarity is entirely coincidental, the passage grave being built some 3,500 years before the advent of Christianity to Ireland.' Can you believe it? What about archetypes? What about Christians being inspired by the ancients as they built their places of worship? What about all the evidence we have that Christianity built upon the past beliefs and rituals of the peoples, particularly here in Ireland?

"And here is one more example. Even when mention is made of pre-Celtic gods, it is of Dagna (the good god), his wife Boann (the River Boyne), and their sons. The time of *Tuatha Dé Danaan* (the race of the goddess Danu) gets only one line. And if you think of the territory covered by the Danube River, named for Danu, you get an inkling of how important that thread of culture is in understanding those times.

"Well, you can see what gets my Irish up, can't you?"

She stops for questions and to take a breath. I must say she left me pondering me own history and the cavalier way I have been looking at it. The wee lass made a lot of good points.

She then continues, "There is a new theory that the site is actually a calendar monument built for a ritual about celestial time. It is now believed that people of this time period in the British Isles used a 16-month and 365 day calendar that matched both the cycles of the moon and the sun. Some of the markings on the stones support this theory and tie it to other sites like Stonehenge.

"You may want to reflect on the mysteries and miracles that these ancient peoples lifted up and celebrated—light after the darkness, new crops after a hard winter, new life among the animals and their own human families. Each spiral and circle that we see will remind you that they did not think in duality. They thought of themselves as part of nature, they integrated mind/body/spirit; they saw and lived their life cycles in accordance with the cycles of the earth and the sky. To me, that is what the 'take home' is all about.

"I better stop here. I encourage you to listen to the guides, read through the extensive and amazing compilation of materials on the restoration, and enjoy the displays. I also encourage you to use your own discernment and your intuition. This place is the quintessential example of an ancient mystery. Ask yourself all three questions:

> Isn't it awesome?
> How did it possibly come about?
> What is the meaning and purpose?

"Let me end with this passage by George Russell in 1897. He was a great inspiration to Yeats, but I discovered him by reading this poem on a *Riverdance* concert program. It's called *A Dream of Aengus Og*.

Aengus Og is a variation of the name Óengus or Angus. You will see it in many forms like we see with Brede, Brigid and St. Brigit. Aengus Og was considered the first child born at Newgrange, then a god of love. Later, St. Aengus the Culdee, a martyred bishop, takes on the name. Please note his descriptions of Newgrange remembering it is written before modern restoration and, in fact, has inspired much of the restoration work.

So it begins:

This was my palace. In days past many a one plucked here the purple flower of magic and the fruit of the Tree of Life . . ." And even as he spoke, a light began to glow and to pervade the cave, and to obliterate the stone walls and the antique hieroglyphics thereon, and to melt the earthen floor into itself like a fiery sun suddenly uprisen within the world, and there was everywhere a wandering ecstasy of sound; Light and sound were one; light had a voice, and the music hung glittering in the air...

'I am Aengus; men call me the Young. I am the sunlight in the heart, the moonlight in the mind; I am the light at the end of every dream, the voice forever calling to come away; I am the desire beyond joy or tears. Come with me, come with me: I will make you immortal; for my palace opens into the Gardens of the Sun, and there are the fire-fountains which quench the heart's desire in rapture. . ..

That took a bit to soak in and ponder. Since I meself have been to Newgrange I could see it just as the man wrote it. Powerful that.

But soon we are off to Newgrange.

The Visitors Centre is already busy. Good it was that Dorrie had given folks a bit of orientation, because we are asked to collect the group and join our guide before any chance of browsing the displays. To avoid vandalism and general wear and tear on the property by so many people coming and going, there is a new system since I was last here. Joining the European Union brought lots of tourism dollars and modern thinking brought lots of attention to the importance of careful archeology. Even though there are local residents and roads still being used, tourists are directed to one central car park. Everyone goes through a gate, and then goes out the other side of the building to board wee vans to the site they are visiting. It feels a wee bit too programmed, but the times change now, do they not?

Before we know it, we are standing in line to enter the chamber itself. I am wishing that folks could have taken in the wide view before we got into the line. Will I not need to remind them to walk around the big mound itself upon exiting? 'Tis now re-sided with what is considered its original white quartz stone, but not too long ago, all caved-in like, it looked like a natural hill on the grassy plain. Only in realizing that, can you understand what Dorrie was saying about all the interpretations of the history of the place.

For now, we examine the doorway, the positioning of the lintel and the roof-box. Aloud, everyone speculates on how the Ancient Ones knew to do such work; advanced degrees in architecture, astronomy, and engineering would be needed today to construct such a thing. 'Tis hard to imagine how they arranged to build it so on the morning of the winter solstice the sun's first rays would enter through that space and illuminate the interior. Truly mystifying. Jake adds to the wonderment by telling us that he read this was built 1,000 years before Stonehenge. I must remark that in the natural order of things, the Irish are always ahead of the English.

The guide warns folks it will be dark and the walls get closer together in the passageway sloping upward into the chamber. He assures us that the inner chamber is large, artificially lit, and comfortable. But I was not prepared for the extraordinary feeling I get when we get to the Center. 'Tis both cave and cathedral. 'Tis the Womb of the Mother and an unimaginable edifice of ancient civilization. The longer we stand, the more the energy of the place builds. I didn't feel this way on previous tours.

When we are all nicely situated, Dorrie signals the guide. He asks that we clear a path going straight from the passageway to the basin in the far recess. We do that. He turns off the lights and we hear Dorrie's voice:

"We come humbly to this place as did those who came
    before.
We stand humbly in the silence of the darkness as did
    those who came before.
We wait for the light and are grateful for its return."

At that moment, a beam of light comes through from the roof-box, down the chamber and rests in the basin, directly on the three spiral design. We know it is a laser simulation, but it is still magical. Beyond understanding. Not a sound is made for what seems like minutes, but is probably only seconds, before Herself continues.

"And as the light fades away again, we return to darkness.
We trust that darkness and trust that it will once again return to
    light.
As the day turns to night and back to day again, so turn the
    seasons. And so turn the seasons of our lives and the
    cycle of our birth, death, and rebirth.
May it ever be so.
Blessed be."

Gordie gives two drum beats from his *bodhran*. The slow, full-bodied sound penetrates the depth of the silent, eerie space and chills me bones.

After nigh on an eternity, Herself makes melodious music from deep within her soul. 'Tis an ancient chant which it appears a number of the women and Rob know. 'Tis simple enough and we all join in, as if compelled by a gentle force to be a part of it all:

> *The earth, the air, the fire, the water: Return,*
>   *return, return, return*
> *The earth, the air, the fire, the water: Return,*
>   *return, return, return*

Aye ay aye ay aye ay aye ay: Aye oh aye oh aye
oh aye oh
Aye ay aye ay aye ay aye ay: Aye oh aye oh aye
oh aye oh.

The guide turns the lights back on, saying his own flustered thanks to Dorrie, saying he has never experienced a ritual the likes of this one and that he will carry the experience with him from here on. Aye, he is not the only one stunned by it all. Finally, our man takes a deep breath and shoos us on out.

By all the saints, 'tis mighty and brilliant altogether.

I remind folks to have a look round. Some walk round the mound, looking at the symbols and the decorative art on the big stones. Others head for standing stones a bit of a distance off. I can sense there is a powerful story, if only we knew more. Would it not be grand to have a real eye into these Ancient Ones and what it was they were really up to doing?

I linger at the stone with the symbol of the triple spiral—to me it speaks to a new day in Ireland, a pride in our past and a connection to the universe that is simple and sophisticated altogether. Give over, shamrock and leprechaun pipe—a new symbol to represent twenty-first century Ireland has arrived.

Back to reality for me now; I have mobile calls to make since I myself am not on holiday as the rest. So whilst the group scatters to the exhibits, bookstore, and the like, I return to the coach to work on coming events.

Coming back for me tea, I join a small group of the ladies who already have their lunch and are gathered on the sunny terrace. Kate's warm smile welcomes me.

"Timothy, please join us. I was just telling everyone how much I love this beautiful sea-green Irish pottery. I would love to take home a set like this. Is it hard to get access to artisan work like this?"

"Aye, we could easily find you a place to buy such a thing. 'Tis modern yet casual, very much in style these days. Do you prefer it now to our Belleek or to traditional Irish china?"

The women buzz on about casual elegance and I tease them a bit just to pass the time. "Have you no appreciation for high tradition? You sound more like country crofters, than the fine gentlewomen that I have come to know."

The shoppers then arrive and we bring tables together and rotate around. Megan wins the prize for number of books purchased, Nathan amuses us with his animal cards and ogham sticks, and Trish displays these beautiful window decals of the triple spiral, gifts for her team at the senator's office.

Rose has in her possession a new purchase that chronicles the *Tuatha Dé Danaan* and asks for me opinion.

"Aye, they say these Ancient Ones lived on the land long before the Milesians and what we now know as the Celtic race. 'Tis all mystery and myth."

"I've read that they are the legendary race of the Goddess Danu."

"Yes, and Marija Gimbutas says you can trace their migration all up the Danube River and across the Baltic Sea. Earlier historians dismissed the goddess figures they found as simply little fertility symbols, but this new wave of thinking acknowledges that they meant much more than that," explains Kate.

'Tis all news to me, but I keep meself still. Let the women have a go, after hundreds of years having been to the side.

"But this book," says Rose, "is more about the myths and legends of these people." She thumbs through it and talks as she goes, the way the wife used to do when we were reading the Sunday papers. Most annoying then and now. But I sit sipping me tea and letting it all go on around me.

"The *Tuatha Dé Danaan* were said to have supernatural powers. How else could people explain how they raised stones weighing a ton or more or built these monuments? So legend has it, when invaders came, they went into the ground, and, thus, into the Other World. When you see these mounds, you can understand that better, as well."

"Aye, legend says that the Dagda (the good king and son of Danu) and his wife Boann (River Boyne) and son

Aengus were the first inhabitants of Newgrange. Their castle, or *sid,* gives the name sidhe to the fairy folk. The three sites then serve his three sons. But as Dorrie was saying, the *Tuatha Dé Danaan* go back even further."

"Ach, you pronounce it either SHEE or SEE and you will find a variation in its meaning. But all the word usages have to do with the fairy lore." I add this in anticipation of questions I often am asked.

Another rotation comes about as Peter, Penny, Dorrie, and Gordie bring over trays and some of the others excuse themselves. Peter is especially enthused, "Dorrie, that was extraordinary. And Gordie, that drum, like the first music, was really a primal experience, eh? Amazing."

"It did go well. You know, I was very pleased, too, but it's the chamber that holds the wonder, not what we did in it, don't you think?" from Dorrie.

"Aye, lass, but to get them to allow the ritual and then to pull it off as you did. Mighty, that."

"The energy in there was unbelievable. I never felt so safe. I've heard the expression 'wrapped in the womb of the mother,' but I never felt it before. I was able to stand there, openly, freely, vulnerable, waiting, just being. And then the light came in. I knew . . . at that moment I knew . . . that I was surrounded by love and light. Grace came to me in that chamber. Does that sound crazy?" 'Tis Sandra sharing that.

Leslie responds, "Not at all, not at all. In fact, it's beautiful." Leslie sounds like her skepticism of all things religious is softening. She adds, "I was seeing it as a pagan site, wondrous in its ability to connect me to nature. So, I must say I am surprised that as a practicing Catholic, you found this site to be so moving, as well."

"I have visited healing centers all over the world, before I got sick and since. Nothing has stirred me like this. Maybe it's the circle of white quartz stones that amplifies the energy, but something made the center of that inner chamber seem alive with magic. I felt that every cell of my body had been touched and healed by a gentle, but powerful force. I just kept soaking it in and sending back gratitude. Had the guide not nudged me to move on out, I would still be there, even in the dark, just basking in the energy of the place."

"Sounds like you see it as a sacred place of healing. Do you think that was its original purpose?"

Leslie directs the question to Dorrie, but Sandra is so worked up she doesn't notice and just continues, "Yeah, when the beam of light entered the chamber, I just shivered. My eyes were directed to the basin of stone in the furthest recess, as the guide suggested. I saw that beam of light rest in the bowl and felt that it was a message directed right to me about my new meditative practices. I've been using a guided visualization that brings a beam of light from above my head down through my chakras. Now, I am going to take this visual experience of the beam of light with me to use in that daily practice. But, I am not answering your question, am I? It sounds corny, but I guess if I had to say the purpose, I would say it was to give hope. Hope that the darkest day was over. Corny, huh?"

"Some of the most profound truths sound corny if heard by jaded ears. I guess that is my experience of the place, in fact a message throughout the trip, is that I need to drop my jaded attitude. But today the message was most direct. Open to the Light. That small beam of hope and faith held so much power. I feel like I was the bowl, the vessel, which received this laser-focused beam of light. Echoes of the Grail. Now, how corny is that?" asks Leslie.

Peter pipes in saying, "This one phrase from my DeMolay days keeps running through my head: 'The sun to rule by day, the moon and stars to rule by night.' Talk about experiencing ancient mysteries, I think we just got a powerful glimpse of what that really meant."

Penny nods as do others and then she adds, "And remember another key Scripture:

The Heavens declare the Glory of God and the Firmament showeth his handiwork.
Day after day uttereth speech, And night after night showeth knowledge. There is no speech nor language where His voice is not heard.

189

"Ah, beautiful," says Dorrie. "It sounds like you guys did Masonic and Eastern Star youth groups."

"That's how we met; but, until this trip, I hadn't realized how influential–fundamental actually–that experience was to the formation of my faith. More so than my church. Much more so," muses Penny.

Sandra speaks up, "I always thought Masons were just anti-Catholic Protestants. Tell me more."

I feel the spoilsport, but it is me that has to say, " 'Tis time for us to board the coach if we want to see Tara in the daylight. Come along now. Ach, and Angie, I hope we are not putting a rush to your sketching. But we must be off." I take a look at the sketch and give a nod of approval as I rise to go. What a talent, that.

I fear Tara can be a wee bit of a letdown, especially to Americans all twisted up in romantic notions of Tara from *Gone with the Wind*. The real Tara was The Seat of Kings, ancient kings, and little is left but the memory. So I come through the Boyne Valley in a well-planned fashion so as people can see the lay of the land and appreciate the entirety of the location.

I take the mike, "Do you not all remember the expression 'All roads lead to Rome?' Well, do you see now that Tara is the Rome of Ireland? High on the hill, Tara was the heart of Ireland, the Throne of the High King." I pull over to the roadside so people can have a longer look.

Dorrie takes the narrative, "There were Five Great Roads that radiated from its hub. If you look closely you can see where they cut through the land. If you take a deep breath, you may even begin to imagine the processionals and parades along the sculpted paths. From every province they came. This was a place of power.

"This was the High Court of the King of Kings, so you know it had the most magnificent building possible in each time period of its use. The names of the gods and goddesses changed, but Lug (Luth) and Medb (later Maeve) are thought to be the most renowned of those residing here. As we drive around, have a look behind. You may be able to see Newgrange in the distance."

Dorrie talks on as I bring the coach into the car park.

"We've repeatedly mentioned the four elements in connection to Celtic spirituality but I don't think I mentioned that legend has it that each element had a sacred object that was highly revered throughout the land. At one point, there was a sacred stone, spear, sword, and cauldron all associated with Tara. Remember we used them in an earlier ritual You'll see the stone, *Lia Fail*, today. I will leave the rest to your guide. The walking may be a bit rough and some may wish to walk longer than others. Timothy will assist anyone who needs it and then be the first back to open the bus for those of you who wish to come back."

The Sour One, Mary Helena to say her Christian name, will have me as her captive for the afternoon. And here at the Mound of Hostages, no less. Would you ever?

The guide is also a sour one. If truth be told, our man is a sorry representation of Ireland and should not be allowed to wear the hat of guide. But we endure. The day is lovely and the beauty of the place makes up for his shortcomings, a wee bit at least.

The man takes us up to the summit of the hill, to the north of the ridge. 'Tis here where we find an oval Iron-Age enclosure known as the Fort of the Kings or the Royal

Enclosure. The old gent gives a dull recitation and 'tis all I can do not to shout out at him. Dorrie tries to warm our man up, but even she fails to get a smile from the old chap. And, 'tis no surprise that the questions trail off since the man has no good answers.

He points out the two prominent earthworks, the two linked enclosures or ring fort and ring barrow known as Cormac's House and the Royal Seat. Then, he brings us to a standing stone, which is believed to be the *Lia Fail*. I pipe in that 'tis also called the Stone of Destiny as people walk into the ring barrow for a closer look. The man takes me hint and explains this is believed to be where the High Kings were crowned. According to legend, the stone would scream if a series of challenges were not met by the would-be king. At his touch, the stone would let out a screech that could be heard all over Ireland.

Nathan nudges me to say, "like the Sorting Hat at Hogwarts!"

"Aye," says I, proud of meself for bein' in the know of the Harry Potter books. To the north of the ring-fort is the Mound of the Hostages, which has jail bars as used in medieval times. Of course, it is actually a small Neolithic passage tomb constructed around 3400 B.C.E. Nathan is proud that he knows this from Gordie's wee lesson and glossary, given in the Burren.

The three banks to the north, are known as the Rath of the Synods. Roman artifacts dating from the first through third centuries were found here, continues the guide.

Some of our group wander off to look on their own. Mary Helena starts back to the coach with nary a word to me. Taking a deep breath, I experience a final moment of enjoyment for the beauty of the day before heading downhill to the car park. One last look at Dublin and the Wicklow Mountains to the south, Slieve na Calliagh and the passage tomb of Loughcrew to the northwest, the town of Kells, and a hill fort a bit further north. There is another cairn-topped slieve, the Mountains of Mourne and Fourknocks Hill to the northeast. And the sea that faces out onto Ionia and Britain/Scotland.

Aye, 'tis beautiful, all round. I hum a few bars of the 'Mountains of Mourne sweep down to the sea' as I see to getting Mary Helena back to the coach.

"Would you be wantin' an arm to lean on going through these rough grasses?" I ask her as she seems to be taking the steepest and most difficult path back to the coach. She begrudgingly accepts and walks without a word all the way down the hill. I open the coach and quickly make an excuse to go outside to the luggage bin just to get away from her orneriness.

I do come back for me thermos and, gentleman that me ma raised me to be, I ask the woman if she wants anything from the snack cart. She does not. We sit in uncomfortable silence until Sandra comes cheerily back to the coach for a rest, she says. She reports the women have gone off to the Maeve Ring Fort and the men up the hill somewhere.

"And what did you think of Tara?" I direct me question to Sandra, not to the Sour One, not wanting to engage such sourness if it could be helped.

"I have wanted to see Tara as long as I can remember. Reading *Gone with the Wind* in school, I found the name itself brought this sense of magic and majesty to my mind. The encyclopedia pages with pictures of the real Tara, of this place, were worn and dog-eared by the time I left for college. So I'm delighted to be here, though it is a bit anti-climatic as so much has to be left to the imagination."

"Aye, true enough, there is not much left to actually see."

"Well, if you ask me the whole day is a big waste of time. Pagan sites with rocks and more rocks and grass where there are no rocks. I don't see the big deal and I don't see anything sacred about it either."

Would it not be smart, I ask meself, to lay low? I lay low and let the two of them have at it.

"Oh, Mary Helena, I beg to disagree. I thought this morning's ritual when the beam of light entered the chamber was one of the most spiritual moments of my life."

"You mean when we were in that dark man-made cave? I thought you were Catholic?"

"What on earth does that have to do with anything? Jesus was born in a cave, Mary Helena. And yes, I am Catholic and I see God as Mother and Father as do many Catholic theologians. Today, I felt the Divine Feminine by whatever name She is called and I am so grateful"

"Hmmpf. How you get anything religious out of that mound is beyond me."

Sandra offers us both some sweets from the wee stand by the gate. I am thinking 'tis more to change the subject than anything and I welcome the gesture. But, right at this very moment, postcards fall out of her wee bag.

Mary Helena takes one look and is set off again. "What are these obscene pictures and why would you buy such a thing?"

Oh me, oh my, are the Wee People up to their mischief?

"They are post cards of a *sheela-na-gig* engraved on a lone standing stone in Tara. It's not the *sheela-na-gig* the group just saw, but I bought a bunch, anyway. Some of those who went off with Dorrie will want one and the snack bar is about to close. Why do you object?"

"Because they are obscene. I have never heard of a – gigg, whatever you called it. But I know obscenity when I see it. Another pagan stone carving. Exactly what I was saying before, there is nothing spiritual about any of this. A waste. An insult."

By the luck of it, the men arrive with crisps and Coca-Colas and more books. Peter takes his tin whistle out of the storage rack above his seat and gives us some tunes until Dorrie and the women return from their time at the ring fort. Nathan, Kevin, and even Jackson join in as they are able. The music is not the best, but it offers up a grand distraction.

The women finally return so we set off toward our lodgings. Surely, our women will be called pagan witches by the Sour One before the night is through. But, I would be having no doubt, not one among them will be fussed by her words.

REBECCA

Leave it to Lily. She finds this bas relief called a *sheela-na-gig* while straying away from our boring guide. She gives out a whoop and draws everyone around it, leaving the poor old guy standing on his own. When he sees what she has found, he is none too pleased either. It is a raised, two-dimensional carving of a primitive woman, standing naked. Her hands are pulling her labia open.

Dorrie explains that these figures are found throughout Ireland in stone church yards and old cemetery ruins. She says that for a while they were thought to be icons to ward off evil in Christian churches. But, it is now known they pre-date Christianity and were symbolic of the goddess. The concept of an open womb was one of strength and hope and love. Reminds me of the relics described in *The Red Tent*; that was the first place I was introduced to the idea of goddesses and the idea that Jewish tribal wives secretly held to such rituals. But, I have to admit they are pretty hideous looking. On first glance, they really could scare away the devil. Dorrie says it really is pretty funny that they are often found in ancient church gardens and cemeteries. She has a bit of that dark Irish humor. We all chuckle as the old guy hustles us away.

He heads north. Fewer follow, but Angie and I hang in a bit longer. He points further north to a narrow rectangular feature known as the Banqueting Hall. Then he allows that researchers now believe it was a ceremonial avenue creating a magnificent and majestic approach to the site.

Rose shivers. She whispers to me that she is seeing a Royal Parade of fifty Royal Fairy Folks coming up the avenue, as if to welcome us. Oy vey. That's too much for me. Thank God, no one else seems to see anything. Certainly, I don't. Then I notice Lily in a position of high alert, like when a cat hears a noise in the bushes. Can't imagine what she is thinking. Actually, I don't get her at all.

There are more ring forts but all begin to blend together for those of us not steeped in all these legends. My mind wanders to images of the desert. Grassy plains are not in my DNA.

Just as the guy wraps up his talk, he mentions that a bit further south of the Hill of Tara is another hill fort known as Rath Maeve, the fort of either the legendary Queen Medb, who is more usually associated with Connacht, or the less well known legendary figure of Medb Lethderg, who is associated with Tara. In spite of all the strange names, I am interested again. But, when we ask more, he looks at us blankly. Who knows whether it is because there is no known answer or because he couldn't care less?

He does find it in him to share that, legend has it, each King had to engage in a ceremonial marriage to Queen Maeve before he could be crowned. I have read about this. It's an old pagan Rite of Spring between the May King and Queen and it represented the power of Kings acknowledging the sovereignty of Gaia, the Earth Mother and receiving her blessing. The Destiny Stone was said to shriek if Maeve was displeased.

His last paragraph of script tells us that Tara is believed to have peaked about the same time Arthur and the Roundtable peaked in Britain. But, as we have seen, the stories all merge together and one character, like Maeve, can span generations, if not centuries.

We thank him politely and then some of us women ask Dorrie if she will go down to the Maeve ring fort and lead a short ritual for us. She agrees. We go off while others go off in other directions.

At the Maeve ring fort, Dorrie invokes the four directions, asks for the guidance and protection from the Goddess, and leads us in a chant. I had heard it before but had forgotten how it gets into my bones. Great rhymes.

After a few rounds, she ask us each to step forward and offer a word that represents the strength of the Goddess as we experience her in our lives. My word is "community." When we all have had a turn, Dorrie closes the circle. We head back.

The ride back to our lodgings is a short one. A bunch of the guys have their tin whistles out. Our group, warmed up from the ritual, leads some chants. Everyone joins in and is merry, except Mary Helena, who for some reason seems more annoyed than usual. I just stay clear of her. I'm so enjoying the sense of community among everyone and I refuse to let her spoil it for me.

I grew up feeling like an outsider. It wasn't the stereotypical story of being teased on the playground for being queer or for even not wanting the newest Barbie. But it was a story of never fitting in. I was the only Jew in a small town school. I was the smart kid who stopped playing board games and such because I could always win. I was the tallest, the first to start my menses; I can go on and on and start a pity party, if I am not careful. But the bottom line is I seldom feel in sync with a group.

Since Dorrie's workshop at Omega, I understand that I am responsible for the energy I allow into my space. I think I have learned to let go of a lot of that feeling like an outsider stuff and to attract a higher level energy. The folks on this tour are so open in body, mind, and spirit that it is like a breath of fresh air. I love it.

Ironically, as I feel more like I belong to the group, I am feeling more distance from Angie. It's really beginning to freak me out. She's not very engaged, is often distracted and seems to almost be hiding behind her sketch pad. It is so unlike her. She is usually the gregarious one. More importantly, she isn't sharing herself with me. I sense her holding something back. I try to shake the worry away, but it creeps back. Joining the others for dinner and socializing after, keeps my mind from fretting more, but the nagging feeling that something is wrong is still there. But we carry on as if things are OK.

Sláinte! How cool to toast in different languages; *Sláinte* is one of my favorites. We had been told there was an honor bar off the lounge. Tonight, for the first time, a number of us gather to partake of a little wine before dinner. Jake's telling a group about two Brits he met over at Tara. They told him that during the turn of the twentieth century, the Hill of

Tara was excavated by those who thought the Irish might have been one of the lost tribes of Israel and they were looking for the Ark of the Covenant. Fits right in with Knights of the Templar stories, he is saying. Who knows? Maybe I have roots here after all, I chuckle.

Dinner is especially interesting tonight because both the nuns and the Road Scholar group are eating at the same time as our group. Baked chicken or fish, boiled potatoes, a medley of vegetables, and the most delicious mushroom soup are served. Dessert is a strawberry whipped thing with home baked cinnamon biscuits, cookies to us North Americans. Good thing we hiked around the Hills of Tara all afternoon. I think I've gained five pounds already. Angie seems herself and I relax into that observation, telling myself I worry too much.

"Who's the guy who looks like Ryan O'Neil?" asks Megan.

"Where?"

"Who's he?"

"I'm surprised you even know who Ryan O'Neil is."

The girl doesn't miss a thing. Our "Ryan" is handsome, getting on in years, but with a twinkle in his eye just like the actor and a way about him that, even from a distance, oozes charm. But who is he and what is he doing here at a nunnery? Kind of like a fox in the hen house, as my dad would have said.

"He's our story teller," Gordie chuckles as he goes to greet the man. So we gather after the meal with the Road Scholar folks. Timothy has even gotten permission to build a fire. We really don't need it, but he wants us to experience the smell of a peat fire. It certainly sets a nice tone.

My fear is that after all that wine and a big dinner, I'll doze off. As I turn to ask Angie to nudge me if I nod off, I notice again how distracted she seems. Something's been going on that she isn't telling me about. I ask, again, but she shrugs off my question as before. I keep wondering if I need to push it. Then I look at Rob who seems to take Peg's absence in stride. Maybe there is a lesson here. I don't want to be invasive or clingy. I decide to wait rather than confront her. There will be time.

The speaker is about to begin. " 'Tis a pleasure, indeed, to meet you one and all and a privilege to be the one chosen to tell you stories, beloved stories from the past that are still known today and we hope to heaven will be told to our children's children and then theirs again," begins Tommy Delaney in his most engaging tone.

"As you well know by now, storytelling is as much a part of Ireland as air is a part of breathin' and stayin' alive. It has been said by the best of us, our stories are all about the same things:

The richness of Place
The richness of Time
The treasures of the Tribe
The treasures of the Ancestors
The joy of the Journey.

"Lovely, is it not? 'Twas a saying of the bards of the Druid tradition who roamed from town to town and entertained kings and common folk alike. Their training required them to learn over three-hundred-fifty stories and to be able to create or adapt a story to suit the occasion. You will be relieved to know I am only choosing three for this evening.

"I will start by talking about the sacredness and the magic of this place, the Bend in the Boyne. I understand many of ye have been to both Newgrange and Tara, both in this very day. Many of the Holy Kings themselves never did that, both in the same day. So you already must be swimmin' in the magic of place.

"But let me take you back…back to the very beginning . . . the time before any of the great mounds of mystery and wonder were even in the thoughts of the people. For 'tis said the goddess or sovereign queen stumbled across the source of the Boyne, which is a place she had been forbidden to go. But we all know what a temptation 'tis to visit the exact thing that has been forbidden . . . and there she was. How could she turn away? And in the moment that it takes her to answer that very question, isn't she just swallowed up by the river? She comes to be one with the river and the river one with her. She is the Spirit of the element Water. You see, she reminds us that emotion and flow and fluency of thinking are part of wisdom. She becomes the source of inspiration; the water that flows from the fountain and the water muse of all poets and bards.

"Now, we know that to be wise, one needs more than inspiration. One needs to attend to all the senses nature has bestowed upon us. And so, if one is truly to be wise, one has to drink not only from the fountain but from the five streams that flow from it. These are the five senses of vision, hearing, smell, touch, and taste. In the story of Finn MacCool, as I hear your young lad told, the old man used his sense of sight and sound and perhaps even smell to find the Well and the salmon. Aye, but 'tis Finn, the lad in the story, who inadvertently touches and tastes the juice of the salmon. 'Tis he then who gains the wisdom. For 'tis the integration, the putting all we were created with together that 'tis needed for wisdom to be found. Do you take my meaning? And that is the story of Finn MacCool and the way he received the wisdom of the salmon."

With that he takes a break, looking down for a bit and then taking a deep swallow of the whiskey Gordie had poured and left standing on a table beside a glass of water.

"T'anks for that. I was findin' meself a bit dry in the throat talking about all that water.

"The second story I would like to be telling if you would be wantin' to listen some more . . .. " He stops to acknowledge all the nods. " 'Tis that of the noble crane. The crane is one of the favorites of Celtic lore. Think about it. She dances in circles, stands in the water and on shore, and flies in the air toward the sun. How could a bird that so embraces the four great elements not be a favorite?

"Like Native Americans, or as you Canadians say, First Nations People, we Celts have long looked to the animals with which we share our beloved isle as sources of animal wisdom. First, what we learn from our brother and sister animals as they live with us in nature. Much can be learned by observation and reflection alone, you see. But more than that, we look to their elemental nature or energy as 'animal medicine,' as something we can take into ourselves for wisdom like with the salmon, our courage as with the eagle, or potency as with the bulls. Then, at a third level, we may pick one or two that stand out for us or our clan and make them our special totem, to walk with us through our journey, protecting, inspiring, and guiding us with their special energies.

"The crane is a bird known in many cultures for its longevity and patience. The Japanese, as you probably know, also revere the crane. In our Celtic past, 'tis connected to the grandmother, the crone, the hag. Now in the oldest of days the crone was seen as all-wise and knowing through having had the patience to live a long life and learn from it. She is also often seen as a gateway to the Underworld and to transformation. A crane's bag, you know, is made from the animal's innards. It was said Finn MacCool himself carried one. Some say his bag was made from a crane who had lived a long life at the Well of Segais, right here on the Boyne. And all Druids are said to have carried a crane's magic pouch on their journeys."

He takes another short break and more than a sip of whiskey. Then with a deep breath and that dazzling smile and twinkle of the eyes, he continues.

"Our third story today, also has to do with the crane and also with somethin' that I hear your young lad, Nathan, here has been studying; that is the ogham. 'Tis an alphabet of lines on and across other lines, where each symbol represents the name of a tree.

"They say ogham was originally only developed for the day-to-day commerce of the people. It was also heard tell that we Irish were late or slow to develop because we had no writing and, then, when we did have an alphabet it was no more than scratching of lines. Such talk comes from ignorance, my friends, and from wantin' to put down the Irish just fer bein' Irish.

"I am here to put the record straight in your minds. Irish is a magic language. The arts of speaking and of deep listening had an alchemy that the Druids did not want to lose. So not only did they maintain an oral tradition, but they forbade written word of anything of importance. Now, the stodgy scholars of later centuries, mind you, them thinking more highly of themselves and less of people of earlier times, got it wrong on both counts. It was not that the Celts were too dumb to develop written history. 'Twas that they chose not to, for they were not wantin' to lose the power and the magic of the word.

"Long before the Celts had read *Genesis*, they too believed that, 'In the beginning was the Word.' They believed that sound and resonance and vibration create magic and hold the sacred. Irish is a magic tongue even to this very day. And that's the way of it.

"And the Druids knew the secret meaning of the ogham. They studied the tree mysteries and they used the ogham to hold and communicate these great Celtic mysteries. The ovates or healers studied herbs and plants, the bards knew their stories and songs, but only the Druids learned the deepest level of story and symbol and magic that was the ogham.

"But I digress. The story you see is a simple one. It is a story of a man lying looking at the heavens when he is inspired to create the ogham. What did he see that so inspired him? Would you believe, 'twas the flight of the cranes overhead, with their feet all crisscrossed. And that, my friends, is how the first written words of Ireland came to be. So with that, I will be leaving you with a wee blessing:

> May your journey to this place and at this time be rich and joyful and may you find yourselves at the very heart of the spirit that is our Emerald Isle.

" 'Tis a good night, I'll be sayin' to ye."

With that, he gulps down the remainder of his whiskey, rises from his chair, and heads to the back of the room. Everyone stands, clapping, and then surrounding him with their personal thanks. Next moment, he is off.

There is still a harpist to come, thanks to the other group. But, we have our own in Lily. Since we have to be on our way west in the morning, most of us say our good nights and go off to pack or turn in early. A few linger, but this time, Angie and I aren't among them.

DAY EIGHT

SLIGO TOWN *CARROWMORE*
QUEEN MAEVE'S TOMB

We leave the Boyne Valley and travel west to Yeats Country and the sea.
Lunch will be in Sligo Town.
Major stops will be at the ruins of Neolithic sites,
including an optional climb up to Maeve's Tomb.
We will arrive at our last lodging, The Sea Side Inn, in
time for dinner and a sunset walk along the strand.

MEGAN

I always thought that once you were thirty, you knew everything. Maybe not all the answers to the big questions, but like knowing yourself and stuff. Now, I wonder. I love these people. They are the coolest group of adults I have ever met, but they all seem flustered. Seekers, Dorrie calls them. They are searching for something or wanting to transform something or change. Somehow it makes me tired just thinking about all that.

Mom says not to get bummed out about it, but to think of it as continuous learning. She says truly healthy people are open to new things and always searching to fine tune meaning and purpose in their lives. Makes sense, I guess, but I hope I don't get old and find I don't know my purpose in life. Or freak out like Peg and disappear from my husband or, the worst, get angry and bitter like Mary Helena.

Mary Helena was so rude to poor Rob at breakfast. I can't believe it. He comes in all cheery-like and she goes, "And, what does a man whose wife is off God-knows-where, doing God-knows-what, have to be so happy about?"

"And, good morning to you, too, Mary Helena," Rob says. I am so surprised he doesn't just put her down or something, but he goes on, "To answer your questions, first I am by nature a person of infinite spiritual optimism, only enhanced by being here surrounded by the beauty of this land and its sacred places. And, as for Peg, she is strong and has a great head on her shoulders. I trust her, I trust our relationship and I trust she is doing exactly what she needs to be doing. If truth be told, it does feel very strange to travel without her, to be packing up her things and moving on to a new place. But, she knows where we are going, and she will find us. Thanks for your concern."

He actually says, "thanks for your concern" like he means it. He isn't rude or sarcastic. I would have been so mad. Someone changes the subject and then in a few minutes we say our "gratefuls" for the day. I say I was grateful to meet and learn from so many people who were actually fun to be around. People laugh. But I didn't dare look at Mary Helena 'cause I really didn't mean her at all. I may be learning from her, but she is not fun.

Everybody scurries around to get ready to move on to County Sligo. Mom makes me help some of the older people bring their suitcases down to Timothy. There is no elevator. I should get extra points for helping Mary Helena, I keep thinking, but Mom says she is just unhappy and that everyone should cut her slack, because she has had a hard life. Dad left us before I was even born so I don't know why Mom thinks this lady has had it harder, but that's my Mom.

Dorrie is just about to begin our morning session as Timothy and I come in from loading the bus. She nods to us and begins.

"As you know, we cross back to the West of Ireland today. We will virtually be traveling a path which is that of the ancient peoples whose monuments we have been seeing. Many believe that these peoples were not only tuned into the heavens but also to crystalline properties in the rocks and electro-magnetic forces in the earth. It's believed that these energy forces move along ley lines. This concept adds to the mystery and wonder of the ancient sites placed along these lines and at their crossing points (vortices or vortexes). So I want to give you a little background before we start out. Are you ready for one more mini-lecture?"

There is a mock groan from the group, but I don't think anybody means it. This stuff is way too cool.

"We have here a couple of maps of the ley lines as they are believed to occur here in Ireland."

She had borrowed a projector from the center and now is projecting maps with lines and diagrams on them from her jump drive.

"Note the straight line from Newgrange to Maeve's Tomb. You will see there are a lot more places named on the map that we will not take time to stop to see; for example, Fourknocks and Loughcrew. They are all of a similar time as Newgrange. Is this coincidence? Is this just the common sense of ancient peoples, placing their temples at places of beauty and majesty and then traveling to them in the straightest line possible? Or did these people know ancient arts, science and magic, that we have only speculated about? The study of ley lines is called geomancy. Many cultures acknowledge them. In ancient China, they were called 'dragon lines.' Native Americans created sacred places at power points where ley lines crossed. Temples in Greece, Turkey, and Crete also show similar attention to these energies.

"The question is, was this part of an ancient wisdom that we have lost? Might we be able to tap into this knowledge and power to heal our present day world?

"Those who read or saw *The Da Vinci Code* will remember the Rose Line, the idea that ancient mystery sites connect through France and up to Scotland on the same ley line. Scholars debate whether it is really true. Some say the Paris Meridian and the Arago markers are only coincidentally tied to this esoteric narrative, but the fact that it is historically documented and that markers are visible today gives me pause to at least wonder about it."

Dorrie points to the next map that shows continental Europe and the British Isles with the Rose Line and another line going diagonally across. She continues: "Note here that Stonehenge, Newgrange, and Maeve's Tomb are on the same line. Coincidence or not?"

She then asks if anyone had traveled to Sedona, Arizona or some of the other places reported to have vortexes and ley lines. Rebecca shares that she had been hiking in a vortex area of Sedona when a bunch of tourists with cameras came trudging through asking where they could find the vortex at Boynton Canyon. She says all they wanted was to snap a picture and move on to the next site. So much for enlightenment and reflection. She adds how grateful she is that our group is not like that at all. She also says that she had felt similar energies here in Ireland.

Dorrie continues, "Some of you may be dowsers who can find water or oil or minerals by using a dowsing rod. Is anyone?"

Penny and Peter raise their hands saying they had dabbled with it. Mom says her grandfather had used it for the well on his farm. I didn't know that. In fact, I never heard of dowsing until Nathan told me he had talked to some of the men about it back at Salmon Lodge. I wish we had more time for me to ask questions, but I will get Nathan to fill me in later.

"Let's save our discussion of Queen Maeve for the bus so that Timothy can get us underway. That will give us more time in Sligo Town where we will stop for lunch. I don't pretend to have any authoritative word on the ley lines but wanted to make sure you saw the maps before we left. You can decide on your own whether they mean anything to you."

We pack up, saying good-bye to the nuns who have been so great, and board the bus in a fun mood for the drive across to Sligo, in spite of the rain. The head nun pinches my cheek as she says good-bye. Even my grandmother hasn't done that to me since I was twelve. But it's okay, just her way.

Everybody settles in, glad the rain waited till today. Gordie says "You can't come to Ireland and not expect rain. But if the Irish can live with it so cheerfully, then so can we."

"Besides," adds Timothy, "You'll be finding the weather to the West is sunny and bright and I predict a rainbow in our future." And just to prove his point, or maybe it is just a coincidence, he puts on U2's *It's a Beautiful Day*. He is so nice and I really love listening to him talk. I wonder if he and Kate are actually together-together?

Penny points out the window to the right and starts singing *"when the Mountains of Mourne sweep down to the sea . . .."* I never heard the song before, but the story of what it means to her is interesting. She tells me, "I came to Ireland when I was your age, back in 1963."

"My mother wasn't even born then."

"Yes, and it was with my mother, our first trip abroad. We were attending a cousin's wedding in Ballyclare, Country Antrim, home of my grandmother and grandfather. You see, Northern Ireland is beautiful, too. You would just love Giant's Causeway, the Glens of Antrim and a closer look at these Mountains of Mourne. My uncle always sang that song."

"Maybe Mom and I can come back before I go to college. I would love to see all of Ireland."

Penny keeps talking. I like it because I love hearing about people's heritage.

"The other day when we were in Dublin, I went in to the Northern Irish Tourist Board offices, driven by curiosity and the loyalty of an Orangeman's granddaughter I guess. They had a brochure on Northern Ireland that shows pictures of dolmens and stone circles. They showed a dolmen located less than two or three miles from where my grandfather lived as a boy. Oh how I wish I had known about Neolithic Ireland when I was visiting or even after, so I could have asked my grandfather about it before he died. Did he go there? Did he know what they were? No one showed me any of that stuff while I was visiting there nor did they ever mention any of it. Grandpa was Scots-Irish Presbyterian all the way. In fact, when I was your age, I used to be so embarrassed that the hot headed fanatic leader of the Orangeman, Ian Paisley, was a Presbyterian minister. Although I was thankful he was from an entirely different branch of Presbyterianism than my family."

I ask her what she means about Orangemen.

She tells me that the name came from "Good King Billy or William of Orange" who wanted the British Crown and came to conquer Ireland as a way to gain power back in England.

"We were church-going Presbyterians. We took Grandpa up to the Orangeman's Parade in Toronto every summer and we listened to his old John McCormick records. I admit to impatience when Gramps wanted to use my hi-fi to play those scratchy, old records. I recall wanting to wear green on St. Patrick's Day. He would say 'so long as you remember, 'tis not our holiday at all' with his strong brogue that sounded fierce, even though I knew he was a softie. He always had a wink and a smile for me.

"Now, here I am studying the three-fold form of the goddess, leaving ale for the leprechauns, and enjoying the hospitality of the South, without a care in the world. I wonder what he would say?"

"Are there still problems, between North and South?"

"Mostly it's only in the border areas now, and certain neighborhoods in Belfast City. In fact, you'll find a lot of folks in the South don't even want to talk about it. But old hatreds run deep and are easily stirred up. It's always sobering to think that folks who look alike could have such hatred and distrust. And, if so, how will The Beloved Community that Dr. King envisioned ever come about?"

"Yeah, everyone is white and Christian, right?"

"Ireland is becoming more diverse—but yes, you're right—the old hatreds that remain are among those who are white and Christian."

Finian's Rainbow is playing on the CD and people are humming or singing along. We both look around, ready to change the subject and get to something lighter. Angie is sketching, Mary Helena is working on a Brigid's Cross needlepoint now and others are just watching out the window. It is getting sunnier. Someone jokes that we have now gone clear across the country and back again, yet Dorrie and Gordie have not shown us a pot of gold. Then, we round a curve and Timothy shouts out, "Will ye look up ahead now? Sure here is your gold." We look out at fields of yellow and gold, the brightest and most splendid splash of color, moving in waves by the wind.

It really is beautiful.

Rob shouts up to Timothy, "What's the crop, Timothy? I've seen nothing like that in America." He says it like he was trying to imitate the way Timothy keeps saying "You have nothing like that in America."

Timothy chuckles "Aye, now, that would be rapeseed, would you not have that in all of America?"

Most of us have never heard of rapeseed. But Peter knows: "A Canadian used rapeseed in the 1970's as the basis for canola oil. That is why it is farmed on a large scale now. Not many were using this ancient plant until canola was invented."

Timothy chuckles, "Takes a visitor to tell me about me own land. Shame on me." He puts on *Fields of Gold* while we continue along the highway. I know it from Sting, but this is an Irish woman singing.

Gordie takes the mike and asks us if we would like to play a brain teaser. It reminds me of traveling with Gram and Grampa with my cousins, but why not? He split us into two teams. The idea is to see how many things we can list that are threesomes, like in the Celtic power of threes that Dorrie keeps talking about. He suggests we take turns and the last team to have an answer wins.

"Who'll be the judge?" someone asks.

"Timothy and Dorrie," he adlibs, looking over at them. They nod that they will.

"What is the prize?" asks another.

"How about the losers chip in for a couple more bottles of mead?" someone else suggests.

Gordie reads some examples from a copy of *The Triads of Ireland*, a listing of over 250 triads, from physical properties like rivers, lake and sea to attributes like "the three things for which an enemy is loved: wealth, beauty and worth." It is supposed to warm us up. But I think it's kind of intimidating.

Lily, though, is not intimidated at all. She pops up with a riddle for us: "What are three things that constitute a harpist?"

There are some good tries but then folks beg her for the answer.

"Well, there is a tune to make you cry, a tune to make you laugh, and a tune to put you to sleep. Easy, huh?" she replies.

Everyone applauds. And so the game begins. At first it's easy and the answers fly back and forth quickly:

"Brede, Brigid, Brigit"

"Earth, Sky, and Sea"

"Maiden, Mother, Crone"

"Father, Son, and Holy Ghost"

"Birth, death, rebirth"

"Mind, body, spirit"

Then someone suggests it become a challenge or quiz, like:

"Name the three Aran Islands"

"Three bays of Ireland"

"Three attributes of Brigid"

It gets tougher, until finally some shouts out, "What are the three cues to indicate a game is over?" Everyone laughs and agrees to stop while we are ahead. Besides, we're near a pit stop.

Once we're going again, Dorrie takes the mike. "Legend has it that all of Tara's kings were required to sleep with Queen Maeve before their coronation. It was no doubt a ritual that harkened back to the days of the Goddess. As we know, most ancient cultures had a *hieros gamos*, a ceremony of union between a representative of the Goddess and of the King. The Power of the Mother meets the Power of Father, Nature meets Man. It was said to ensure fertility and a good harvest. As Maeve morphed from Goddess to Queen, she retained the power and sovereignty of the Divine Feminine throughout Celtic times.

"Symbolic of her influence, you will soon notice a mound on top of a far-off mountain. That is her tomb and it can be seen for miles and miles. It is a bee-hive structure, like Newgrange, with corbelled roof. Some say it looks like a nipple on a giant breast, but I want to talk about how it looks like a beehive. The symbolism of the bee was important to the Celts. The names Medh, Maeve, and lots of its variations mean bee. Remember when Timothy brought us mead the other evening? It was made of honey.

"We all know that the Queen Bee is in charge, the beehive is to protect her and that there is only one in the colony. So the legend that the Queen, the Mother, the Goddess was sovereign and that her sanctuary was womb-like and dark with light coming in and out at strategic moments made sense to ancient people dependent on the land. Maeve's Howe in the Orkneys of Scotland is even bigger and more clearly demonstrates her importance to the Neolithic peoples.

"As people start organizing by kingdoms, not just tribal communities, the need to remind them of the power of the Mother and the sovereignty of the land created the requirement that Queen Maeve travel to Tara for the marriage or sexual meeting with each would-be king. Like the rites of May, where a maiden was taken to bed by the prince, this was seen as necessary for the land to thrive and be fertile. The pervasive sense of women's sovereignty and the need for men to partner with them for the land to thrive and be fertile is played out in subtle and not so subtle ways within Celtic Ireland. Here, people never subscribed to the belief in dominion over nature.

"You might have heard of the *Cattle Raid of Cooley*. In this famous tale of pagan times, Queen Maeve, representing her province of Connaught against Ulster and its King, do battle over a white bull. There are many renditions, but they all play on this notion of male-female power. The bull, of course, represents power and potency and its symbol is Taurus. It is fun to think about the millennia that we know about and how the astrological signs (going counterclockwise around the Zodiac) correspond to the animals most sacred and symbolic to that time period and what that means. Gemini, Taurus, Aries, Pisces, Aquarius: The Twins gave way to the Bull which was followed by the Ram and then the Fish and now the Water Carrier; each the symbol of an epoch."

Wow, I really have to think about that one! And also about this thing about sovereignty; it's new to me and something tells me it is important. I'll ask Mom and Kate.

As Dorrie finishes, Timothy adds that the May Day celebrations and the fairs that are held throughout Ireland, but especially in the West, are linked to Maeve and to the celebration of the sovereignty of the land and its bounty. He puts in a CD with old Irish tunes and everyone joins in singing, *"She moved through the fair..."*

I kick back, thinking I will journal some of this amazing stuff.

When I next look out, I see another mountain to the North of Sligo Bay. Timothy speaks up to tell us it is called Ben Bulben, the legendary home of the Fir Bolg. I, of course, have to ask who they were. Timothy says they were an ancient warrior group. Dorrie adds that it is also Yeats country. She points out the place on the rock cliff which is said to be a fairy entrance to the Other World. Amazing.

Kevin offers a famous Yeats poem about the place.

Under bare Ben Bulben's head
In Drumcliff churchyard Yeats is laid.
An ancestor was rector there
Long years ago, a church stands near,

By the road an ancient cross.
No marble, no conventional phrase;
On limestone quarried near the spot
By his command these words are cut:

Cast a cold eye
On life, on death.
Horseman, pass by.

Kevin is such a great guy. I would love a dad like that. Stupid Jackson can't even see it.

Even Mary Helena joins in the oohing and ahhing as we catch sight of Sligo Bay. I'm probably the loudest. I so love the ocean.

Gordie takes over the mike, "This indeed is Yeats country. Tomorrow, if you want, you can take a longer tour and steep yourselves in the story of his life and the stories in his literary works. But, the shorter version is right here in Sligo Town. His statue is just a short walk up the main street and the museum is around the corner. Yeats may have been born in Dublin, but he felt most at home here. In his autobiography, he says, '*I longed for a sod of earth from some field I knew, something of Sligo to hold in my hand.*' Of course, he meant the whole countryside not just the town of Sligo. Nonetheless, the town's energy and prosperity was much enhanced by his return and the name recognition it has today is because of him."

When we are off the bus and on our own, Mom and I walk slowly across the bridge. I am glad she hadn't asked Mary Helena to join us. The Garavogue River rushes below us. It is peaceful and energizing at the same time. I love water. It is kinda like the Ballykissangel place, but the river here is much, much wider and stronger.

Kevin is already up at the Yeats statue when we get there. He describes how he can picture Yeats strolling along. The skinny man in bronze is cool. Mom takes pictures of Kevin and then of all of us, including Jackson, who shows up just in time. Then I am ready to move on. Mom agrees I can go off exploring.

Lunch is at the big old hotel right in the town center by the river. No way I can get lost. I walk by the hotel before I hit the shops, just to make sure I know where I am. Looking into its windows, I can imagine all the people from Mom's postcard gathered over tea in the salon. It will be a great place for lunch. Meantime, I look in shops. We have done almost no shopping! But mainly, I think a lot about what is going on.

At lunch, I find that Mom saved me a seat at a table with Trish, Kate, Natalie, Angie, and Rebecca. Perfect! I had all these ideas that popped up while I was walking around and I wanted to talk about them. I had gone into an internet café just to see who was around. No kids were there, so I looked up stuff online about ley lines and stuff. "I really get now that history, science, psychology, religion; even mythology and magic have to be seen together. And people have to know their biases and open themselves to different thinking. I can't wait to get to college 'cuz only one of my high school teachers even gets this."

"That hurts to hear, but often it is true that teachers are too caught up in old curricula," Melanie lets the thought trail off.

Kate jumps in, telling me, "More and more college faculties are offering interdisciplinary programs. In fact, when Dorrie was talking this morning, I thought of a new program called archeo-astronomy I just read about. Make sure you look into schools with innovative programs that will challenge you in new ways like that. Oh my, am I sounding too much like a teacher or too much like a mom? Or both?"

But both Mom and I thank her for the advice. Mom even suggests we talk to her about selecting schools next summer. All of them make me feel so good about myself and they are so cool, each in their own way. So I continue, "I want to be the Joseph Campbell of my generation."

They all applaud right there in the dining room and I am mortified. But they go on, talking about Campbell and his influence, ignoring my blushing. Rebecca, pitches journalism by pointing out that it was the journalist Bill Moyers and PBS who brought Campbell's work to everyday people. Everyone has read *The Power of Myth* and agrees it was one of the best books ever.

I keep going, "I always thought that cultural anthropologists like Margaret Mead were kind of b-o-r-i-n-g, but the more Dorrie and Kate talk about historiography and patriarchy and the Divine Feminine, the more I see that it could be interesting. I googled a lot of this and found out more about that amazing woman from Lithuania, Marija Gimbutas. You know, she was the one who first showed that the Goddess and matriarchy were there before all the invading tribes took over. Did you know she came to America and taught? Did you know Joseph Campbell said she was awesome and that he wished he had known her work when he wrote? Why doesn't anyone ever talk about all this stuff?"

The older women agree that if they ran the media, different choices would be made; same for educational policy and schools. Mom laughs and says, "All this talk is charging my batteries for my work back on the Hill. Maybe, I should get a focus group of NetGens like Megan to shake us up some."

"Good idea, Mom!" I reply.

The others agree and add, "Not just like Megan, but including Megan."

That feels really good and I start to talk again, but Mom interrupts: "You are like the Energizer Bunny today. Maybe you need to give everybody a break."

But the women urge me to keep going, so I do. "Remember when we first talked about *sheela-na-gigs* and then I found that booklet? The writer is criticizing the sixteenth century monks for their take on them, but he is blind to his own biases. Kate, you explained to me then about historiography, about studying the historians themselves and how the lens of their time and upbringing, gender, class, etc., influenced their work.

"And now this ley line stuff, OMG! Energy and magnetic and electromagnetic forces. Most historians and anthropologists didn't even consider that the placement and the design of ruins had more to them than just being forts."

Kate reluctantly interrupts me to point out Timothy and the rest of the group are leaving for the bus. She suggests we continue this later. I think she really means it.

Carrowmore and Maeve's Tomb are only about five miles from the Town of Sligo. This seems strange 'cause, after having looked at it from a distance for what seemed like hours, now it is actually too close to see. Perspective is a funny thing.

Then we pass them by. What? Dorrie explains that we were going to Carrowkeel first. She explains that the climb up to Maeve's Tomb might leave people tired and dirty and wanting to go directly to the Inn. Timothy says it only means backtracking ten to fifteen miles.

Dorrie gives us an overview of Carrowkeel as we pull in: "I know some of you have probably seen enough rocks for a lifetime, but I can't let you miss this place. We'll be seeing remains of a village of huts as well as cairns and passage tombs. Here the main points of alignment are with the moon and also with Croagh Patrick, seventy-five miles away. At one time historians said the place was established as a burial ground for unbaptized children. But we now know that is not true. In fact, some speculate that it was an ancient observatory of some sort. No one knows for sure."

I am particularly intrigued by the light box that lets the sun in a month before and a month after summer solstice and lets the moon in a month before and a month after winter solstice. How did they know to do that? And why? Dorrie shows us the Croagh Patrick Stone, shaped like a mountain. She says the sun sets here on both Samhain and Imbolc (November 1 and February 1). How awesome is that?

We then go to Carrowmore. More rocks. Dorrie tells us this is the oldest and largest of all the Neolithic sites in Ireland. We don't take the official tour but we wander around with a site map. There are like thirty tombs. The huge center dolmen with a ring of stones around it is amazing. Then there is a pyramid made with five standing stones that is also cool. Some of the stuff is restored, others parts are untouched and then other parts have been messed up by people who didn't really know how to do archeology. I would get so bored sifting through dirt all day, but I am intrigued by people who do it and what they find.

We hop back on the bus and over to the parking lot at the foot of the trail that goes up the mountain to Maeve's Cairn or, you know, Maeve's Tomb, which we had been driving toward all morning. It is on the top of Knocknarea Mountain and it just shouts "pay attention to me."

Both Dorrie and Gordie warn everyone that the climb of about two and a half miles is a little treacherous in places; nothing dramatic, but certainly not a quick romp in sandals. It will take about forty-five minutes. They suggest though that all those thinking of climbing Croagh Patrick should definitely think of this as a test run. I'm not sure I want to go to Croagh Patrick when I can be at the beach, but I can't wait to get to Maeve's Tomb. I've only been staring at the little mound at the top of the far-off mountain all day. No way would I miss going up.

Timothy is taking all the non-climbers to the shore, just a few miles away. Our hiking group heads up by foot as the rest of the group heads down on the bus. Timothy is driving them down a beautiful path to the sea. I wish I could do both.

Mom goes to the ocean. She says she just felt like some alone time walking the beach. When I ask her about it later, she just said everyone got out, walked the beach, put their toes into the ocean and just sat and watched the birds circling with the air currents. She never really told me what had been on her mind.

I keep looking for them as I climb, but the road curves too much. Kevin, Nathan, Dorrie, Gordie, Jackson, and I get to the top first. It is gorgeous. When Rose arrives, she and Dorrie find a bank which probably had been used for rituals. Rose says she can almost see the ceremonies. Dorrie nods. Then we sit and watch Nathan and Jackson climb to the very top of the stone pile–all forty feet, like mountain goats or a kind of King of the Mountain.

When we get down the hill, the bus is waiting for us and I hear a chorus of *The Water is Wide* by Enya. Now I really can't wait to get to the ocean. Finally, the slackers arrive and we are off.

Timothy tells us, " 'Twill not be long now, 'tis not far. We are headed directly, as directly as any Irish road 'tis known to be, to The Seaside Inn, an old distillery, now a wee oasis of a lodging place by the sea."

The owners are actually there to greet us as we get out of the bus. There are four of them, two brothers who married two sisters. They tell us they quit city jobs to do this inn thing. They sure do seem happy about it. I'd love to hear more, but everyone is anxious to get their room assignments. And I can't wait to go to the beach.

They really spoil us, too. Dinner is this scrumptious buffet of seafood, oysters, salmon, and fish. The table is beautiful, with flowers and candles. They light our table candles during dessert and I love the dessert. It is this layered meringue, whipped cream, and strawberries called Pavlova Cake. Penny says the Irish call it a "company dessert," you know, for "tea time." And Mom promises me she'll make it for my birthday.

We get to see an amazing sunset. I love seeing the sun set on the water. And the moon was bright and getting bigger. Walking along the beach, the strand, as they call it, is so great. If only I had a cute Irish boy to share it with. But other than Jackson and Nathan, there are no other boys around. Bummer.

The biggest surprise, though, is that Gordie has arranged for the Inn to show *The Secrets of Roan Inish* on the lounge flat screen. It is one of my favorite movies. It's the reason Mom and I had even thought to come to Ireland. And then he follows it with *Ondine,* with Colin Farrell. I love it.

ROSE

A year ago, I never would have imagined a trip to Ireland, and certainly not this kind of trip. Yet, here I am in

Yeats country. As my dad used to say, "The world works in mysterious ways." I had Jack and the company he works for to thank for the opportunity. While the recession has burst the economic bubble of the Irish Tiger, the company my Jack works for is still pleased with the business opportunities here. I was just lucky to find this tour at exactly the time he would be off golfing and hobnobbing with his international clients.

I had always collected fairy figurines and pictures. They used to be harder to find, but now they are everywhere. Just a few years ago, I came across a wonderfully enchanting book that got me into them again. This young woman stumbles upon a portal to an ancient land of fairy. I was so smitten with it, that I started thinking about my fairy collection and about my childhood. And right about then, I came across a flyer about a workshop on "Providing Sanctuaries for the Fairies" in the Charlottesville area. Under the guise of visiting my sister, so I didn't have to explain to Jack, I traveled down to attend. Actually, my sister went with me, which was fantastic. Now we are both hooked on truly learning about the Fairy Kingdom and how we can help keep it alive. I asked Sis why she never showed any interest in fairies when we were children. She just shrugged and said that the family thought of it as Rosie's thing so she paid no attention.

It sure was my thing. Everything I owned had a fairy on it. I had a fairy lunch bag, notebook, and purse. When things could not be found with fairies already on them, I added fairy stickers. I had a Tinkerbell collection, a fairy princess, and magic castle collection, too. Wisely, my parents stayed out of it, neither encouraging nor disallowing the near fixation that I had about everything fairy. What they did not know was that my brother called me Tinkerbell and teased me unmercifully.

Nor did they know my big secret. I had a true fairy friend, Elsbeth. I confided everything to Elsbeth and Elsbeth taught me all sorts of things about the garden and flowers. Then my brother heard me talking to her. He really ridiculed me after that. Finally, I couldn't take it anymore. I gave in and gave up Elsbeth. I remember my mom asking why I was so sad. But I never told her. In my heart of hearts, I had lost my best friend and I knew it was my fault. I had abandoned Elsbeth, my dear and loyal friend. Eventually, I grew up and moved on but I never forgot.

Now, I am realizing, as Dorrie said, folklore around the world includes fairies or little people. And, there was Yeats. He seemed to believe in what he was capturing in Celtic lore. They say it was one of the reasons he revived the stories from Irish peasants so the *sidhe* would not fade out of Irish consciousness.

So now I've come full circle and was wondering again if it might be true that there is a Fairy Kingdom and that we can communicate and interact with it if we believe it to be so and are open to it. Even if it is just a metaphor, it is a metaphor that needs to be promoted. That's my latest conclusion. It reminds us that we are all connected and that our precious environment and all the living things that make it up must be believed in and protected.

I went back and attended a second workshop on elementals and the Fairy Kingdom just before the trip. It went into a lot more detail about the different kinds of elementals such as fairies, dwarfs, leprechauns, sprites, elves, gnomes, devas, etc. The workshop leader was joined by another woman who played a number of instruments and sang the most magical music. Then together they led what they called a fairy journey, I was swept away and could imagine every step of the visualization. It really got my creative juices flowing and my sense of wonder was rekindled.

Later in the workshop, we discussed how to lead these fairy journeys, but I was so overwhelmed that I didn't get it all; it was too much to absorb and process. Then, I got busy getting Jack and my things ready for the trip and sort of forgot about it.

Since stepping off the plane, though, I have sensed that Elsbeth is at my side. Remembering all the ridicule I had suffered as a child, I decided to remain quiet about the whole thing. Jack would have locked me up. But then, on the first night of the tour, I decided I would open up a bit about all this.

That third day, the one with all the options back at Salmon Run Lodge, I made an appointment with Dorrie. Talking with her, I worked through some of my hurt at the sense of ridicule I had felt as a kid and explored some of my thinking with her. She was great. She reminded me that lots of people spoke about angels these days, and out of body experiences, and that seeing fairies, channeling, etc., were all very subjective. Just because they could not be proven did not mean they were not real. While some people won't believe, more and more people are opening to the possibility. Dorrie added her personal belief that the different manifestations of Spirit come to people differently according to their world views. All are real in their own right.

Dorrie encouraged me to trust my heart and my "still small voice within." She also said to always ask that the contact be in my Highest Good and in the Highest Good of all involved. It is her belief that spirits will leave if you tell them to do so and that they have to honor you when you ask for the Highest Good.

It was at Glendalough, where I first had the experience of seeing other fairies besides Elsbeth. When Dorrie gathered the group for guided meditation, I could not believe what I saw inside my mind's eye. A dozen or more fairy people, dressed in finery and looking very regal, were greeting and blessing the group. I could tell Lily was greeting them back, but I couldn't tell if anyone else saw them.

When Dorrie sent everyone off for personal meditation, Elsbeth and I went over and behind some nearby bushes. There was an open space. I sat there and was rewarded by a view into the Other World with Elsbeth as my guide. I marveled at the sense that this parallel kingdom of earth, water, and sky was so beautiful and bright and peaceful. I felt lighter than ever before and was entirely speechless.

Later, I realized that this had been the kind of fairy journey that I had been introduced to in the workshop back in Virginia. Now, here I am in the midst of Yeats country. Ever since we arrived in County Sligo, I have sensed the Little People around me. I keep getting shivers, a kind of shared excitement all the time. I see blurry movement out of the corner of my eye all the time now, too. And Elsbeth says a leprechaun is asking her for a formal introduction. So watching the movie just now has really blown me away. Are there actually roans or selkies? Would they present themselves to me? What all is in store? Will I ever settle into sleep?

ROB

"I must go down to the sea again."

This line of poetry just keeps repeating itself in my mind all day. I'm not sure why, but I can't shake it. Neither can I shake my anxiety about Peg. I have been pretty calm up until now, but it has been a long time with no word at all. And, I miss her. Packing up without her today was especially strange.

So here I am in Yeats country. Headed to the sea. Hopefully, so is Peg. She so loves the sea. If she is not there yet, I will really begin to worry. I so hope the song's words *and there my true love shall be* will pan out.

I've been doing my work, my psychological work. I can only hope that Peg has done hers as well. For me, it's all about coming to terms with what the phrase "emergence of the Divine Feminine" really means, in general, for me, my ministry, and my life with Peg. I've always been able to change; to really make deep paradigm shifts, and to do so rather quickly and painlessly. I just need to be exposed to the new models and concepts. I'm not good at conceptualizing things alone. I tried to explain this to Kate. Not sure if it made sense to her, but I found it clarifying some things for me as I talked them through out loud.

I've gone through lots of changes in my life. My family came from Spain, during the Fascist movement, with good educations but no money. We were different from everyone in the neighborhood. Some people saw me as a very complicated guy. But I didn't think so, even though I didn't fit any stereotype. I wasn't predictable, and that made some people uneasy.

But, in my mind, my life took a natural progression. As I sought a path to spiritual maturity, I found I had a gift for helping others do the same. Helping people get in touch (or stay in touch) with who they are and find flow in their life is my ministry.

As a college student, I got involved in liberation theology. It mainly took hold in South America where the priests and their people questioned their impoverished circumstance and the role of the Church. I came neither from poverty nor South America, but by speaking Spanish I was privy to many personal stories of injustice and pain. I listened and took them all in, knowing it made me a better man.

Then I began thinking of becoming a priest. I soon realized that not just the hierarchy and privilege bothered me, but the theology did, too. I could not picture God. Who would this God look like? I did experience a sense of something greater than myself and something deep and meaningful within myself. When I read Emerson's idea of the Oversoul, I knew I was on the track of finding a theology that I could accept. His writing led me to seminary and UU ministry.

And now the notion of Celtic soul is affecting me in a similar way. I had always heard that a trip to Ireland stirred the Irish soul; I've read Thomas Moore and most all the Celtic mystics. But I didn't expect it to get in my blood like it has. At the Well, I asked to be open to new ministries that met the needs of this new century, this new time. Now, I'm experiencing my answer.

I learned long ago, you cannot change other people; you can only change yourself in relation to others. I know Peg believes that, too. I know that's why she went off alone, without my counsel or support. I get that it was a segment of her journey toward wholeness that does not include me. What surprises me is how very hard it is to just wait.

When Mary Helena made her sharp comments this morning, there was no way I wanted to try to explain all this, but certainly I've kept thinking about it. I hate being alone. And Peg's absence is making me realize how much I rely on her. Perhaps, this time has even been good for me, but, whatever, I just want her to be there when we arrive.

I must go down to the sea again.

I'm getting more and more anxious. Is she already here? Will she come tonight? Can she get transportation way out here? I enter the Inn. Taking a deep breath, I ask the desk clerk if she is here.

"Aye, the lady checked in two days ago. Here is a key to the room. She says to tell you she is on the strand."

It is all I can do to put our luggage in the room, leave my socks and shoes behind, and run to the beach. I find her down the strand, walking a make-shift labyrinth in the sand. She looks vibrant, she looks wonderful. She sees me just as I begin to move toward her. We run into each other's arms like kids, but the embrace between us is very adult. Neither of us says a word. Neither of us wants to pull away.

When we do break the embrace, we wander hand in hand further down the beach, away from the Inn. I spot a secluded place on the back side of a rather high sand dune. We stop there.

The emotional charge between us is matched by the sounds of the sea, creating a trance-like sense of timelessness. Rolling waves, steady, gentle sounds of nature coming in to thrust themselves upon the shore. Crescendo, echo, silence; cyclical, gentle, but piercing rhythm, like being rocked in the soul of Abraham, like being home in the womb, soothing, healing in its steadiness, its constancy, its fullness. The rich sound, gentle yet strong, present yet non-intrusive. Change creeping in slowly, penetrating, ever moving; steady, firm, certain. With these sounds our coming back together is affirmed, our reunion complete.

DAY NINE

AT THE SEA *YEATS COUNTRY TOUR*

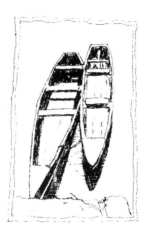

Today offers a day of respite and reflection for those who wish to relax by the sea.
We also will offer a half-day trip through Yeats country with a visit to his gravesite.

DORRIE

"What's with you?" I ask, experiencing what I call Gordie's shadowy side.

"Nothing. Why do you ask?" he responds curtly.

"Well, you practically bit my head off back there. And right after yoga, to boot. Did you just wake up on the wrong side of the bed or is something bothering you?"

"Just that we have this bus tour and most people are not going to be doing any touring for the next three days—that's one quarter of the trip. What if they hate just hanging around? What if they start fighting with one another? I'm getting antsy myself, and I have more control over the process than they do."

"I thought it was just wonderful to see so many people out doing spiritual practices at the beach."

"So?"

"So? That is exactly the snappishness I mean." I answer. I'm learning to answer back and not take it personally when he gets challenging like this. So I take a deep breath and continue, "I know you say I always see things through rose-colored glasses, but people seem really in the flow to me. Do you see any signs of trouble?"

"Not really."

"So let's just let it unfold. We can watch for indications of people wanting something they're not finding." I think he is just uncomfortable when not doing something, but if I say that when he is in this mood, he will just accuse me of psychoanalyzing him. And, maybe my intuition is off.

Fortunately, Timothy arrives just then. Timothy is always so upbeat. He brings balance back to both of us. I feel better. Breakfast is a hearty buffet of eggs, fruit, oatmeal and homemade breads, including Irish soda bread with raisins. It's my favorite. Since it's close to the end of the trip, I give in and take two pieces. Even after last night's seafood feast, I'm ravenous. Blaming it on the sea air, I eat every bit of everything.

Penny comes over asking if we have a minute for a suggestion. "I keep wishing I could be part of every single conversation at meals, on the bus, everywhere. There are so many resources and interests, so much expertise and so much passion. So I thought why not put together a series of mini-sessions where people could talk about what they are thinking and learning. You know, kind of like bulletin board courses."

Gordie pipes in right away, "That certainly would give people something to do in their down time, especially if they are not going to Yeats country today or on the hike to Croagh Patrick tomorrow."

"I like the idea. It fits in with my sense that the group is developing into a learning community, not just random folks on the same bus tour. But I also know how important reflection and play are. So I'm torn," I offer as a way of continuing the dialogue without committing until I get a better sense of it.

"I think we can take that as a yes, right?" pushes Gordie.

"Let's test it out," is the best response I can give.

We generate a potential list. First we write down all the things planned and then all the other possibilities.

"This is too much, even for me," I say. "We don't want to force things. If, indeed, the knowing is within, we need to leave more time for people to go within, don't you think?"

"Not all of us want to sit around contemplating our navels all day," from Gordie.

Ignoring his sarcastic tone, I answer, "Yeah, but it's so hard to find the balance, so hard to get the right mix. I know how to help individuals and small groups with balance, but a whole bus full? I just don't know . . .. "

Gordie jumps in with "Well, I do, Penny. I think you should go for it. Talk it up with others and we'll get something going."

So much for my leading the program part, I think. But, I need to switch gears anyway and focus on my final session with the group. Maybe I'm being egocentric to think people should want to listen to me again, while I am thinking they might not want to sign up to listen to others. This train of thought, along with the snarky vibe from Gordie, unnerves me. I take a walk around the outside of the Inn to center myself before entering the Blue Room where folks are gathered. When I arrive back, I am relieved that I easily connect with the collective energy of the room.

I dive in: "We are meeting to talk about pilgrimage today so the hikers can get off to Croagh Patrick right after breakfast tomorrow for their climb. The Croagh Patrick excursion is a quintessential pilgrimage, but the Yeats tour today and the labyrinth Peg made in the sand for us can also be forms of pilgrimage.

"A pilgrimage is an intentional journey that creates opportunity for opening to Spirit, taking in that which is needed, and letting go of that which is not. Some pilgrimages require great physical effort such as climbing Croagh Patrick or walking the *Camino de Santiago* in Spain.

"In the example of Croagh Patrick, we have the Celtic rhythm of coming full circle as we have with the labyrinth. We go to the top or to the center and then we return. In some instances, we release the old, find the new, and solidify the changed state. In other instances, we begin with intent for the new, we find it, and we release that which is no longer needed on the return. Pagans talk about going sunward (clockwise) and widdershins (counterclockwise); the first as a sign of manifesting (as the sun builds heat through the day), the second is a sign of demanifesting or releasing. But mostly, I think, it is conscious intent that matters.

"When you walk the labyrinth or even use a finger labyrinth, you are meant to think about your approach and then follow it through. The beauty of the labyrinth is you know you are safe. You know you cannot get lost. Yet, you get turned around at unexpected times. This is meant to free your mind from the mundane and give Spirit space to enter.

"Labyrinths have been found all over the world. There are outdoor labyrinths like one I visited that overlooks the Arctic Ocean in Norway or indoor ones, like the floor of Chartres Cathedral in France. Peg, would you like to share anything about the labyrinth you created on the beach? "

"Ah, well, Dorrie, I am not sure where I would begin. The process of making it was part of my taking off alone to work through some childhood issues that had surfaced. Somehow, actually digging the path in the sand anchored and grounded the mental and emotional work I had been doing the last few days. Plus, it was a joy to see it complete and to share it with you all."

"Thanks, Peg, and let me add we are all delighted to have you back with us."

Everyone applauds for Peg, who graciously acknowledges them with her hands over her heart and a slight bow.

I continue, "Long pilgrimages like the Camino de Santiago require setting aside time, committing to a sometimes arduous yet always simple activity of constancy. The path and goal are clear. The activity has an evenness to it, for one usually follows a trail, and one always is given signs for the direction he or she is traveling. There is an end point in this linear trip and a sense of reward for reaching it.

"In later years, for many in the western world, the concept of suffering entered the picture. The narrative became 'Christ suffered for our sins, and so, we, too, must suffer.' Extreme hardship and penance were added to the concept of pilgrimage. People were told to climb or walk on their knees to prove their true devotion. You won't be surprised to hear that in today's world of instant gratification, pilgrimages lost their appeal. But, there is a resurgence of interest now as seekers, rejecting the notion of suffering, return to the notion of mind/body/spirit integration and fully present intention.

"Pilgrimages can also take the form of a visit to a site or place of special meaning, which is why I said today's trip to Yeats Country could be a pilgrimage. Again, it is the intentionality.

"Vision quests, shamanic journeys, guided visualization, angel visits, and fairy journeys are all in the general family of pilgrimage. In each, you are led to leave your place of security and control, suspending judgment and control, and allowing something outside of yourself to enter."

"But, I thought you said those things were spiritual practices?" comes a sharp question from Mary Helena.

Maybe she is trying to trip me up, but at least she is listening. "You're right, Mary Helena, I did say and write that. I think the difference is simply about intention and magnitude. Pilgrimages are usually major, long-planned, one-time efforts. Spiritual practice is meant to be a daily way of achieving centering. For example, you walk the Camino over a number of days and miles as pilgrimage. You do a slow, intentional meditative walk every morning."

"What about these guided visualizations, fairy journeys, and all that talk I hear some people discussing? Certainly that is not prayer," she continues.

"Good question. Meditation is a form of prayer but visualization is not necessarily prayer. A guided visualization consists of listening or reading a series of steps that lead you into an experience of your imagination, like onto a beach or into a garden. Good ones appeal to all five senses. As for the other part of your question, I would not advise shamanic, fairy, or other journeys unless you know your guide is pure of heart and is very experienced in the process. And, whatever visualization or prayer, always ask for your Highest Good and the Highest Good for all involved."

I get back on track, not wanting to take too long. It is so hard to know what the right balance is. But this is my last talk.

"We know that swimming dark underground passages were part of Egyptian mystery schools and snake pits were part of Greek mystery schools. But, more likely in today's world, our challenges and wisdom learnings come in non-physical ways. The author and men's retreat leader, David Whyte, suggests today's equivalent to facing the monster in *Beowulf* might be saying 'no' in the board room. Remember the all too real story of the Challenger space craft disaster? One engineer insisting on being heard during discussions on the safety of the O-rings might have avoided the tragedy. Today's tests of moral courage are not the romantic pilgrimages of The Knights Templar, but they are still fraught with danger and opportunity. So whether or not you plan to pilgrimage to Croagh Patrick tomorrow, I invite you all to ask yourself these questions:

What are my challenges?
How might I create an intentional opportunity to meet such challenges?
Do I need something to strengthen me? Or cleanse me? Or guide me?

"Ask whatever question you most want answered. Then, open yourself to hear the Universe's response. These next few days are designed to give you time to take in that which you most need from the gifts that Eire has given us.

"Let us be silent together while we contemplate those gifts."

Gordie steps in at the appropriate time to remind people that Kevin will be talking about Yeats at 11:30 and that those wishing to go on the Yeats tour should meet Timothy in the parking lot at 1 p.m.

Just about everyone takes their break on the beach. The sun is shining now and it is gorgeous. In fact, I am debating skipping the Yeats tour to enjoy the beach myself. My earlier fantasy had been that Gordie and I might get away together. Given his prickly mood, I now think being alone would actually be better. As much as I enjoy all this, it is taxing. I need to keep in balance.

Trish, who we are learning is quite the shopper, found kites in Sligo town. She brings them out now, one for each of the kids and another for the adults to share. Megan, city girl that she is, has never flown a kite and the boys get great pleasure in showing her how to catch the wind. I take the first turn with the fourth kite. I think the kids are surprised to see my bright rainbow-striped kite above theirs, riding an air current, diving and soaring high in the sky. They have no way of knowing that flying kites is my favorite pastime. When I was a kid, I used to imagine that I could fly, too. After a few bruised knees, I learned to let the kite fly for me. And now, it is so Zen. I just love it.

It's hard to go back inside when the beach is so luscious. But Gordie gently, but authoritatively, gets everyone back to the Blue Room. I don't envy Kevin his time slot, but he seems really excited for the opportunity.

He begins enthusiastically: "We have heard about Yeats as leader of the Celtic revival, we saw exhibits at the Abbey Theatre about him as playwright, and we have enjoyed a number of his poems on the trip. Now, we are to meet the Yeats of the West of Ireland—the preserver of legends, the guide to the twilight times, and the friend of the Fairy Kingdom.

"I thought this morning we might look at one poem in some depth to really appreciate these aspects of his work. I want to play you the musical version of his poem, sung by a local woman, local to me in Delaware, that is."

Folks laugh at the realization. We have actually been gone long enough that we have to qualify what we mean by home. Kevin puts the words of the poem up on the screen and begins a CD. Thankfully, the displayed words make it easy to follow. The title is *The Song of Wandering Aengus.* Remember Aengus was the first son of the *Tuatha Dé Danaan* and god of Love. So it begins.

> *I went out to the hazel wood*
> *Because a fire was in my head,*
> *And cut and peeled a hazel wand,*
> *And hooked a berry to a thread;*
> *And when white moths were on the wing,*
> *And moth-like stars were flickering out,*
> *I dropped the berry in a stream*
> *And caught a little silver trout.*
>
> *When I had laid it on the floor*
> *I went to blow the fire aflame,*
> *But something rustled on the floor*
> *And someone called me by my name.*
> *It had become a glimmering girl*
> *With apple blossom in her hair*
> *Who called me by my name and ran*
> *And faded through the brightening air.*
>
> *Though I am old with wandering*
> *Through hollow lands and hilly lands,*
> *I will find out where she has gone,*
> *And kiss her lips and take her hands;*

And walk among long dappled grass,
And pluck till time and times are done
The silver apples of the moon,
The golden apples of the sun.

Deep, deep silence fills the room. Then he asks what we heard and are feeling:

"Beauty."

"Simplicity."

"Longing."

"Inspiration."

"Magic."

"Passion."

"Haunting."

"Mystical."

"What do you notice about his imagery?" asks Kevin and folks offer their interpretations and thoughts.

"The story of the well, wisdom, and the salmon."

"The elements were all there, especially fire."

"The Wand is a magical device."

"It is also in the tarot and this had that sense of stepping out like the fool."

"The woman was like a Muse."

"She was a spirit."

"The fairies and the *sidhe* come in to what, at first, I thought was a simple love story."

"Well, there you have it; Yeats the mystic, the dabbler in the occult, the man who lifted folklore and fairy tales to a new light of respectability in the world of the intelligentsia who had deemed it beneath them.

"With his works, we all are asked to ponder the degree to which the 'superstitions' of the country people had meaning and message. When they refused to cut an ancient tree, remove stone piles to build a road, or level a field, they were protecting the fairy tribes, the world of in-between and the Celtic way of being in the world. Without such protection, our bus tour would not be what it has been.

"This is Yeats country. We could visit each place he wrote about and check off a list, but his soul is all around us and in all the places we have already visited. I would like to suggest a poetry reading on the beach tonight at twilight. We can see for ourselves the magical light variations that Yeats saw as we read *Twilight*. There also will be an almost full moon tonight, which is especially fortuitous.

"Some of you have heard me say that I studied Yeats, the man and his works. You may not have heard me say that my wife and I spent our honeymoon here and traveled every inch of Yeats country. Yeats especially loved being here in County Sligo. We visited his uncle's house where he practically took up residence. We also went to the church cemetery outside Drumcliff where his tombstone reads, 'Cast a cold eye on life, on death. Horseman, pass by!' But, I have to say, I felt closest to the man and his work when I simply enjoyed the countryside as he had done. Like today, sitting along the strand, in this magnificent weather with his poetry in hand."

Gordie interrupts with an observation and a question. "You know, Kevin, you make a good case for just kicking back at the beach today. I get the sense that we all are struggling with the pull of this beautiful day and its invitation to experience what Yeats writes about versus the desire to drive around to the places he lived and worked. I guess I would just like to ask how many folks really want to take a bus tour this afternoon.

Well, that's a surprise. Yet, it is also typical, too, when I think about it. Just when I get most exasperated with Gordie, he does a 180 degree turn. And, even though, he didn't consult me on this, I like his spontaneity. Plus, from people's body language, I think he is totally right.

"I really prefer a walk on the beach," says one.

Another replies, "I need to stay out of a bus for one day."

"I would rather do the poetry."

"If there is walking, I'd rather not go."

I laugh and say, "It seems then Drumcliff is not in our cards for today."

Gordie gives me a look I can't really read, but he says nothing. I nod and offer a slight smile. I don't want to further skew the outcome of the discussion. Gordie continues by asking for a show of hands. None go up. So, people are on their own until dinner and the twilight gathering.

My instincts are on track; people are okay with some downtime. Gordie, too.

But, back to Kevin's presentation. I am so pleased Kevin picked up on the fact that so much goes on in the in-between time. And he framed our free time in a creative way that I had not thought to do. The Celts really did understand the in-between as well as their concept of the 'Mountain Behind the Mountain.' Hopefully, people are getting that. Hopefully, they catch some of the magic. So Kevin finishes up on a high note, encouraging everyone to spend some time in contemplation and even in fantasy for the rest of the day.

I don't pretend to know how everyone will spend their free time, but I can tell the teenagers are up to something. All huddled together around a single activity, although I've no idea what. Nathan may be the youngest of the three, but he clearly is the leader when it comes to organizing activities. He coordinated the tin whistle music lessons with Pete. He got permission and guidance from Gordie about a website he and Megan are preparing. Now, he has them planning something new. I smile thinking about the ways people would use their "free" time. I also made a mental note for Gordie to check on them. He reads and deals with teenagers better than I. In fact, maybe that's why he is so testy today, maybe he is sensing that free time equals trouble because of these kids, or kids in general.

Free time for me also means time for individual meetings with those who expressed an interest. My first appointment is with Angie. I put some Celtic harp music on for background. After lighting a candle and centering, I encourage her to begin.

"I think I am over my health scare crisis; but, something funny is still going on. I did the visualizations and meditated on the questions you gave me. I wasn't quite prepared to tell Rebecca, but finally I did. She had sensed something was going on. In fact, she thought I wanted to break up with her. I felt so bad I had shut her out. We had an intense talk. It went really well. We both were clear and honest with each other that neither of us wanted to have a child."

"Was that part of the issue, do you think?"

"Yeah. It was a huge relief, so it must have been. I realized meditating on your questions about my sacral chakra that I was in a silent turmoil about having another baby. It's not something I had thought I was worried about. It isn't like I might accidentally get pregnant, but the clock is ticking. I realized I do not want to have another baby and that I feared that Rebecca might expect me to."

"Yet, that doesn't feel like all of it?"

"No, I still feel something is blocking me, I think it is about using my creativity and moving forward, but I don't know what or how. When I went through the questions you gave me, I realized I've never stepped out into something on my own. I've always followed: first, my family; then, my husband; and now, Rebecca. I feel like I'm never going to take a proactive step in my life on my own, for myself. So how can I apply my creativity? Hear a calling?"

I decide to try to get her out of her words, "Take a few deep breaths and then try to visualize the block. Okay, good, now what color is it? What size? What material?"

After a bit, she replies, "It's orange . . . a giant orange wall. It is really close to my face, almost touching me. It looms over me. It feels powerful and intimidating . . . .. I can't go forward without running into it. It might be plastic, it is smooth-looking, solid, but not brick or stone."

"Can you step back away from it or push it away?"

"No! I don't want to go backwards."

"Okay. I understand. You do not have to go back. Just see if you can put some distance between you and the wall. No need to retreat; just get a look at it from further away. Like you have a video camera and can adjust the wide angle lens."

"Okay, yeah, I can. Wait. Okay. It is a giant orange cone, like a traffic cone."

"Does that have any meaning to you?"

"Warning. Danger. Slow down."

"Okay. This is an important message within you. Accept it as such. Know you can keep it and you can heed it. Yet, you can also put it into a new perspective so that it works with, not against, other important lessons of your life. Okay? Okay, then. Take deep breaths. Now try to make the image of the cone even smaller. Can you put it even more distant? Okay, can you snap a picture of it? Now can you make it three-dimensional so that you can hold it? How do you feel? What are you getting?"

"A message to be careful taking risks, to watch out for hazards of construction."

"Does anything say stop or do not proceed?"

"No, just to be cautious."

"Great work. Now you are beginning to see the cone as a reminder rather than a block. Keep this image. It is important to hold on to it, knowing that it is within your control, rather than controlling you, okay? Now, look again. Does it still bring fear?"

"No. It is just like a flag or signal now. That's it?"

"That is a lot. Good work; but, I notice your shoulders are still tense and you are still braced for danger. Can you relax your shoulders, letting all the negative energy flow from your shoulders, down your arms and out your finger tips? Okay, good; let yourself feel the heaviness and let the tension flow on out. Continue until you are feeling and seeing light throughout your body . . ... How does that feel?"

"Liberating."

"Good, now can you look at your orange cone again? How does it make you feel?"

"Not fearful, just, I guess, guarded."

"Hold onto your picture of a small orange cone as a caution sign: see it as an aid in your work of transformation as you go forward. Use it to help you use just the right amount of caution and discernment as you enter this new stage of your life. This stage is not about being in roles defined by others, but creating for yourself, co-creating with the Universe. Trust that you can do this new work and relax into it."

"Do you seriously mean this is all there is to it?"

I laugh at her expression. "Well, yes and no. Life is an on-going process of discovery, but I think for now you have done what you needed to do. And you have turned a block into a tool to help you move forward rather than stop you. Good work. And you still will have those medical tests, right? Just to be sure."

"Yeah, I will." With tears, she hugs me, thanks me, and is gone.

I go outside to get a stretch break before my next appointment. Someplace nearby, Lily is playing the harp and singing. She is so amazingly gifted. Every cell in my body feels her magic. I really have to find a special way to thank her for her contribution of music throughout the trip. And I have to get hold of some of that music she calls interdimensional.

TRISH

Lily's music is so enchanting. It takes me back to my meditation at Glendalough. And the walk back when I saw Kevin with his arms wrapped around the Cross of St. Kevin, sobbing. It brought back all the pain of my split with Mr. Blues. I know the hurt of a lost relationship and the fear and loneliness of raising a child alone. But I can't even imagine the heartache of losing your soul mate or of having a son who demonstrates loathing and disdain toward you when you reach out to him.

That day, I gave him time to collect himself before approaching. After a bit, I went over and asked if I could join him. He nodded, but remained silent. We sat together in silence on that bench for quite some time. That's when I remembered the postcards. In Dublin, I had found a great postcard—black and white sketched profiles of Joyce, Shaw, Wilde, Behan, O'Casey, and Kevin's beloved Yeats. It had just one line "A few words from Ireland."

It was perfect for not just Kevin but a couple of my colleagues who are literary sorts. They were still in my bag and so I pulled one out for Kevin. He held it and looked at it and finally a slight smile came to his lips and a barely audible "thanks."

Tears came to my eyes then and do now. I was moved to reach out to this man, this man with the poet's soul. But, I couldn't. I couldn't then and I can't now.

I walk the beach, the labyrinth, and then the beach some more. I never have this kind of time for myself. Never take time. Lily is playing again, or still, when I get back to the Inn. Again, I am mesmerized by her sound. It has a lightness of being to it, an Other World quality and the words are chilly in their simplicity. She tells us the songs were written by her friend Gabriella. This one now is the most compelling.

> *Come with roses in your heart,*
> *if you want to take your part,*
> *In the circle of the stars in which we gather.*

> *Weave the stories of your fight*
> *into tapestries of light*
> *For the healing of the body of the Mother.*

Oh, my.

The magic of the afternoon lingers well after Lily stops playing. The light is perfect when we gather after dinner for Kevin's Twilight poetry session. The color, the softness, the sense of magic in the air is perfect. They say the Celts loved the in-between and what better example of in-between could be found than to be on the strand of beach between water and land at twilight on a day when both sun and moon appear.

241

Megan and I made luminaries out of little brown candy bags filled with sand and votives. We set them out to guide everyone down the beach to the place Kevin had chosen. They aren't much to look at now, but it will be dark when we end and they will be brilliant, to use that wonderful Irish expression.

Kevin looks so calm and self-assured as he welcomes everyone. "Yeats had always loved the West of Ireland, especially Sligo, his childhood home. His efforts to capture and write the old stories of the Gaelic tradition before they were gone and to write them in plain English are best illustrated in *By the Roadside*, from *The Celtic Twilight*. His aim was to bring the arts, imagination, and magic back to the people. His belief was that the Church took over control of all culture in medieval times and that the true Celtic spirit needed CPR. He breathed life into it again. Tonight I asked some of the group to read a sample of his works to us."

Peter reads the first poem.

The Hosting of the Sidhe

The host is riding from Knocknarea,
And over the grave of Clooth-na-bare;
Caolte tossing his burning hair,
And Niamh calling, "Away, come away;
Empty your heart of its mortal dream.
The winds awaken, the leaves whirl round,
Our cheeks are pale, our hair is unbound,
Our breasts are heaving, our eyes are a-gleam,
Our arms are waving, our lips are apart,
And if any gaze on our rushing band,
We come between him and the deed of his hand,
We come between him and the hope of his heart."
The host is rushing 'twixt night and day;
And where is there hope or deed as fair?
Caolte tossing his burning hair,
And Niamh calling, "Away, come away."

We sit in silence. Then Lily plays the harp and we sit a little longer. Beautiful.

Penny's voice softly pierces the veil of silence among us. "These words are from *Deidre,* one of his plays:

> *I have believed the best of every man, and find*
> *That to believe it is enough to make a bad man show*
> *him at his best,*
> *Or even a good man swing his lantern higher.*

Then Gordie reads:

> *Had I the heavens' embroidered cloths.*
> *Enwrought with the golden and silver light.*
> *The blue and the dim and the dark cloths*
> *Of night and light and half-light,*
> *I would spread the cloths under your feet.*
> *But I, being poor, have only my dreams;*
> *I have spread my dreams beneath your feet;*
> *Tread softly because you tread on my dreams . . .*

Another musical interlude follows, only this time Lily is joined by Peter on the tin whistle and Gordie on the drum.

Kevin, who has been sitting in the sand soaking up the words of his favorite poet along with the rest of us stands. Must be the end of the program I think with a tinge of disappointment.

"This last is from *The Stolen Child,*" Kevin tells us:

> *Come faeries, take me out of this dull world,*
> *For I would ride with you upon the wind*
> *And dance upon the mountains like a flame.*

We sit in silence. Then Lily plays the harp and we sit a little longer. Beautiful.

Lily, takes it from there. More inspiring than ever, she leaves us spellbound. The stars and the moon seem to sparkle as if they, too, are enjoying the melodious sounds.

We are all reluctant to break the mood, but finally begin to stir. Gordie speaks, "We have found an oldie but goody for you tonight, folks. For your cinematic pleasure we will be showing *Darby O'Gill and the Little People*, in the main lounge. It is a vintage Disney movie, made before a good number of us were born, 1959. It was a favorite video of my childhood and seemed worth tracking down since we are here in the land of the leprechauns. I ask when you see it, you not throw popcorn. Take the hokey, corny, clumsy special effects as part of the entertainment. And here's wishing you and our leprechaun friends will find it to be a good *craic*. It will be followed by *Finian's Rainbow.*

I remain on the beach with Kevin, not talking, just enjoying the sound of the waves and the moon as it begins to shine on the water. Finally, I break the silence, "That was so beautiful and I really admire your willingness to keep an open heart." I am surprised at myself about the open heart bit.

"I have a son, I had to keep going, it hasn't felt particularly courageous, but thank you."

"I think allowing yourself to be vulnerable after such a painful loss is the height of courage. Did your love of poetry help?"

"At first, I was too shut down to even think of it. But later? Yes. Now? Absolutely."

We sit quietly together. "I think I know a little about what you mean. I was pregnant when Mr. Blues and I split. It was creating a life for the baby I carried that got me through."

"Yeah…'Fake it till you make it' was my motto. And, what about you? Sounds like you are still angry and hurt though. Has it been hard to let go?" remarks Kevin.

"I had to let go of my feelings for him just so we could survive. Letting go of my anger, though? Mostly, I only get mad when I think about how he let Megan down."

"Does he have any contact with you or Megan?"

"No, he showed up a few times while she was still a baby, but he was either high or begging for money or both. I finally told him I would send him to jail for non-support if he came back."

"So we each had to let go in different ways, huh? I remember how hard it was to tell Jane it was time; that we both had to let go, that Jackson and I would be okay. God, it was the hardest thing I have ever done in my life. But she was struggling and in such pain at the end."

"I can't even imagine."

Silence, again. "What do you say we take a walk along the tide line as it comes in?"

"I'd like that," I say, as he takes my hand.

TIMOTHY and KATE

John and Melanie's silhouettes can be seen walking along the strand to the south of us, and Gordie and Dorrie have just come back to the beach and headed to our north.

"Dear Kate," says I, fumbling a wee bit as I go. "I have here a poem I meself found thanks to Kevin's help this afternoon. But, I canna see it in the dimness of the night. Will you come back to me lodgings so I can read it to you properly." I am made nervous by Kate's laugh, although it is a sweet enough laugh.

"Is this the AARP version of 'come back to see my etchings?'" she asks.

Her meaning 'tis not at all clear. But, she takes me hand and for once I know to keep mum and just walk on. I think we both knew we were taking a big step, just perhaps not how big. We get cozy. I open and pour us some wine. I have just enough light to read the poem I have researched and rehearsed:

When You Are Old

When you are old and grey and full of sleep,
And nodding by the fire, take down this book,
And slowly read, and dream of the soft look
Your eyes had once, and of their shadows deep;

How many loved your moments of glad grace,
And loved your beauty with love false or true,
But one man loved the pilgrim Soul in you,
And loved the sorrows of your changing face;

And bending down beside the glowing bars,
Murmur, a little sadly, how Love fled
And paced upon the mountains overhead
And hid his face amid a crowd of stars.

"That is beautiful, Timothy, Just beautiful. You dear, sweet man."

"Kate, I do not want to be the man who hid me face, I want to grow old with you, lass, and I want to see your changing face."

"I don't know what to say."

"No need for talk lass, no need for talk. We can save all the talking for another time . . .."

DAY TEN

THE PILGRIMAGE to CROAGH PATRICK

The choice is yours today—
an excursion into County Mayo to climb Croagh Patrick or a quiet day at
the seaside.
Currachs, jet skis, and other water options can be found at the nearby
harbor.

PEG

Today is the pilgrimage to Croagh Patrick, but I'm certainly going to pass. I've been having my own pilgrimage these last few days. They've been hard days, but good days. Now I am just enjoying the people and the sea and, of course, being back with Rob. He has been such a dear about everything, as I knew he would be.

When I left the tour in Dublin, I barely knew everyone's name. Now, I can see folks have gotten to know one another, shared stories and experiences, and bonded with others in the group. I know I won't catch up, but I do want to get back involved. It is such a different kind of involvement than with my congregation, colleagues and family. Fun role to just be one of the group, stepping in and out as I want.

I told Rob the overall, short version of my time away yesterday morning before we headed down to breakfast. The rest we have been discussing in bits and pieces. It's so nice to be back with him. We had a wonderful reunion. It was beyond what I imagined possible or felt I deserved. I am truly blessed to have this fine man as my soul mate and partner. Talk about gratitude.

I know that over time, the story of my abrupt pilgrimage will unfold in greater detail, depth and nuance, but now I'm just anxious to rejoin the group. I was glad Dorrie gave me an opening yesterday to speak about it. That brief bit was ideal for naming the elephant in the room and letting everyone know it was okay to talk about it. Of course, Mary Helena had been dying to hear all the details. She certainly didn't wait for permission to probe. In fairness, we had had some conversations of depth. Nonetheless, I pushed her off until today. Maybe that was why she was so much on my mind. I promised to meet up with her after we saw the bus off to Croagh Patrick.

This morning, I lingered in bed, trying to remain in that dreamtime, the time between sleep and wakefulness when the veil between worlds lifts. The in-between as Kevin and Yeats called it. I was floating, that sense of being above your body, floating. . .almost awake…absorbing the beauty around me . . .. Waking, I felt thankful for the renewed openness I was experiencing, an openness to Nature, Mother Nature, Mother Earth. My attention went back to the dolmen . . . healing energy coming in . . . wondering how to help others open to the power of Spirit . . . magic wand . . . magic words . . . magic touch? How to get this great healing spirit of Light and Love to others? Then I fell back into a deeper sleep. In my dream, I saw a woman turning her back, shutting out the light, curling up in a fetal position. That can't be me, can it? After all the work I have done? Am I still denying or resisting something? Am I afraid to move forward? Near panic, I asked myself all these questions from my lucid dream state.

My inner dialogue said, "No, no, not me . . . but still, another woman shut down, wounded, too hurt to see the Light and Love around her . . ." I knew that I was being called to witness this and to respond with help. How could I get through to women in this kind of pain? The images of the Well, the dolmen, the Celtic cross came floating by again, all promising healing, renewal, and restoration.

I was getting such a firm sense that part of my ministry needs to be helping create space and support for women to find the Nurturing Mother, both within themselves and in the feminine form of god/goddess... I saw a *sheela-na-gig* . . . I knew what they were from my reading, but I asked to understand their true meaning. The answer came in gentle tones, "She is not just a protector to ward off evil, but an invitation to openness in its most real form, to open the body to love and communion, to birth and rebirth, the ultimate channel between life and death. From whence we come and from whence we return to come again."

At that point Rob woke me. In spite of our "no talking until teeth are brushed rule," I started a conversation, although a foggy one. "Oh, Rob. I was dreaming...yes, I am all right . . . I was dreaming and thinking about what I need to be doing to help other women release stored grievances and heal wounds."

"Haven't you always done that, dear?"

"Somehow this is different . . . maybe more intentional . . . and guided . . . I don't know, but I think I will just lie here a bit longer and try to make sense of what is swirling around in my head."

He just nodded, bending down to give me a quick kiss of good morning. I took his hand as he straightened up and just held it for an extra moment or two.

When I did head for the shower, Rob was already dressed and anxious for his first cup of coffee. I always teased him that it was silly to have coffee before meditation, but he was not to be swayed. He said he would meet me at sound toning and left while I dressed.

It was during toning mediation that I realized Mary Helena was the woman in my dream, or at least, represented the women I was to help. Seeing her bitterness and imagining her story had prompted me to deal with my own. Yet, she was still in pain as were so many others. How could I convey to her what I have learned these last few days? How could I be able to help her open herself? Learn to forgive and trust again? I had promised myself that my ministry would now, more than ever, begin to address forgiveness and reconciliation, but I'd had no idea that I would be asked to give it a go so soon. Mary Helena, I knew, could not move forward unless she practiced forgiveness. I asked the Divine Feminine, Goddess, Saint, Spirit for help and support in helping Mary Helena and others like her.

So I now am in a bit of a daze as I leave toning. Rob is engaged in a long conversation with Dorrie. Rebecca, Angie, Kate, and I walk companionably on to breakfast. Angie is just about to tell us about her guided visualization, when Mary Helena charges over to our table.

"There you are," she scolds Kate. "And tell me, just how was I to know you weren't drowned or something? You have been late, waking me after pub crawling and the like. But staying out all night this time! That takes the cake! Hmmpf!"

I am stunned. Not that Kate had spent the night with Timothy, which is the obvious guess, but that Mary Helena is so rude. I try to think of something to stop the nonsense and reduce Kate's embarrassment. But, Kate clearly doesn't need my help.

"Mary Helena, that will be quite enough. I am not your teenage daughter and I do not need to account for my whereabouts to you. Judge me all you want, but I do not intend to listen to your scolding. You are out of line and I will not have it."

"Well, I never . . . I mean, I just thought . . . .."

"I think the kindest thing any of us can say, Mary Helena, is that you must not have been thinking or you would have known better. I think you better drop it now," says Rebecca firmly.

We sit in silence for a moment. Then I ask the others about their preparation for the pilgrimage. Not that the conversation was completed by any means, but for now I think it best to switch the subject. After all, this isn't an encounter group.

As soon as we finish breakfast, we gather to see the pilgrims off. Dorrie asks the climbers to step forward. She suggests they each silently name and visualize their intention for the pilgrimage. After giving them time to crystallize their thought, she invites them to form a tight circle and to hold hands. She motions for the rest of us to encircle them. She then offers a beautiful Irish blessing.

"We gratefully acknowledge the presence of Spirit as this inner circle of pilgrims journey forth. Those of us in the outer circle offer our love and support. Pilgrims, you have set your intent. Now allow Spirit to guide you in the release of that which is in your way and in the attraction of that which is within your grasp. In the words of an old Irish blessing:

> *We wish you not a path devoid of clouds, nor a life on a*
> *bed of roses,*
> *Not that you might never need regret,*
> *nor that you should never feel pain.*
> *No, that is not our wish for you.*
>
> *Our wish for you is:*
> *That you might be brave in times of trial,*
> *when others lay crosses upon your shoulders.*
> *When mountains must be climbed and chasms are to be*
> *crossed,*
> *When hope can scarce shine through.*
>
> *That every gift Spirit gave you might grow with you*
> *and let you give your gift of joy to all who care for you.*
> *That you may always have a friend who is worth that*
> *name,*
> *whom you can trust and who helps you in times of*
> *sadness,*
> *Who will defy the storms of daily life at your side.*

One more wish we have for you:
That in every hour of joy and pain you may feel Spirit
close to you.
This is our wish for you and for all who care for you.
This is our hope for you now and forever."

We each place a hand on the back of one of the pilgrims, sending them off with love and support. My heart goes out to Melanie who is clinging to John for the longest time. Timothy gently, but firmly, summons them and they are off.

Kate, Sandra and I get coffee and head for the Strand Room. For a while, we just look out at the sea. Kate breaks the silence, "Before any of the others come in, I just want you two to know, I did stay with Timothy last night and it was even more wonderful than I could have imagined. He is amazingly tender and sweet."

I just simply say, "I had no idea, Kate, but he does seem like a great guy." And then I add, "Even if I had had ideas, I wouldn't have expected an Irishman to move so fast. Is there more?"

Kate blushes a bit, shakes her head. I give her a big hug.

Penny and Mary Helena enter. Mary Helena immediately inserts herself, directing her energy to me: "So are we still scheduled to have our chat? You said you would tell me about your little private pilgrimage."

It is hard to know with her whether she is being sarcastic or if it is just the way she says things that can rub me the wrong way. But I take a deep breath and reply, "Yes, I will be glad to. Why don't we remain right here, some others have also asked to hear more."

"Well, I thought . . ."

"I think it will be better this way. Fewer times to tell the tale, as it were." I purposely cut her off. I don't feel like giving in to her after the way she has treated Kate, plus I think it might take the edge off the earlier incident if we are all together.

"So tell us what happened? What did you do?" Mary Helena asks in her most penetrating voice.

"The logistics were actually much easier than I had thought they would be. That first night I stayed in Dublin, right on St. Stephen's Green. The next morning, I took a bus from Dublin to Limerick and then got a room at a bed and breakfast on the side of town where my great-great grandparents had lived. I took a local bus there, had tea and talked to a few locals. None of them knew any of my relatives, though. That actually was okay. I wasn't really looking for that. I simply wanted to know more about the context of my family's past and to understand it better."

"Are you saying that was all there was to your leaving the tour so abruptly?"

"No, I am just saying that the actual decisions to visit the family home went well. My reasons are much too personal and complicated to go into here. Basically, they were old family issues that I had buried. All this Irish stimulation brought them back to the surface." I had intended to find an elegant way to help Mary Helena through the telling of my own story; instead, I find I'm just holding my own to say it at all. Trying not to be defensive but protecting my personal sense of privacy.

"We can certainly appreciate your desire not to rehash everything. Please tell us the pieces you feel like sharing," Kate breaks in, deflecting Mary Helena's continued grilling.

"When I decided I wanted to return to Brigid's Well, I asked Moira, the bed and breakfast owner, about a local bus. Moira said it was a place she had always meant to visit. She posed that, if I didn't mind the company, she would drive me out. What a bit of luck. She was a thoughtful, non-intrusive type so I took her up on it. Her driving saved me navigating instructions and travel hazards, and allowed me to totally give over to the experience.

"The Well is where I had first felt overwhelmed. It was where I needed to return. What was it Dorrie said? Brigid represents fire, light, and transformation. I felt a fire of burning anger that I had not realized was in me. It was like I had a dark spot that I was finally allowing to be in the light. The fire of anger pointed it out. It gave me warning. I was fortunate. If ignored, I think it would have consumed me. So when I returned to the Well, I asked to be released from the anger and the resentment I was holding."

"Was it like a sudden release?" Mary Helena asks.

"Yes and no. Were you ever treated for a kidney stone? It felt like that. The light broke up the dark spot and reduced it like a laser reduces the size of a kidney stone. But then the remainder was released more slowly."

"So then what?"

"I thanked Moira and returned to the bed and breakfast for a final night. I was too exhausted, mentally and emotionally, to do anything else. The next morning, I realized that I wanted to get to the sea, to look out as I had at the Cliffs. And, to let the sound of the sea heal me. A sandy beach would be even better. The idea came to me to check if there was a room here at the Inn. Sure enough there was."

"How did you get here?"

"The bus system here is amazing. Only two buses and I was practically to the door of the Inn. Riding in silence interspersed with listening to fellow passengers and telling them parts of my own story, I smiled for the first time in days. All these lovely people were part of my healing. The stream of consciousness thinking that is part of a good, long bus ride was like a balm.

"But it was the sea that helped me release my stored up grievances and address the deep injustices to Spirit that were hidden away inside. I had picked up a Thich Nhat Hanh book on forgiveness at a Limerick bookstore. It became my companion, teacher, and aid."

"Didn't you want to talk to Rob through all this?"

"Not this time. I needed to do this work alone. I thought about him a lot and, of course, hoped he was okay. Poor guy. A lot of men would have hit the roof or sent the police out to find me. I knew it was unfair of me to leave him like that on our vacation, but I also knew he would understand."

"It is a little hard to imagine what you mean without specifics, but it sounds like you overcame some long-held resentments," is Sandra's summary.

Now that I have struggled through telling my story, I start thinking more about how I could be of help to Mary Helena. I carefully offer, "Yes. You no doubt followed the scandals within the Boston Catholic Diocese of sexual abuse, going back to the 1950's. Now, as I am sure you know, just recently, it has heated up again. The Pope himself has acknowledged the problem here in Ireland. It is ghastly the number of priests who abused their power. And my anger at the Church hierarchy and the whole Irish Catholic conspiracy of silence about alcohol and abuse was buried deep inside me. I had thought I had dealt with all the feelings I had about it long ago, but coming here stirred them up again."

Mary Helena hits the roof, "I am so sick of everyone trashing Roman Catholicism. It is not just the Church that has these problems. They are everywhere. And why bring up things about decades past and why bring them to Ireland for God's sake? All I hear is everyone criticizing everything Catholic we see here. I have prayed to St. Patrick and to St. Briget all my life. And this whole damn trip, you people won't accept them for who they are. I have heard more blasphemy here in ten days than in my whole life. And calling these blessed saints by pagan names and saying they are only myths. How dare you!"

I am taken aback, as are the others. I hit a nerve for sure. So I take a deep breath, reminding myself to check my own reactivity, "Yes, I have talked against certain Roman Catholic church practices, especially those that glossed over abuse. I have also expressed how my own theology has changed from my Catholic upbringing. But, I certainly respect believers in the Catholic faith. I believe in religious freedom and honor the truths that can be found in all religions. I apologize if I gave you reason to think otherwise."

"You aren't the only one. It is the entire sniggerly tone of this group," says Mary Helena defiantly.

"Mind if I respond?" Sandra asks as she continues to speak. She directs her words to all of us, but it is clear she is trying to reach Mary Helena. "Jake and I and others in the group are Roman Catholic. Speaking for myself, I just want to say I have not felt disrespected at all. I have enjoyed and welcomed our open discussions of different interpretations of history and theology. Through these conversations, I've gained insights into the history of my own religion. I haven't an Irish bone in my body, but I have especially enjoyed hearing about Celtic mysticism. The messages of the women saints of the Catholic Church are honored more here than in my parish at home, let me tell you."

"Tell us more about that, please," Kate encourages.

"Well, you know, as I have already told some of you, when I got cancer, I started going to a spiritual director, a referral made by the hospital social worker. Ironic that it wasn't the chaplain, but the social worker, who suggested it. It was she who got through to me. I was a little leery at first. But I went and the spiritual director was wonderful. I attribute a huge part of my remission to her and the work we did together.

"I had converted to Catholicism for Jake when we married. I was an Episcopalian, so it wasn't that hard a transition. But, after the kids were grown, we drifted off. The new priest was pretty old school, and there just seemed to be lots to do on Sunday, our only day together. Anyway, Sister Ann accepted me where I was, listened to my fears, and just affirmed me in a way the Church had not done before.

"Peg, that book you mentioned, the one about Christ as pastor not victim, really resonated with me. Sister talked that way, and she introduced me to Sophia. I had never even heard of Sophia or knew she was a Biblical figure until then. She gave me a book by a nun who called Sophia *The Star in Her Heart.* I read that thin little book over and over. Thinking of Sophia and wisdom and the opening of the heart gave me a new sense of myself as a woman. I prayed every prayer, did every activity, and lingered on every word. Later, I started reading more voices of Catholic women and stories of the women saints and all. But at the time, this one little book was like magic.

"I really didn't think beyond myself at the time. I was just focused on healing. I understand, now, that these books were about the reemergence of the Divine Feminine. It is happening within the Catholic Church and within the Episcopalian. My friends talk about the woman Episcopalian priest at Grace Cathedral in San Francisco who rediscovered labyrinths and actually got the hierarchy of Chartres Cathedral in France to move back the chairs and feature its ancient labyrinth, which is built into its marble floor.

Now, coming here and hearing all this, I am so excited. When *The Da Vinci Code* came out I was thrilled. It didn't shake my faith. The Church's reaction seemed ridiculous to me. No book of fiction is going to convince me to really believe that there really are descendants of Jesus and Mary Magdalene or that they are being protected by some secret society. But I do believe women and the feminine side of God played a bigger role in the early Church than we are led to believe. Having read about Sophia, I even guessed the secret code in the movie." She chuckles at the thought, then finishes by saying "Thanks for listening."

I give her a hug. Such a brave and unassuming woman. Mary Helena says nothing nor does anyone ask her for her thoughts. Before going our own ways for lunch, Sandra suggests we take a few minutes of silence to send healing energy and prayer to our pilgrims, especially Melanie. We can only hope things are going well over at Croagh Patrick.

I have volunteered to coordinate the final party. Having missed so much of the trip, this seems like a way to plug back in and contribute. It will be fun and it will give me a way to catch up with some of the folks. Rob helped fill me in and guide me towards some of the talent. Gordie is taking care of the logistics. In fact, he arranged a special prawn and standing rib roast buffet and a wine and beer bar in the banquet room. It will be a pay-as-you-go bar, which to me is always wise, not just economical.

Angie and Rebecca offered to do decorations. They have two ideas. One is to decorate within the theme of threes, picking up on the great triad game they said they played on the bus. The second is to make take-home quality, individualized place cards, using a Celtic knot motif. I am thrilled.

Peter offered to organize the "Boys Band" with their tin whistles. Lily, of course, will play her harp. Where did Lily go, anyway? I can never figure out her comings and goings.

The teenagers have a short video they have been planning. Gordie is already seeing that they have what they need, so basically, at this point, I just need to write up a program.

So I decide to walk the labyrinth, something I hadn't done since the group arrived. Rob was tied up with his men's group, and I really need to work through this issue of Mary Helena. I feel a need to help, yet clearly I seem to be alienating her rather than helping. Perhaps, that's part of the process. But I want to think it through. There are lessons here for me, too, I know.

Penny gives me a shout. "May I join you?" She is further along the water's edge and I hadn't seen her.

"Sure. We haven't had much time to get to talk to one another."

"I want to thank you for sharing so much of yourself this morning and to apologize for not speaking up when Mary Helena started in."

"No problem. It would have been awkward if everyone had rebutted her point. Sandra's story said it all."

"Actually, there is another aspect I would love to explore with you. I am trying to start a women's healing center in the Ottawa area. Your reference to family abuse, alcoholism, and conspiracies was so passionate. I think that needs to be a big part of the work of the center I envision."

"There certainly is a need. Am I right that you are talking about holistic healing and spirituality as well as traditional social services?"

"Exactly. Your reference to ministries of forgiveness and reconciliation resonated deeply within me. Might we talk more about that, too?"

"Sure, but why do these connections always come toward the end of a trip? Well, if we run out of time here in Ireland, we can continue talking back home. I share your sense that we have things to learn from one another and would love to share more."

"Great, so we'll talk later. Right now, I need to write some postcards and get them out before we leave. Even now, we'll be home before the cards arrive."

"Postcard writing is a dying art. Good for you. See you later then."

So I arrive at the labyrinth, my original destination. I want to enter the labyrinth with the intent to sort out what I am to do or not do about Mary Helena and to leave with a better understanding of my role and ministries. The talk with Penny started the ball rolling. Now, to focus and clean up the questions, I repeat them aloud as I enter and again silently as I walk: For the Way In: What are my learnings? For the Way Out: How might I apply them to helping Mary Helena and others?

The lessons come in the twists and turns, but I make mental notes: Avoid judgment and forgive those who lash out, it is their pain talking. Step back out of the spiral of negativity that develops.

The thoughts tumble on: Remain non-attached to outcome. Continue to show up and to offer unconditional love and support.

Then on the straight stretch in the winding path, it hits me. Whack! I left my family for the convent, then marriage, and moved to the other side of the state because I felt like I was drowning. I fled for my life. My guilt is that I have never gotten to the forgiveness part for myself. I had walked out, not stepped back. Understandable, but not complete.

As I enter the center, I experience a deeper calmness than I ever remember feeling. Fixing Mary Helena, who had not asked to be fixed, is not the issue. I have been fixating on her because I still had my own work to do. I need to reenter my own family with forgiveness and find reconciliation. So obvious and so simple, now that I see it.

So I weave my way back out of the labyrinth making a plan to visit Boston, to call my brothers and sisters, to visit the house where we grew up, and reconnect to the family circle as best I can. Only then will my pilgrimage be complete.

THE PILGRIMS to CROAGH PATRICK

ROSE

After that emotional send off, we are silent as we drive the seventy miles southwest to Croagh Patrick. Timothy says to "relax, the mountain rises over 2,500 feet so 'twill be no missing it." We already know that the site was Neolithic, before becoming an important place used by the Celts for pagan rituals or even later, a Christian holy place. Dorrie has taught us to see the three-layered history of these places. I particularly love that aspect of the trip.

"So, Timothy is there a church and monument to St. Patrick up on top?" asks a voice from behind us.

"Would they be able to name it for the Blessed Saint and not have a wee chapel? But, truth be told, I have never climbed up to see it for meself. Did you know that until well into the mid-nineteenth century, it was a pilgrimage only for women? Just like the group today. We men folk never seem that keen to come.

"Now, do you all know that Christian legend has St. Patrick banishing the snakes and dragons and demons in 441 A.D., starting at the very place we're going? And, did you also know that 'tis a place where the country folk honored Crom Dubh, a local deity like. And 'tis always been here that 'tis considered the main site for the Lughnasa ceremonies. While 'tis back at Knocknarea, you will find the site best known for Beltane."

"They are pagan holidays, aren't they? Do people still celebrate them nowadays?"

"We would simply say they are Celtic holidays. You would be surprised, especially here in *Gaeltacht*, how much the old ways still are practiced. The priests and those who attend chapel strict-like, of course, call 'em Saints Days and, aye, folks still like a good celebration.

We had already discussed that the story of the snakes may have meant ridding the place of the goddess and pagan worshippers. Whatever the interpretation one gives the story, the mountain now carries his name, but also continues celebrating the celestial light worshipped by the ancients and blessing fertility as practiced by the pagans.

Rebecca, Angie, Leslie, Trish, Melanie and I return to our private thoughts as we approach the foot of the mountain. Mostly, I think most of us came out of curiosity and a desire to support Melanie. But, with Dorrie's encouragement, we each had also given thought to our own needs and reasons for coming. I hope to connect with the elementals of the mountain. Angie says she still needs something. Is it Inspiration? Clarity? Direction? She says she plans to ask that what she needs to know be told her as she climbs. Rebecca says she is just supporting Angie and Melanie. Leslie wants to explore her new call to do environmental work. Come to think of it, Trish doesn't share what she has in mind.

We disembark from the bus, say good-bye to Timothy and regroup at the trailhead. Without planning it, we stop to focus on a special send-off for Melanie. I half-jokingly say that we need to tell the goddess and St. Patrick, respectfully, that none of the rest of us want to be pregnant, thank you! The local practice, especially for women wanting to get pregnant, is to sleep overnight at the summit during the festival. Of course, for Melanie it is not going to be an overnight, nor on Lughnasa. Nonetheless, she is obviously eager to do this, calling it the most important journey of her life.

I think I read that over a million people come here each year. Today is a week day, though. We seem to have the place practically to ourselves. So we form a healing circle with Melanie in the center. We surround her in healing energies and words of hope. Then, we joyfully start our climb in earnest – each at our own pace and with our own thoughts.

As I walk, I am feeling a war of energies building within myself. One feels like St. Patrick chasing out the demons. My Roman Catholic upbringing talking, I guess. The other feels like the energies of the *sidhe* and the affirmation of my newfound interest in the fairies. I reach the top exhausted, but do not enter the chapel to sit or kneel. Instead, I take in the breathtaking view. Clew Bay looks as still and serene as the pool at Brigid's Well, the hills patched in every shade of green imaginable, mixed now and again with splashes of yellow or purple. Then I hear a whisper. "We are One," the voice whispers. "St. Patrick knows that now; all is well, all who follow the Father, know we are One; Brede knows also, those who follow the Mother are One. The Father and the Mother are One. The gods and the goddesses are One. You of this world and We of the Other World are One. Do not fret little One, Where it matters, it is known. All are One."

I sit in stone silence for a long while. By the time I know to start back down the mountain, I am singing. Singing Molly Scott's *We Are All One People*. The words have even more meaning now.

ANGIE

Dorrie's advice is front and center in my mind. Let go, let God. I repeat it to myself periodically all the way up the mountain. I try to release any feeling I identify as binding or weighing me down. I get in touch with old feelings of failure, of inadequacy, of discouragement, and try to shed them, step by step as I climb.

Years of therapy have taught me that I am okay. But I don't think my body has caught up with my mind. So today has become a physical pilgrimage, for healing of my body. I sense the elemental forces within me are strong and stubborn, plus I have to admit I don't attend to them as well as I do my mind and heart. So I offer thanks to my body. I see that it is the vessel for my spirit. It is my temple. I reclaim my wholeness step by step.

At the top, I see nothing but beauty and possibility. I don't even ask myself what I should make of it. I simply am in the moment, free, taking it all in. Relishing the breeze, the view, all of it. Then, I see Rebecca off in the distance. I just stare at her, so grateful that this caring and wonderful woman is waiting for me.

REBECCA

I get to the top first. I think I needed a workout more than reflection. Besides, there is nothing I love more than sitting on a mountain top, looking out to sea. It reminds me of childhood, before my parents split. Today, I am the happiest I have been since those early days. I know in my gut that Angie will get a clean bill of health. I pray again in gratitude for our health, for our life together.

"Hey, there you are."

"You're just in time. I was just wishing you would get here in time to sketch the sheep over there."

"It's so magnificent. Sheep or no sheep. The beauty is all around," Angie twirls around a couple of times to take in the 360 degree view before sitting down next to me. "May I share this rock with you?"

"You may share everything with me, my heart."

"Remember the wonderful Navajo prayer about beauty you taught me?"

"Sure:

Beauty is before me,
And beauty is behind me.
Above and below me hovers the beautiful.
I am surrounded by it.
I am immersed in it.
In my youth I am aware of it,
And in old age I shall walk quietly
The beautiful trail.

"Hmm, nice. The Celtic and Native American sensibilities are a lot alike, aren't they?"

"Yeah, in fact, I was just thinking our next trip should be to Sedona. You know—to the medicine wheels and vortex sites."

"For sure, but for now, how about lunch?" We eat our box lunch, quietly enjoying the surroundings.

Angie breaks our silence, "Are you really certain about the no kids thing?"

"Here we are on the mountain that promises fertility. For days we have been surrounded by all these fertility signs, symbols, and goddesses who bless the process of birthing. If I'm not getting the vibes to procreate here, then how could I be more certain? Besides some of us have to think about the population explosion."

"Good, but you know what?"

"What?"

"I want us to create something together."

"Oh my god, what does that mean? I thought we just said no kids?"

"We did, and it's not that, but we need something that is ours to share and shape and express ourselves, you know, besides the house."

"You mean, like get a dog?"

"Oh, no. Not a pet. I mean, like a project. Something creative that engages us, where our gifts get shared and where someone benefits besides ourselves."

"Tall order, but I like the idea of co-creating something."

"Let's think about ideas on our way down. It's getting cloudy and chilly."

MELANIE

I read about Croagh Patrick in *Trinity* way back in college. At the time, I was struck by the story of 'The Troubles,' the Irish conflict. As a young African-American all of a sudden surrounded by people referencing ethnic stories and pieces of history to which I had never been exposed, I discovered historical fiction was a fun way of learning more.

I started with *Exodus*. It had helped me understand the stories of the Jewish experience post World War II. That led me to *Trinity* and I fell in love with Conor, its young hero. I remembered reading of his mother's struggle with infertility and then her faith in the patron saint of Ireland, St. Patrick. At the time, as a non-Catholic who certainly was not interested in getting pregnant, those aspects were irrelevant. I was just caught up in the story of the woman's deep faith and, of course, perplexed by these Christian white people having a civil war among themselves.

So now, as John and I try so desperately to have a child, I am here as Conor's mother was here, to climb to the top in hopes of a child. I know now I should have shared my plans with John. He was so hurt and angry that I hadn't, 'cause I was so afraid he would dismiss the whole idea. So I just convinced him that a relaxing trip to Erin would be good for us both. His grandmother used to work for an Irish-American family and he and the boys in that family spent summers together at the family's Catskills camp. He knew more about Ireland than most black kids, that's for sure. So I knew he would enjoy it. Then I sweetened the deal with the suggestion of three days of golf at the end of the tour, and he was sold.

My mistake was in not sharing all of my reasons for coming. He was so angry when he found out from Mary Helena in Dublin. He was livid. I can still hear his angry complaints. "The pressure we are putting on ourselves is the problem," he kept saying. "Now, even on our vacation. And you know very well that faith is inside and with God, why are you doing this silly legend stuff? Pilgrims on hands and knees to punish themselves! What kind of God asks that? It is superstition. It is beneath you. It's witchcraft. You duped me into coming. I do not support this." The tears roll down my face just thinking about all he had said that night after the theatre.

Stop it. I need to clear away those thoughts and emotions if this climb is to mean anything. So I focus on Brigid's Well, my resurgence of faith at Glendalough, the magic of the first light and first sound at Newgrange. Then I can hear John's apology and promise of support. Once again, I can hold the sense of well-being our united prayers and our love bring to me.

The little ritual at the base of the trailhead really helped, too. I feel their support here on the mountain even though I am alone. I remember the quotation that pilgrimage is 'seeking what the heart holds sacred.' I hold in perfect intent the vision that a healthy child will be born to us in nine months.

When I reach the summit, I hear music in the chapel and it draws me in. I kneel at the picture of Jesus with the little children and the lambs, remembering that picture from childhood, and I just sob. I cry out the pain of my barren womb, as the crones used to say. I cry for the ache in my heart and in John's that we have no child to share their love. I just plain cry until, finally, I have no more tears to shed. Then, I simply pray and pray some more.

When I feel I have done all I possibly can do, I pick myself up and go out into what has become a cloudy and dark sky. Asking once more that my prayer for a healthy baby be granted, that I leave Ireland pregnant, and that our child be born in the spring, healthy and whole, I start down the mountain.

THE MEN MEET

John, Peter, Jake, Gordie and Kevin join Rob in the Seabird Room. Rob starts them off. "First, let me just acknowledge that we're a pretty liberated group of guys. Who else would come on this kind of trip? But, I also realize that we men don't come together much to talk about the topics we are here to talk about today. I have a clergymen's study group and I have led some men's groups at church, but still it is new territory in a setting like this.

"I thought we would begin by exploring our relationships with women briefly, then talk about our worldview/religious beliefs and how we relate to the images of whatever form we experience and name as the Divine Feminine. How does that sound?"

"Daunting, but let's give it a go," laughs Gordie, nervously. Others nod.

"So how about some ground rules? First, that it is okay to pass. Second, that what we say to one another stays in this room. Third, we are not trying to fix or judge one another. We just will listen and learn."

"Okay, let's do it. I need this kind of conversation. You guys have a lot of experience with women and relationships that I would like to hear about," offers Gordie.

"How many more days do we have?" quips Jake.

"Let's start with women's roles in our lives: mother, sister, spouse, friend, colleague, soul mate. How do we differentiate these roles and expectations? Remember the old cliché that men see women as whore or Madonna. That always seemed too simplistic to me, but then, I lived with a bunch of sisters, my mother, and grandmother. What about it? And how does seeing the Divine as Father or Mother or both fit into any of that?"

Jake speaks up, "That is way too much to even think about, let alone talk about and I am not used to sitting around like this, so let me jump in first. Besides, I would guess I am the most traditional of all of us. I confess that when I was dating and first got married, I just expected Sandra to do the things my mother did for me, plus be the princess I had courted and the sexpot I had lusted for. She says I got pretty macho and demanding. I know I felt a lot of pressure to be the breadwinner and all. It actually was my mother who took me aside and told me to lose the attitude or I would lose Sandra.

"But it was hard competing in a dog-eat-dog world and then coming home to be all sharing and all gooey. Finally, with Sandra's encouragement, I started my own firm, where service, not competition, was the culture. That helped. But then came the next hurdle, having kids. Seeing my wife as sexy and the mother of my children and an equal partner all at once were not things that came easily to me. But it wasn't something you talked about in those days.

"Frankly, it was not until Sandra's recent cancer scare that I paid much attention to the nuances of our relationship. She did all the adapting and cajoling and teaching me to come around. I feel guilty to this day, thinking that all I put her through probably led to her getting cancer.

"As for the God part, I never thought about it until this trip. I guess having the image of God as Father fits with my being entitled to certain things by virtue of being male, you know, like God, the Father, Our Maker. Again, I never thought much about it. Truthfully, even in this trip, like at the Well, I just got bored after a while. You know, like what's this got to do with me?"

Then Kevin takes a turn, "I think some of this is slowly changing. Like Jake says, things are different now. I think each generation faces a different experience. A lot of what women like my mother did during women's lib helped men and women my age be better partners in marriage. Jane and I were doing great till her cancer. Then, this male protector archetype kicked in and I acted like a jerk. I wanted to fix it, control the situation. When I couldn't, I deflated like a balloon and took a long time to come around to a place where I could be with her as her partner. It was awful. And, as you can see, the issues with Jackson around it all – are still a mess."

John goes next, "As I said before, being a black man in America gives this all some extra spin. Like a lot of kids in my neighborhood, I was brought up mainly by my grandmother. I had a dad but he was real old and sickly and died when I was very young. My mom worked all the time. But my grandmother always put me first. Until this day, I worship her and know she is responsible for my survival, not just my success. So I was always around strong women, but had no trouble with separating and differentiating all these female roles.

"As for how relating to Melanie goes, one of the things that attracted me to her is how together she was. She comes from a two parent professional family. She has great common sense and wants to be of service to others in her work. It doesn't hurt that she is beautiful and bright, too. I like to think I am pretty flexible about roles and power and stuff.

"Listening to all this, though, surfaces some of the fears I have about kids changing things. I don't want to lose my soul mate and lover to this mommy thing."

Gordie weighs in, "I really don't know where I'm at with all of it. I guess that's why I'm still single. I just don't trust myself to get it right. I get super critical of any woman I get serious with and I know I like to be in control. I just don't know if I can be the kind of husband and father I want to be. My childhood family life was pretty screwed up. I made a lot of promises to myself about what I would not do or be, but don't see much to tell me how to do better."

Then from Peter, "All this goddess talk got me thinking about the stuff on the three stages of the Goddess and the three stages of women: maiden, mother, and crone. I am realizing of late, that I have now lived all three stages with Penny. Thankfully, I had a houseful of aunts and sisters to learn from. I thought of them during the Lughnasa play. They were tight with each other and just as fierce. I was the spoiled little boy, but I learned a lot. Going off to college was so necessary for me to separate from them. I had good mentors and waited a while to marry. All that contributed to Penny and I becoming good partners to one another. Plus, we had the Masonic and Eastern Star foundation from our teens. I now see how much that opened me up to the kinds of things we are talking about."

Rob speaks again, "Finding Peg and then our discovering our ministry together has been similar to what you are saying, Peter. Opening to different forms of the Divine and opening to differing roles in work and family do go hand in hand in my way of seeing things.

"Like, here's an example. Early in my ministry, I was preparing a sermon on creation stories. Peg challenged me and made me see how gender impacted the entire theological discussion. It truly changed my thinking and reminded me that I don't have all the answers or even need to have them. It's a more subtle thing than the medieval chastity belt invented by men so they would know a child was theirs. Or even the experience I had when my kids were born and I felt like a fifth wheel, being made to cool my heels in the waiting room. But, it comes from the same source. I realize that it was men who created the notion of dominion over nature and men that got us in so much trouble environmentally, needing to be makers and masters.

"I guess I am trying to express why I am excited about this reemergence of the Divine Feminine in this new century. I believe it will help us find balance and become the partners and co-creators I believe we are meant to be."

Jake responds, "I wouldn't have been able to say it like that, but, yes, I think there is hope for us to learn a better way. When my wife had our first child, wow, did I have trouble relating to her sexually. Then I resented the close bond she and the baby had. I started working late and going drinking with the guys. It is such classic and stereotypical behavior that I'm embarrassed to think about it. Now, I watch my daughters and their husbands. They have moved beyond all that. I see a much healthier picture.

"As you said earlier, Jung talks about the animus and anima in each of us. I think I have seen women, especially in the workplace, much more comfortable with their male side. We guys are playing catch up, I sometimes feel. But the balance is coming."

Kevin reenters the conversation, "Since the beginning of Jane's illness, I was forced into addressing my feelings and vulnerability for the first time. They say that women deal more readily with emotion. You see the tie-in around these goddess stories, women connected to the moon, her monthly menses like the moon cycle and all that. Some say that women are more comfortable moving from light to darkness and back to light again than us guys. Some generalize that they trust more because they embody the cycle of birth, life, death and rebirth. All I know is that my grief counselor asked me to look at what emotion and darkness meant to me. I realized it was like going into a cave without a light, just a deep hole with no escape. I thought of that a lot when we went in Alliwee Caves back in County Clare and then, of course, Newgrange and our ritual there. This ritual of going into darkness is missing for men especially in this day and age. I think we men suffer because of its absence.

"I can see this emotion thing being played out with KJ. He has been so angry with me for being weak. The male/female gender role stuff has already kicked in. He always went to his mother for comfort and sharing feelings, not to me. Even as a little boy, he had to show me what a big man he was. Then, it turned. He sees me as a big wimp for expressing my grief and trying to help him do the same. Man, it's complicated."

They sit in silence for a while. Rob gives a questioning look to Peter who looks pensive.

"I guess none of this was ever that hard for me, partly due to family dynamics. Partly because we Canadians do not live the Marlboro Man stereotype quite so strongly and partly due to the fact that Penny is my soul mate. We have learned together, grown together and now are growing old together. But I am thinking a lot on this trip about the cultural impact of all this, about the world my grandchildren experience.

"Rob and Jake, you'll remember when we had drinks together in Dublin? Gordie and John, just to fill you in, we talked about the book *The Great Turning*. Do you know the book? The more we see on this trip, the more we talk, the more I am burning to find ways to help us do this turning, personally, in our communities, and globally. How do we get the message out? How do we free our children and grandchildren from the stereotypes that have hurt us all?"

Rob agrees, "You know, for me, coming to Ireland and being with the land and the elements of fire, water, air, and earth in such an intentional way, in this Celtic spirituality of cycles and rhythms, I realize my justice work and sustainability work have been missing this spark of the Divine Feminine. It was a little dry and always issue-oriented, rather than soul-felt. I see I can change that. It has, in a way, already changed. As the chant goes: 'She changes, everything she touches changes.'"

Feeling more relaxed, Gordie adds, "So we just need to bring everybody over for a tour? What a gift that would be to the inner city kids I work with. But, short of a trip like this, everyone needs to have the experiences and rituals that are so lacking in our culture."

Peter is enthused, "I keep mentioning the parallel male and female youth groups that Penny and I belonged to. They really wove the ancient mysteries and the rituals of light and dark into us during those developmental years. I never realized how central they were to defining me until Newgrange. How do we do that in today's world? How do we compete with YouTube and video games?"

"Perhaps, we need to find a way to do retreats like Robert Bly and the men who started the men's weekend work," offers Kevin.

"You know I sound like Goldilocks, but Bly is too high-brow for the men of the neighborhoods. Yet, a group like the Promise Keepers is too Fundamentalist for me. We need something in the middle, that would be just right," quips John.

Rob notices the time, "We better end here, but let's talk more. Let's take our ideas to that workshop some of the women are leading tomorrow on 'A New Story for a New Time.' We can meet again after that, if we want."

They all agree, thank Rob for convening the group and head to the lounge for "pints" and to meet the others.

Afternoon tea gives way to cocktail hour. Wine and cheese is spread out to encourage the group to gather together. Most of the guys bring their beers from the bar as the women delight in having good wine available. Dorrie reappears and gives all the credit for arranging our cocktail hour to Gordie. Underlying the cheer and camaraderie, there is concern and worry. The sky grows blacker and blacker and there is no word from the group on the mountain. There certainly is a big storm brewing and it looks like it has already hit to the south of them.

Since there is nothing they can do but wait, the men continue their discussion.

"You know, intellectually, I understand when women got excited by books like *A God that Looks Like Me*, but not until this trip and the prominence of variations on the theme of the Divine Feminine did I have firsthand experience of how different it would feel if things were reversed. It's kind of like being in a minority for the first time; it helps you realize what you miss when you are even a small player in the dominant culture."

"You got it, Rob. Being black, I always had trouble with all the pictures of Jesus as a tall, bearded white guy or God as a stern, old white man. I never could see the Divine personified. And, now the women want to talk goddess to me. So being a black man in America just got even more complicated," he laughs, but he means it.

Kevin adds, "I really never thought much about the power of religion or our religious constructs to influence male-female issues before. But it makes sense when I do think about it. "

"I think it's a mighty powerful lens," contributes Peter.

Rob adds, "I've been thinking of how the differences between the way men and women see the Divine Feminine is like looking into a mirror. Looking at the same thing and identifying it, yet, being opposite. Remember learning to shave in a mirror? This feels like that." Everyone laughs in agreement and Rob continues, "Or think about the word ambulance written so it can be read in the rear view mirror. From straight on, it looks like gibberish. But through the mirror, it's clear."

Kevin pipes in, "Jung hypothesized that we all have an anima and an animus. Yet, the male in the female and the female in the male sure do play out differently."

"I think I am getting why I find it positive, even though I don't always get it. It's like being right-handed but learning to do lots of things well with your left hand. Bringing both the male and the female views of god/goddess or energies of the Divine will serve us well as a culture," contributed Gordie. "But, the part about finding it within ourselves is going too far in my estimation."

"Yeah, identity stuff is complicated enough. Rob, as a man of ideas and words, this all might make sense to you, but I can't go there. Of course, I agree we want a culture that no longer demonizes women or relegates them to second class citizens. But, not if it messes with my identity as a man to get there! No way...and I say again, especially for black men in America, there is enough baggage already without taking that on. I loved my momma and grandmother, but this feminine within stuff...No. No way."

Jake jumps in, "My daughters think I'm a dinosaur, but I have come a long way in understanding their women's right issues by watching them at school, in sports, looking for jobs. I speak up when all women are expected to cook, but only men are expected to be top chefs and all that. But, this stuff. I am still their daddy not some weird combination of mommy/daddy. I'm with John—that's going too far."

Rob chuckles, "Never would I dream of that for myself either. No. I think we are in closer agreement than our statements suggest. Let's drink to our identities as enlightened, yet still manly-men. I don't want to mess with that either. As long as we honor the fact that not everyone experiences gender the same way. And let's drink to the male gods of the Celtic pantheon, too!"

They all hoist their glasses in solidarity and then order another round.

COMING DOWN THE MOUNTAIN

ROSE

Trish comes upon me as I descend the mountain and we travel back down the last of the trail together.

We are the first to return. We find Timothy napping, but he wakes as we near the bus. He is none too pleased when he notices the darkening skies. He sends out some sharp blasts of his horn, hoping the others will hear the warning and hurry down to the bus, saying that storms can pick up fast in these parts.

ANGIE

Rebecca and I skip down the trail. I haven't felt this light and playful since my health scare. But, after today's trek up the mountain and the serenity we experienced up there, I feel great. All the way down, we've brainstormed ideas for creative projects. Finally, I think I have it. "Let's do something with my sketches, let's tell the story of our trip by making greeting cards or stationery with them. You could write the prose or find the quotations and I can do the marketing and bookkeeping."

"Do you think we would find a market for cards like that?"

"Sure, if we bring out this theme of Celtic spirituality and the Divine Feminine, I think so. It would be a fresh perspective and it would resonate with a lot of people."

"But, no one sends cards much anymore."

"These would be specialty, high end stuff. That always sells. Some could be the knots and triple spiral stuff we are doing for the party, too. They would be beautiful and smart looking. Besides, it is about doing something creative together. It's not as if we are quitting our day jobs."

"True, and if we do a lot of online stuff there's no overhead. You know, we could make sketches and photos available for websites, screen savers, and wall paper, too."

"Let's stop and write some of these ideas down before we forget them."

"I don't think that's wise. Look at that sky. I think we better hightail it down, right away."

"You're right. Hope the others are ahead of us."

MELANIE

The storm has come up fast, the wind is whipping brush around, and the rocks are becoming treacherous. I guess I am the last to leave the summit. I am alone and still pretty high up the mountain as the storm worsens. The sky darkens and looks more threatening. Why didn't I notice this sooner?

All of a sudden, the blackest of the clouds bursts wide open and dumps all the darkness that it has been holding. The rain is coming down so fast and furiously that I can't see a thing. I am afraid to put one foot in front of the other. I am afraid to move at all. Coming up the mountain the trail seemed wide enough and safe. But now?

A brief moment of lighter sky allows me to see some rocks to the inside of the path. I find a bit of shelter under one of them. I don't mind the wind and wet so much now that I am firmly seated in what seems like a safe place.

I wonder where the others are and if they are in danger? Or worried about me? But I can't risk moving. The rocky path is too slippery and it is still too dark to trust myself not to lose my footing . . . especially if I might be pregnant. Please God ...

Don't panic, I tell myself. After all, this isn't the Himalayas. It isn't even winter. But it does bring me up short. Granddad's notion of when you know you are going to meet your Maker comes to mind. He also used to say I was way too dramatic. That is what I need to remember. I really know I will be okay, but it is one of those times when you ask, what really is important? What is my life really meant to be?

The answer for me is that John is the love of my life and my work with troubled teens its purpose. Where does a baby fit in? At the center, as an extension of our love, not as a way to prove I am a woman. I know I have enough love to give a baby, or babies, as well as those who need me. I vow that if indeed I get pregnant, I will not swerve from my calling to help youth. I remind myself I am strong, and I summon all the courage I have to stay calm and let the storm pass. If this is a test from God, I will pass.

After the wind dies down some and the rain softens, I start picking my way down. But, I slip in the mud. Once down on my fanny, I decide I might as well stay down and try sliding down this next bit of trail on my butt. Not very pretty, but at this point, who cares? There still are huge, dark storm clouds hanging overhead. They will lift soon, won't they? Or will it worsen? I just don't know the weather patterns here. So I guess I should move on before the rains come back in full force.

TIMOTHY

The Reek is another name for the mountain here. Although at this moment, the name is taking on another meaning altogether. 'Tis wreaking havoc. Wreaking havoc whilst I slept when I should have been looking out for the lasses. All are back now, but wee Melanie. All back, waiting and getting more frantic by the moment. Sure enough, when a storm hits this area, it comes fast and fierce. I keep kicking meself again that I was napping instead of looking at the sky change. Had I seen the storm coming, I could have warned the lasses. Dark it is already and not even tea time. We can only hope and pray that Melanie had the sense to stay put, not try to move among the rocks in this darkness. Now, I ask the others if the lass is a city girl or does she know her way in the out-of-doors? No one knows.

So I get into me hiking boots, and get out a wrap, first aid kit, and me torch. Luckily, it is charged up. But little good it does as the rain comes down even harder, in sheets now. 'Tis pelting me so fierce like that for a time I cannot see me hand in front of me face. I must simply stand and wait for it to blow past. Patrick, keep her safe and sheltered I pray as I wait.

When the worst passes and I once again can see the trailhead through the torchlight, I commence up the path to find her. I leave me coach keys with the women so they can turn on the heat or run for help if need be. I also ask them to call Gordie in a half an hour if I am not back. They'll be able to see the storm at the Inn, even if they are not in it.

Calling out Melanie's name and shining the light ahead of me, I climb; but not a soul is to be found. No other cars left in the car park. No other hikers along the trail. I call again. Finally, I think I hear a reply, but it could have just been the wind. I keep going, praying that the lass has the rightness of mind not to stray from the path.

Finally, I hear an answer to me call. "Stay put!" I yell. "Okay, okay," I hear in return.

I find the wee lass huddled amid the rocks, having sought some protection after traveling a good bit in the mud. She looks like a wet puppy dog, waving with all her strength. God bless her. She falls into me arms. Only when she has settled herself, do we begin the journey down the mountain, letting the light of the torch guide us on our descent.

The women at the foot of the trail run to meet us, taking the lass into their arms for the last bit back to the bus. Once inside they take over, stripping her of wet clothes and wrapping her in a clean, warm blanket. We have a bit of me tea whilst we calm ourselves. Melanie is bruised and exhausted, but nothing seems broken. They clean up a few of the scrapes with antiseptic from me first aid kit. Then the women continue to fuss over her while I call Gordie to say we are okay and are headed back. As claps of thunder echo off the mountain, I turn toward the Inn. With the soothing flute of James Galway in the background, we all watch the waves throw themselves upon the rock. The contrast between the hard, pounding surf and the light, angelic music is not lost on any of us. Glad to be inside the wee coach we are, that 'tis for certain.

JOHN

I started fretting as the storm grew in strength and seemed to hang right over Croagh Patrick. Gordie delayed dinner while we waited but even the extended cocktail hour didn't help. I just hope and pray Melanie is all right, that she hasn't taken unnecessary risk. What a relief when Gordie says they are headed back.

So now the bus pulls up and everyone disembarks but Melanie. Where is she? Finally, she comes down the steps, looking like she just came through the car wash, but not hurt, thank you, Lord. Thank these Irish gods and goddesses and Jesus and Patrick and all the saints. And to think I have been pouty and pissy with her these last few days.

She collapses into my arms and shakes so hard I think it will break my heart. Finally, I whisper a question whether she is hungry and she just shakes her head. I tell whoever is standing there not to expect us back for dinner. I think we both are in a daze. But I manage to make our way through all the well-wishers, up to our room.

I help her get out of what little she has on under the blanket and into the shower. Then, I join her, holding on to her from the back as she leans into me. I soap her and rub her skin as she soaks and as the steam rises in the shower stall. Next thing I know, my arousal is obvious to us both. We rinse each other, touching gently at first. Then the contact becomes as heated and steamy as the atmosphere around us. Our need for one another is desperate.

We move to the bed. Melanie cannot or will not let go and that makes me want her even more. Finally, I am spent and we fall asleep connected; connected at more levels than I had ever thought possible.

MARY HELENA

Dinner is good. Everybody is relieved that the bus got back okay; but now I am restless. I usually am exhausted and read myself to sleep while everyone goes drinking. But today was so slow and I just am not tired. I wander out to the strand. The clouds have blown off to the east and the sky is calm now. The full moon is shining brightly on the water, which has tamed itself. I feel a soft sensation, gentle like the moon glow on the water, like a crème rinse gently rolling over my body in the shower. I sit quietly and just allow myself to feel the gentle wash of light.

Perhaps it's a message. I have prayed and prayed to St. Brigid for guidance and for healing. I want to be well. I'm beginning to realize I need to heal my heart emotionally as well as physically. I know I am resisting. I was downright rude to Peg. But it is so hard. Letting go. If I let go of all this anger, then what? Nobody ever talks about that part. And then what?

Sandra said that her faith had helped her heal through cancer. She had suggested a spiritual director, saying many nuns do that kind of work now. Maybe I should try that. I can at least give it a go. Gentle and easy seems to be the message of the moonlight. When have things ever been gentle and easy? But maybe a slow melting of the ice that I've built around my heart, a gentle fire from St. Brigid is the answer to my prayer. In the distance, I hear what sounds like the wailing siren of the roans. I don't believe in roans or selkies or any of this fairy nonsense. Yet, there is magic here on the strand tonight. I will just stay out here awhile, just watching and listening.

TIMOTHY

A hot shower and a good dinner and Kate's smile of relief and love revives me just fine. So I need not disappoint those wishing for a trip to the pub. "So folks, 'tis your last night to be comin' out for a few pints with me!" I shout out, laying on the thickest brogue I can muster. They all laugh, listening to the particulars, "The boys playin' tonight have been travelin' I hear. This is their first night back in a fortnight, so the pub will be packed. I suggest we leave right away if we can."

Realizing it would be the last night out as a group, I am preparing for a big group and a late night. I even arranged for the courtesy van at the Inn to pick up those who wanted to leave when the band broke for intermission. That encouraged some to come who otherwise might have passed.

So off we went for a night of hand-slapping good fun, wonderfully spirited music and a few good reels of dance. Before the end of the first set, I ask the boys to play *Wild Rover*. Most now know the chorus and sing "No, nay, never" loud enough for the folks back at the Inn to hear us. Kate gives me this look of fun and joy and playfulness. And all me clouds are lifted away.

I get back to business, arranging for some local lads who speak Irish to come over to the tables to talk to our people. Not a soul should ever leave *Gaeltacht* without hearing the locals in their native language. The lads are shy, but after a whiskey and some assurances that they can talk about anything—their sheep or the sea for all anyone would know or care—they come round. Just the sound of the Irish is what I am after, I say, givin' them a second whiskey. And it works fine.

People love it, and the lads have free whiskeys the rest of the night.

Peter pairs himself with Nathan and challenges Kevin and Jackson to a game of darts. Trish and Megan smile that smile of, "Well, finally." I call the Inn to cancel the courtesy van, for it looks to be that all will stay to close the place. And so, we party on. Then the boys play their final song, *"I'll Take You Home Again, Kathleen."* Everyone looks toward Kate who is becoming a lovely shade of crimson. I add to it by coming over, standing behind her with me hands on her shoulders, singing the loudest of all.

A full moon, glistening on the water beckons as we return to the Inn. For some of us lucky souls, the night 'tis not yet over as time slows and the moon grows bigger and brighter.

DAY ELEVEN

ON THE COAST

Our last full day
This is a free day with a banquet and party planned for our
last evening together.
We encourage you to look through the background materials we have
provided and ask any questions you may have.
Please also provide release slips for photo exchanges and contact
information before the end of the trip.

JOHN and MELANIE

Tantric sex, and here in Ireland. Who would have thought it? John chuckles to himself as he awakes to the rising sun. Once awake, of course, he has to go to the toilet and there is no way to break away from his bond with Melanie without waking her.

Melanie's first thought upon waking is a resounding, 'Yes! We're pregnant!' She is immediately certain she can feel the stirrings of life within her. She also senses, knows, that they will be all right, no matter what. They had not made love to each other with such abandon, with such passion and intimacy in years. Something wonderful would come from that . . . they had surrendered to one another and to something bigger than themselves last night. Good things would follow . . . how could they not?

John offers to go get breakfast and bring it up to bed. She loves the idea. She loves to be pampered, but more importantly, she wants this seed which she knows he has planted to take root. She isn't going any place this entire morning.

John comes back with tons of food. After they gobble down enough food to satisfy the gnawing in their stomachs, they linger over the rest of it, enjoying the luxury of breakfast in bed. Then, he runs his hands over her body, imagining her belly already swelling and her breasts enlarging. He kisses her navel and all the places he has just touched. So beautiful, he keeps whispering to her. They make love once more with the same passion and abandon as last night. If they did not make a baby last night, then surely they did this morning, thinks John. Both fall back asleep in each other's arms.

DORRIE

I get up way before sound toning and slip quietly into my sweats so as not to disturb Gordie. The beach and my journal beckon. I had never imagined that this trip would be so rich with ideas. It is truly an example of how we learn from one another. I love it.

The blue paper of my journal matches the blue grey of the sea and the sky: A muted place in time and space to quietly capture the nuance of my thoughts. There is almost a mystical quality to the strand today as the gentle waves lap the shore. I relish every minute of it.

I'm a little anxious about the session we're doing today, Creating a New Story for a New Century. It's the working title of the book Kate and I have been talking about writing. I am more of a speaker than writer and Kate the opposite. I think that makes us a good team. The idea of inviting everyone to come and brainstorm ideas was Megan's and she was so enthusiastic. I think both Kate and I wanted to encourage her and, selfishly, to also benefit from her youthful exuberance. She designed a poster and offered to write up the quotation she shared with us in Sligo Town. I came up with a creative format that I hope will work because I know both Kate and I can get too academic for a lot of people

I'm going to jot some of the ideas down in my journal to have as backup. But with this group, I doubt I'll need to look at it.

Serendipity: See what happens . . . be open to Spirit. The Kate meets Timothy story.

Synchronicity: Things happen and connect–watch for signs, The way I keep seeing and hearing the word 'story' everywhere.

We Are All One People: That wonderful song by Molly Scott and the way we all have bonded.

Intersections of Science and Religion: The astrological alignment of these ancient monuments.

Emergence of the Divine Feminine: Brede, Brigit, St. Brigid, Mother Earth.

Acceptance of Mystery and Wonder: How did ancient peoples know and do what they did???

More is Not Necessarily Better: The enduring thing is the simplicity and beauty around me

Quantum Thinking: Holograms, relativity, wave and particle, sound and light, and all the potentialities in all this.

I know Rob has a list of things, too, like interconnectedness. And then there is Rose. I know Gordie, and others, are really turned off by the fairy talk. But, how can one experience Ireland without a bit of magic? Fantasies and stories that open the heart and mind. What could be more Irish?

I also want to collect real human stories for the book. Like the story Angie told about being in the Peace Corps and working on a project where for the first time the money was given directly to women for projects in their village. How, like, they had a simple water system built and took care of health needs, etc. Before that time, the male leaders had squandered the money or outsiders had built unneeded roads, etc.

There is a lot of table-hopping at breakfast as people make plans for the party. We all notice that John and Melanie are missing and everyone just smiles. So when we get to the round of gratitude at our table someone suggests we also send energy to Melanie and John for a bit. We do, each in our own way. That's a great thing about this group. Each in our own way. I also love this ritual, especially since it emerged from the group. Intention and gratitude, powerful practices, for sure.

And, I love the lyric quality of these West of Ireland folk. Timothy is telling the group what "a soft Irish morning" it is. Grey, foggy, and drizzly would be the words used back home. In fact, it is even a little greyer than when I journaled. But everyone is okay with it. Even Mary Helena is rather pleasant, even cheerful, talking about tonight's party.

Megan goes into the meeting room early and posts the wonderful quotation from Thomas Berry for all to see:

> *It is all a question of story. We are in trouble now because we do not have a good story. We are in between stories. The old story, the account of how we fit into it, is no longer effective. Yet, we have not learned the new story.*

Kate asks Lily to play something that will stir people to think about the new. Sounds like Lily is getting it just right, too. People are coming in and sitting quietly listening to the music and, it appears, really thinking about the quotation.

I go first, "When we stop to think about it, we all have been living the story of the Holy Grail for the past millennium. It is the story of the individual, one hero, one savior. He goes through trial and tribulation. In the end, he triumphs. Yet, the Grail remains elusive. The Summerland, the Kingdom of Heaven on Earth awaits another hero, another coming of the messiah.

"Our whole psyche, our archetypes, our personal lives, our communal lives, our governments are built upon the story of the triumph of the individual. It has been a great source of strength. It is also leading to our downfall and destruction."

Kate takes over. "The reemergence of the Divine Feminine is reminding us that we have lost our way, we have lost our balance. The individual hero is important and equally important is the community from which he or she comes and to which they return. The circle, the family, the earth must not be disregarded or overpowered for the sake of the individual. The Round Table part of the Arthurian story has been lost. The flock that Christ came to shepherd has lost its voice. We no longer are served by the quest of the individual alone, not when it is at the expense of the community. We need leaders and models of community, where the individual remains whole and contributes in collaboration and partnership.

"Remember how much ridicule Hilary Clinton got for saying that it *Takes A Village*? But belonging and learning and working together are keys to our future, to our twenty-first century storyline."

Megan is next, "The three of us are really committed to working on a project to provide a new narrative, you know, a new story that will help people see that they sometimes have blinders on. When people don't see that, they keep getting stuck and never change. We want people to stand up for themselves and not wait for some hero-type person to take charge. Because sometimes the people who think they have the answers really are too much a part of the system to fix it.

"Young people especially notice awesome things that seldom get reported or discussed—things that could change the world. Like the true story Mom and I heard on NPR radio about a group of women who trekked to the North Pole. They waited for one another so all could touch the place and plant the stake together. Or the story of the young boy with Down's syndrome in the Special Olympics who was winning the race when one of the other racers fell. He went back, and so they all went back and then they helped the fallen racer up and walked together to the finish line.

"Then look at what Live Aid did. Like, during Michael Jackson's funeral, they talked about what a big deal getting the *"We Are the World"* project was. Now we get global action immediately with *"We Are the World 25* for Haiti 2010" on YouTube. I could go on and on."

Megan is trying not to cry as she steps back, deferring to Kate and I. So I move us on, "I never dreamt when we sent out the flyer for this trip, that all this would be happening." I feel tears slide down my face as I continue. "So the question is what are some of the components and ideas you have for what a twenty-first century story might include? Rather than just talk about it, or even brainstorm a list, I thought we might create a collective story. You know, where one person offers a paragraph, then another adds onto it, until everyone has had a chance and the arc of the story comes to an ending through improvisation. Everyone up for it?"

There were a few sounds of nervousness. I remind people that they can pass and we don't have to go in order. I know it will take off because we clued a few people in ahead of time so they can be ready to get us started.

"I'll begin with a paragraph and then I invite you to chime in one by one as you are moved to do so."

"Once upon a time, in the not so distant future, there was a Band of Merry Travelers known to peoples throughout the world for their visits to towns and cities everywhere. It was rumored that the places they visited were never the same again; though, there seemed to be no predictable pattern to where they went or what they did when they got there. Yet, many legends were already building about the good they did wherever they went." (Dorrie)

288

"Ach, and for transport and lodging, they were very self-contained. They had a wee caravan, a futuristic high tech version, mind you, of a Travelers wagon. In it seemed to be all they ever needed, and you would be dazzled to see the things pulled out of it on demand. No one ever reported being asked inside and no one knew quite what to make of the vehicle. It appeared the whole lot of them slept within on nights too cold or rainy for them to camp out under the stars. You could be sure they always had a campfire going. For part of their magic was their knack for getting folks to tell their stories to one another. I am told, even when in the city centers, they got permits to make it all legal like to have a fire. Never would you pass by that a group was not around the fire. The kettle was always on. There was always music. You were always encouraged to join in and maybe have a pint with them." (Timothy)

"The Band of Merry Travelers were a marvel to watch. Like an all-star basketball team or Wimbledon tennis doubles champions. They covered the whole town as if it were the team's court. They were always in the zone, alert yet casual and steady-paced. They shared leadership, seeming to work through the town, one-on-one and teaming up to get people to share stories. Always engaging, listening, and offering comments that egged people to get to the big stories of their lives, their hopes and dreams. When they took airtime for themselves, it was to tell stories of how others had made things happen, how people had found ways to overcome the barriers and limitations they recounted. Sometimes when you passed the campfire, you would see small groups of people who shared lots of similarities. Other times, there were obvious mixes of ages, the sexes, race and color. But always, it seemed people were sharing stories and finding commonality in their hopes and dreams." (Rob)

"They also used questions to prompt people to share their visions of a better future. Questions like 'if you could do just one thing, what would it be?' or 'what one thing would change this town for the better?' Before long, a community vision began to emerge. No one realized the Band of Merry

Travelers had been the catalysts. In no time, a plan came together. People gathered much like barn raisers of past generations to begin a new community center." (Gordie)

"Someone suggested that it must be green. So the whole project was stopped until plans were completed to use the best of recycled and innovative materials and state of the art water, heating, and septic systems, including solar panels and a windmill. It was so green that it was called the Emerald Isle of the Future, not to take away a thing from Ireland, of course."(Leslie)

"Then, the youth started a Rave in the Commons to demonstrate that the center needed to have a sound system and stage for bands. And it needed to be techno-savvy if anyone under thirty was expected to use it." (Jackson).

"Soon every group started demanding and advocating ideas and needs. Some, like issues of accessibility, were key, others were pure craziness. The town leaders became paralyzed. Homeowners and business groups got nervous about the cost and pushed back. School leaders were afraid the money would come from their budgets. The project was about to stall out and die. But then, the Band of Merry Travelers started to spin their magic. People began asking each other a new question: In what ways might we make it happen? Thanks to the BMT, as they were affectionately called, people started looking to themselves as well as looking for examples far and near to inform their work." (Trish)

"People started contributing ideas, tangible resources, and promises to sponsor parts of the project. Enlightened leaders righted the sinking ship and stayed the course once it was righted. Coached, emboldened, and supported by the BMT, they took charge and brought modern-systems thinking to the forefront once again.

"They worked together, not only training and educating people as they worked, but empowering them, as well. A wonderful building was completed in record time. But the best part was that other green buildings and renovations popped up all over. Kids, who had been in and out of jail, learned to help put up solar panels. Entrepreneurs partnered with unemployed workers to start new projects that brought life back to old neighborhoods and paychecks to people who were willing to work. The town began to prosper." (Kevin}

"And within the center itself people began to share their gifts and talents. Murals were painted on the walls; a sound and light system and stage were designed for people to play music and hold concerts or receive satellite transmissions. Poetry groups, parenting groups, craft groups, study groups of all sorts started. High tech, high touch was the theme as relationships deepened and new technologies were available to all. A steering group saw to the choice of murals so the whole community felt represented. A huge peace quilt, where each person or family who wished to be represented could add a square, was created. Scenes of sacred sites and community rituals from various cultures covered one wall. Present day pictures of people and activities covered another." (Sandra)

"The area that would become the healing center and meditation room had a Tree of Life theme. Symbols and pictures of nature and rites of healing were tastefully added. From the main window, you could see the labyrinth that had been created and the ancient oak tree that had been saved." (Rebecca)

"As people worked side by side, offered their talents, and received the benefits of the gifts of others, they started to get along. Old grievances were forgiven, wounds began to heal, and trust was building." (Peg)

"People had a sense of belonging. And as they felt they belonged, they started reaching out to others. Social networks—face to face and virtual—sprung up fun-to-do good deeds. The arts and artisan works were promoted and young people were encouraged to appreciate art and to express themselves creatively." (Angie).

"Retired people found a place to contribute meaningfully to their community." (Jake)

"And a garden was planted which brought butterflies and fairies and joy. Under the guidance of the elementals, it flourished." (Rose)

"A community garden was added and shares given to the poor. More and more, the older people sold their big, rambling homes and moved into new condominiums built for elder living." (Penny)

"And, yeah, the Church took the lead in getting elders and teenagers to help single mothers get through the rough patches." (Mary Helena)

"Teens felt affirmed and part of the wider community. Teen pregnancy rates even began to go down. News of what the town was doing went viral. Nobody could get enough of the good news stories. Then the bad news junkies started making up rumors and conspiracies about how unreal all the good stuff was. Someone came up with holding a virtual town meeting every Saturday where people could tell their part of the story. YouTube picked it up and people from all over started watching, asking questions and seeking support for their projects. It was awesome." (Megan)

"The trouble, though, was that the parts didn't make a whole. There was more to the story than people realized as they repeated the steps they had taken. Like good jazz improvisation, there was more to it than most people see and it was hard to replicate without the Band of Merry Travelers. They needed to learn for themselves the value of building a holistic community." (Peter)

"Then it began to come together. It was about the weaving of the energies and the wisdom of all. Men and women, young and old created the continued transformation. They began to see that and celebrate it." (Kate)

"What no one realized was that BMT also stood for Band of MAGICAL Travelers. Their alchemy was to bring people and science and religion and faith and history and the future all together in a way that made good things happen and that changed people's thinking." (Nathan)

"And they took their magic throughout the land so everyone would remember. Remember to listen to one another's hopes and dreams and honor the gifts of every being in the Spirit of Love and Light. So the story never ends." (Lily)

Silence prevails.

"Whew! That was wonderful. May it be so. Thank you all. Let's just sit with all this and embrace it for a minute. There is so much to think about. Let's just pause a bit longer in silence. Then it is break time. Coffee and tea have been set up in the garden. How about meeting back here in thirty minutes?"

The three of us are speechless as we hug each other and get hugs from the folks also caught up in the excitement of the story we had created together. Ah, if only this creative, positive thinking could be bottled. I say a short, silent prayer that we will be able to capture it on paper.

MEGAN

Nathan is asking me what it was like to be part of the group and praising the work I did.

"Thanks," I say. "It was kinda scary, but really great to get a chance like that."

"Yeah, it wasn't like a school presentation, you were really getting the adults thinking. Sometimes they keep going on and on about the past and making a big deal of stuff that's just too obvious, like that technology is changing things . . . duh."

Just then Gordie comes over. "Great job, Megan," he says to me and then turns to Nathan, adding, "Still hanging in there, Nathan?"

"Yeah, it was really good, but I don't really want to go back in for more of people sitting around talking."

"I know what you mean. So, I've got a proposition for you two and Jackson, if we can find him in time. You'll have to get permission from your parents, though."

"What is it? Where are we going?" we both question him at once.

"I was just talking to one of the inn keepers and they have a charter boat leaving for a tour of Sligo Bay in forty-five minutes. There are four extra seats. Want to come with me?"

Nathan jumps right in, "Sure!"

I don't know what to say. Will people be mad if I left now that my workshop is over? I stall around and finally ask, "Do you think it's rude of me to leave now?"

"Not at all," Gordie replies. "Everyone would jump at the chance if there were more seats. Besides you two have been such great travelers, I'm sure all the adults will want you to have this, kind of as a reward."

"Okay, then, I'll go ask Mom." I say happily.

Nathan groans, "I forgot. My mom's going to be talking about the environment and she'll expect me to be there."

"Actually," replies Gordie, "this boat trip was chartered for a group of economic leaders from the European Union that are studying eco-tourism so you guys will be doing something that is all about the environment. You can tell her all about it."

"Will we have to listen to lectures and will we have to be all formal?"

"We'll stay out of the way of the official part. Besides, you kids have proven yourselves. I'm not worried. Go check with your moms and tell them to give me the okay. Then, get your jackets and rain gear. It might be cold or misty out there. Now where can I find Jackson?"

"I think he went back to his room. He said he wanted to finish that book he was reading at the start of the trip," offers Nathan. "Oh, what about lunch?"

"It's all taken care of. Just meet me at the bus in ten minutes."

So Gordie finds Jackson, we get our permission and meet at the bus. Timothy is driving to the small nearby fishing harbor where the charter boat is waiting for us as part of the deal with the Inn. Most of the European Union people are men and most are a little bit serious, but I'm used to that because of Mom's job. Nathan and I answer a zillion questions and even Jackson is polite.

The EU folks ask if our group is on an eco-tourist tour. They like it when I tell them about visiting sacred sites and how, to us, that had a lot to do with the environment and connecting to nature. Then they go back to talking business.

Nathan says his mom and her friends should think about sponsoring eco-tours. Gordie agrees while Jackson and I just watch the shoreline go by.

The harbor is like the TV set for *Murder She Wrote*, only Irish. For one thing, the fishing boats are different. The Irish boats kind of look like old rowboats, but painted all sorts of bright blues, greens, and reds, just like on postcards. And there are lots of bigger fishing boats and activity. Timothy said most of the fishermen would have come in with their catch by this time of day, but people are still working around, cleaning the boats and stuff. Off to the sidelines are sailboats and a few motor boats. They are so tiny compared to the big party boats on the Potomac. It scares me to think of being out on the open sea in any of them.

Ours is a tour boat so we can go inside and sit at a table and look out through the glass. The EU people already went in and are having coffee and a presentation of some sort with a guy pointing out things as we move along. The four of us stay on deck watching the captain and his first mate. Being at the rail also gives us a closer look at the sailboats as we pass by. Before long, we come to a really interesting sight that none of us understand so Gordie calls the first mate over and asks him about it.

"Aye, you would be lookin' at the oyster raceways that are part of the mariculture here in the West. Fish farmin' you might say, but not the kind with cages. The seawater flows through and 'tis all quite natural seemin'. 'Tis the wave of the future, so to speak, and lots of EU people come for a look. We farm clams and mussels, too, and up above in the estuaries are the salmon raceways as well."

"Is that what the folks downstairs are here for?"

"Nay, the ones below are lookin' at our eco-tourism. 'Til the monies ran out, we had ourselves a program called Green Box to help local artists, bed and breakfast folks, and all. They would think up things like bike trails and festivals and nature walks, that sort of doin's. These ones are lookin' at the waterside possibilities of such efforts."

As he spoke, one of the little boats, *currachs* he calls them, came into view. "Do the fishermen actually take those out on the sea?" I ask. "They look so small."

"Lots of rocks along the shore as you will see. 'Tis the width and flatness of these ones that helps keep you from disaster. You see, lass, the sea is a hard mistress. 'Tis no safe place when a storm whips up, no matter your boat."

"May I ask you a question?" Nathan, too, is intrigued by this salty Irish seaman.

"Aye, away with whatever is on your mind, lad."

"I read that very few Irish fishermen actually know how to swim, is that true?"

"Aye. 'Tis icy cold, the water. The likes of me never had the urgin' to learn. Now today, they have some seaside pools and school programs for the wee ones."

"I also read that the Irish knit sweater patterns were different in each family so that if your body washed up they could identify you. Is that true?"

"Aye, sadly that was the case. See, if you were caught out in a big one, would not much matter if you had a vest or were a swimmer. You were a goner. And you understand, 'twas fact that the fish would not be able to eat the sweater. But enough talk of such. Do you see our lighthouses now? That 'tis the safety feature that matters. Up and down the West coast and around to the North they are. We have many a visitor just for the lighthouses. During the Big War, the Allies relied on them and used the northern route above Ireland and between Scotland and Norway into the North Sea. Some say the war was won on account of these beauties, if you take me meanin'. Here we come to Oyster Island. Do you see it now?"

Jackson and Gordie are fascinated by the big lens and the mechanics of the lighthouse. I think they are disappointed the boat doesn't stop. But I see the sea lions gathered and that's all I care about. They are so fun and so noisy. Nathan asks if they are selkies. But, Seamus, our first mate, chuckles and says the Irish are more likely to call them roans, if they are. Of course, I know that from *Secrets of Roan Inish*, but to think I am actually here in Ireland seeing sea lions in the bay. Wow!

Wish Mom was here to see this, but I am taking lots of pictures.

We circle around, past the Metal Man statue. It reminds me of Gloucester and the statue there. You know, the one on the frozen fish packages? Seamus also points out Coney Island. I never thought about how our Coney Island might be named for an Irish island. That's a cool idea. Thinking of Coney Island hot dogs reminds Nathan and me that we haven't had lunch yet. Nathan's fries sure would be nice right now. We go below to get warm and to eat the box lunches the Inn has provided. Sadly, "No, sausages," says our Nathan in his best Harry Potter imitation. What a funny word sausages is with an accent.

I couldn't see if Gordie and Jackson were really talking or just hanging out. Whichever, I'm glad. Gordie seems to get that Jackson doesn't need to be fixed, he just needs a friend so he won't take his anger out on everyone. Gordie seems like the guy to get through to him.

All of a sudden while we are eating, I remember the video we are doing for the party. "OMG! Nathan we still have to get the video done. Will we be back in time to finish it?"

"Actually, I think I've got it mostly done. I brought what I did last night along for us to look at. We need to decide about background music. Timothy has lots of stuff we can borrow. Plus, Gordie made us promise he could preview it. Want to do that now?"

"Yeah, let's look through it first and then call Gordie and Jackson down to look, too."

So we spend the return trip looking at the video and looking out the window so as not to miss a thing. We would be back in plenty of time to finish it and get to dinner.

BACK AT THE INN

Rebecca is set to begin after break. Dorrie steps in just to tell everyone about Gordie and the young people going off with the EU eco-tourism leaders. Everyone is happy for them and amazed at the serendipity of the kids having an environmental experience while the adults talk about it. Leslie steps up with an announcement, too. The environmental group has decided they want to wait and meet over breakfast in the morning. They want us all to have more time for people to think about twenty-first century strategies.

Rebecca begins, "I also changed what I was thinking of doing so people could get outside this afternoon. After all, this is our last day. I thought I would offer a guided visualization rather than a mini-lecture.

"By now, you all know of my interest in exploring opportunities for people of different faiths to see the commonality in their spiritual practices, their symbols and rituals and their deepest truths. My own view is that right now most interfaith groups form around common ground issues of justice or service projects. They advocate together on issues of agreement rather than having meaningful and heartfelt discussions of faith. In fact, I think most of us avoid talking about religion because we don't want conflict.

"Yet, I think it is our common experience as spiritual people in right relationship that is needed to make this a less conflicted, more peaceable world. That is what this trip and learning about Celtic spirituality have been about for me."

There are lots of heads nodding agreement as she continues with a question. "Did everyone get to see or try Nathan's ogham sticks? They symbolize the importance of trees and tree lore to the Celts. As you know, I've been thinking a lot about the Celtic Tree of Life and how it compares to the Kabbalah Tree of Life, which is a key to my own spiritual practice. I'd be glad to talk more about that with anyone who asks. But for now, I would just like to offer the visualization.

"Let's start with a deep relaxation. I invite you to take deep breaths, sinking, sinking into a state of deep relaxation. Let your body sink into the earth. Let your limbs go free. Let your spirit soar.

"Imagine yourself here in the West of Ireland, long, long ago. Imagine yourself on top of a knoll overlooking a green valley. Perhaps it is dotted with a blue lake and punctuated by the sounds of birds calling to one another. See a tall oak tree on top of the knoll. It is three times taller than the biggest tree you've ever seen; its trunk is three times wider than your outstretched arms. Its branches create a circle around you three times greater than the hut where you live. It is the tallest thing you have ever seen. It is the biggest living thing you know. It provides food, shelter, building materials. Just experience being beneath that tree for a while."

She pauses, waits a bit and then continues, "Now, imagine that you live during that same time period of long ago, but you now are traveling across the hot desert, surrounded by sand dunes for as far as you can see. The sun beats down on you. You are thirsty and hot. You long for shade and a drink and a place of rest. Far ahead, you see something on the horizon. It seems to rise above the sand and call to you. You start toward that distant tall object, you know it will be a tree, you know you will find shade, you know water will be nearby.

"Earth, water, sky. You will find them all meeting at the tree, the Tree of Life. You find the tree. It is a tree whose roots go deep into the ground and drink in the water of life. Its branches lift into the sky with leaves blowing in the wind. Its trunk connects earth to sky like a pole, like the *axis mundi.* Its height catches lightning and creates fire, becoming the burning bush.

"Imagine the tree half green and half ablaze.

"Imagine the Tree bearing fruit and nuts to sustain us. Apple tree, fig tree. Imagine the Tree of Life.

"Stand under the tree and take in all its facets and energy.

"Give thanks to both the trees you have seen in your visualization and to all the trees that keep our planet green.

"And when you are ready, return your attention to this room and to our time together."

"Lovely. Thank you so much, Rebecca," says Dorrie as everyone murmurs approval and then claps. "Let's end the morning with a song," suggests Dorrie. How about a green song? Everyone know the *Garden Song* ? she begins and others pick it up, *"Inch by inch, row by row, gonna make this garden grow . . ."*

Lily just beams as she makes joyful poetry of the gestures that go along with the words. What an experience, what a morning. Heads are spinning with ideas, and hearts are full of gratitude.

KATE and TIMOTHY

Kate and Timothy take a picnic lunch down the beach to have some time alone. It is still a bit damp, but not windy so they are comfortable laying out a blanket and sitting quietly.

"What a beautiful spread," remarks Kate, "one of the perks of dating the man with wheels, I see."

He loves that laugh. He loves the ease she has with herself.

"Kate, my luv, what are we doin' come tomorrow? Would you be after stayin' on for the *céilí*?"

"I'm not ready to say goodbye tomorrow, Timothy, but neither do I have a clear picture of what staying on would look like, or feel like. If we were in the States, we would go back to our homes and daily lives and I would just show up at your family party on the weekend. But here in Ireland? It feels awkward. Where would I stay? What do we say when your children ask who we are to one another? Do we even know ourselves?"

"Aye, you bring up good questions . . . questions that I really had not gotten to yet, Dunno . . . dunno."

Silence, for what seems like an eternity to Kate.

"What I do know, Kate, is that if you lived here in Ireland, I would ask to be courting you with the idea that we would marry in the spring, hearts willin'."

"Timothy Mulhearn, I believe that is a proposal."

"Aye, 'tis, I think we are grand together, do you not, as well?"

"I do, Timothy, indeed I do. But it would be such a big step . . . and what if . . . well, we have known each other less than two weeks."

"Do you love me, Katie girl?

"Yes, you charming Irishman, I do."

"Well, then. The rest will work itself out now, will it not?"

They proceed to make plans for the next steps they know they want to take together. She will stay in the room with Mary Helena tonight. That will give her a chance to pack up. Besides, he has to get up extremely early to prepare for their leaving. He will get her a room in a small inn near his home for the next few days. Not a bed and breakfast where they might feel they were being watched, but still a nice comfortable place. She can do some touring while he spends a few days with his son, who is arriving tomorrow evening.

Then she will meet them all in a small family dinner before the big *céilí*. She can meet the whole clan at the *céilí* itself. After his son flies back to his home, Katie will move in to Timothy's house. She will tell her family and friends that she is staying for the summer. She will say that she met a man she wants to know better, a relationship she wants to pursue. They will want to know what that means. They both will just say honestly that they do not know yet. Then, come fall they will decide what comes next.

"Aye, then, we will give it a go to the fall equinox, a Celtic Thanksgiving, the time of the second harvest. If we are as happy then as we are today . . . ach, Kate, are ye not giving me a second life for which I am grateful, indeed?"

"I'm feeling a little shaky with all this planning, Timothy, let's just walk a bit and enjoy this place, this moment."

"Aye, woman. You have the right of it; 'tis in the moment where love resides."

ROSE

Over the last few days, I have talked more and more about the Fairy Kingdom. Most people hadn't stopped to realize how many countries have fairy traditions. But when I ask them to remember childhood fairy tales, they realized there were gnomes, elves, sprites—a long list and from cultures as varied as Scandinavia and Japan. The more I see of Ireland, the more I see how the energy that keeps them alive in people's minds and hearts works. But even here they are now in danger. Old forests are disappearing and brambles, bushes, and hedgerows are being cleared away to widen backcountry roads for lorries and tour buses.

Ever since the day we came into County Sligo, I've been saying I want to lead a fairy visit. Now it is the last day and I am finally bringing a small group of us together to do it. I decide to wait until the kids get back from their boat ride. Nathan and Megan were so excited to join in and they had already gotten permission from their mothers. I didn't want to exclude them.

I asked just a few people. I am too new at this to have strong or dark energies and would be self-conscious if Dorrie joined. So it will just be Rebecca and Angie, Leslie and Trish, and their kids. I had asked Lily if she wanted to participate, but she said she couldn't possibly. Then she changed her mind and said she would play the harp if I wanted. I still don't get who she is or what she is doing but I'm glad she's coming.

I decided to skip the beach location I had planned to use. The kids would be getting back too late. By using my room, we would have more time before dinner.

So here we are. When everyone gathers and settles in, I give them a little orientation: "Thanks so much for joining me. As you know, a fairy journey is a lot like a guided visualization, only we will be guided by a fairy who takes us into his or her world. You may just imagine it or you may feel totally like you are part of the Other Kingdom. The key is to relax, remain open, and go where it takes you. There is no right way to do this. In fact, it might not even seem the same to everyone. But that's okay.

"I'll tell you what our guide says and generally describe what I'm experiencing. Please feel free to add what you are getting. Not everybody sees, hears, and senses everything, or anything even, especially at first. That, too, is okay. In fact, probably some of you might get one sensory channel, but not the others."

Leslie interrupts, "I don't think I am any good at this, I'm afraid I'll hold the group back."

"As long as you are open and relaxed, it will be fine. Just come along on the journey. Fairies don't like negativity and intense emotions, especially anger. Just be yourself. The rest will take care of itself."

"What about the stories of children being snatched by fairies? And what about impressionable teens? Are you sure it is safe?" asks Trish.

"Remember what Dorrie taught us about always asking for the Highest Good? And to say no to anything that feels wrong or hurtful? I will begin with an invocation that includes safety. In fact, if there are no more questions, we will begin with that now. Oh, but I forgot to finish what I was saying about the process. I will repeat what I hear or see for those of you who are not getting a direct experience. Those who are getting things, please chime in and add your observations. Okay, here we go.

"As Lily begins playing her harp for us, let us begin with our own cleansing and relaxation. Breathe in relaxation. Breathe out tension. Deep breaths, clearing yourself of any anxiety or negativity. Listen to the lovely music and let yourself open, open to the miracles of Life and Love, gently, freely, open.

"I want to begin with a quotation from a fairy visit chronicled by Terry Frank, one of my workshop leaders in Virginia, 'The vibration of how it was everywhere, faintly shimmers here.' As we begin our fairy journey, may we listen to the vibration of our own bodies, may we attune our bodies to the Universal vibration, and may we be joined by those beings who see to our higher good as we travel this life, this precious gift of life that we have been given.

"Today, we specifically ask to be open to the vibration of the elementals who lovingly serve this planet and to whom we owe so much. Today, may we gain insight into their world and, by doing so, gain insight into our own world as well.

"May we do so in perfect safety for ourselves and for those we encounter on the journey.

"So let us now close our eyes again and silently tune into the vibration, with the help of Lily's harp until our guide arrives."

I am so excited to be doing this that it is hard to calm down and relax, but I do. Soon the others relax as well. Then, all of a sudden, our visitor appears—at least to me.

"Dear lady, I am MacRafferty, ambassador of the royal *Sidhe*, here to guide you. Let me say 'tis an honor to meet you and your lovely friends."

"An honor to meet you. Did you say Mack Rafferty?"

"Nay, 'tis all one word, if you please. MacRafferty. If you be needin' a second name, then let us say 'tis Rowan. So 'tis MacRafferty Rowan, as you say. That would be the way of it."

"Can anyone else see or hear MacRafferty?" I ask the others.

"I am picturing him kind of tall for a fairy and in a fancy, silky white suit. Is that right?" pipes up Nathan.

"And, I'm imagining the suit all glimmery with shimmery threads running through it in rainbow colors and a sea green ruffled shirt. And I think he is young," adds Megan.

"Could be," is my reply. "I mainly hear and sense these things, particularly at first, so you keep those visual images coming."

"Rose, is it? Since it seems for the moment that only you can hear me, will you please act as a translator? Would you tell your lovely friends that I can hear them and that me clothes are the latest in fashion in me land and I have been around many a year. No young lad am I."

I repeat what he just said. No one else says anything for a bit.

"Are you ready then?"

"MacRafferty asks if we are ready to go on a journey with him to the Other Kingdom."

"You mean like pick up and follow him?" asks Leslie.

"Well, in whatever way you wish to follow . . .. He says he will provide the way."

"How about a coach like Cinderella's?" Megan blurts out.

After a pause to hear his answer, "He says he knows that story and yes we can all ride in a big pumpkin if we want."

Silence. Then I feel like I am floating off, going higher and higher into the blue sky until I become lightheaded and even a bit queasy. Finally, I feel like we descend. I envision the sea and beach, then mountains and green hills. In the center is this lush jungle-like area where plants and flowers abound. It looks like Ireland, but like, Ireland on steroids. It is beautiful. The weirdest part is that the forest, the lake, the mountain, the sea, the moors are practically on top of each other. Like the countries represented at Epcot, I could walk into each area within an hour. It doesn't seem right for all those scenes to be in view at once.

MacRafferty must be reading my thoughts because he says to me, "Ach, but you seem to like your man Disney, now. I have seen the wee story boxes and the big story walls you have. Did you know now that Mr. Disney was a frequent visitor to these parts?"

I just stammer, "Yeah, I've always loved Disney." I hadn't realized he would be reading my thoughts.

Then I turn my thoughts back to the group and ask what they are seeing and hearing. Trish says she is getting the sea and the roans. Rebecca is sensing a deep woods with tree elves. Nathan is seeing fire-eating dragons. Angie says she hears flutes. Leslie is silent. I now am seeing the *sidhe* court and butterfly-like, yellowish winged fairies flying around like honey bees. Leslie then allows as to how she feels a flutteriness around her but that's all.

"But, Mom, you are here. I see you sitting on one of the big rocks of a cairn and there are little fairies all around you. They seem to really like you," offers Nathan.

"Maybe, that's the magic, Nathan, that we all see what we are thinking about or expecting."

At that point, I sense the group pull back. I continue on with MacRafferty.

"Would you please be tellin' your people that the reason now that you would all be seein' different sites or all the sites of the Faery Kingdom here so close together all at one place is because you would be witnessing a Convocation, a very special coming together of all elementals—air and fire and water and earth ones, all together. They have all come for the Grand Gatherin', so 'tis but necessary to provide accommodations in the natural environments of all these beings. So we *Sidhe* create this place every, every ten of your human years. Consider yourselves very privileged to be seein' this. Right now is the Faerie Fair. Soon, we will be startin' The Big Meetin'. Just you watch now."

I repeat what he said, or at least, as much as I can remember. Everyone in the group remains quiet. Finally, Nathan asks, "MacRafferty, MacRafferty. Will we be meeting some of your people? Will I get closer to the dragon?"

I repeat the reply, "Nay, lad, 'tis only an observational journey today. In point of fact, as soon as the opening ceremony is over and before the actual beginnin' of the formal reports, I'll be needin' to ask you to return to the wee coach. You can watch and listen from within, but no distraction is allowed to interrupt the meetin'.

Just then, Lily's background music gives way to a stately blast of horns and tympani and cymbals, summoning the crowd to attention. The pageantry begins. I never imagined all these beings existed. There are so many differences and they all seem peaceful. Wow, this is amazing.

The pomp and circumstance come to an end. "Would you be getting into the wee coach now, if you please. We can observe the meetin' from within for a while, before I return you to your own place."

I gather us together and the coach is moved to the top of a nearby hill where we can watch and still hear the goings on. Everyone is still interested but one by one their engagement seems to fade. I am determined to continue, I will report to them later what I experience.

It seems like representatives are reporting in and getting recognized or credentialed, all in a quiet, orderly manner. What a privilege to witness this, unbelievable. Then the upbeat, joyful mood seems to go flat, then gloomy, then downright dark. I can feel fear rise up in me, and, of course, that makes it harder to know what is happening. I hear a part about honey bees disappearing. They are saying the bees are needed to help pollinate the flowers. They talk about water disappearing and icebergs melting. They talk about how they are in even greater peril than humans. They say that if humans do not wake up soon, the whole blue-green planet that they work so hard to keep beautiful will be ruined.

Then, all at once, the mood turns back to a lighter and brighter place. Beings begin to sing and then dance with the music, lighting up the entire crowd and the sun shining brightly.

"What happened? What happened?" I ask MacRafferty in an urgent tone that scares the group. I have to pause to reassure them. Then I turn my attention back to MacRafferty.

"Ach, lass, we are hopeful beings. We are hopeful that your people will listen, hear and be moved by Spirit to change your ways. We must hope. We must bring hope. And, now, lass, I must take you home. Home so you can tell our story, for it is your story, too; we are all One."

Group members seem to sense we are done before I say anything. We will talk about it in more detail later. For now, I want to make sure everyone is okay and that we thank MacRafferty properly. Lily is still playing harp, which is calming. It helps me re-enter. After we all express our thanks and say good-bye, I see MacRafferty go over and kiss the top of Lily's head, saying "Goodbye, Tiger Lily."

She keeps playing as she replies, "Good bye, Raffi. Love to you all, dear Beings of the Light. Love to you all."

What an experience. Not everyone got what I got and I don't even know all that I got. My head is spinning. I check that everyone is okay. They all seem to be glad they came and interested in talking about it later, after dinner. That sounds fine to me. I am exhausted and I want to journal a little before dinner, while everything is fresh in my mind. I have a strong feeling MacRafferty will be back and that my work is just beginning.

I am working really hard to switch gears and get ready for the party. I finally get myself down to the banquet room. The buffet is a feast worthy of royalty, I think. And that immediately reminds me of MacRafferty, but then I get my focus back. The tables are set up so we all can mix and mingle throughout the night yet still see forward to a raised platform stage. The Inn has provided candles, flowers, and a generally festive ambience.

The name cards are amazing; Angie and Rebecca printed everyone's name in beautiful calligraphy and added borders with intricate Celtic knotted designs. Each is different. John and Melanie, for instance, have the classic Celtic design of the snake with the egg in its mouth. Rob has a salmon with hazelnuts. Nathan has ogham, as well as salmon. Not all are as obviously matched, but all feel like the person whose name is being highlighted. They are truly take-home mementos and a gift of love.

Angie, with help, has decorated the walls with sketches of things in threes: three shamrocks, three spirals of Newgrange, three rings, three salmon, three trees, etc. The style is fun and whimsical. People start challenging one another to a short round of the triads game, but there is too much going on for anyone to want to think too hard for too long.

Peg opens by saying how much she loves the line *"My life goes on in endless song, how can I keep from singing?"* She says it is in her congregational hymn book, but also an Enya CD. So she projects the words on to the white wall that is the movie screen for the night. We sing along with Enya as a warm-up to the talent show. She is right, it makes a wonderful opening.

A number of people have come forth over the last two days offering to sing or play for the group. It really makes a nice program. The young people's surprise is amazing. They put together a ten minute video of their trip, all the sacred sites and at least one really good shot of each group member at a site of special meaning to them. We clap, cry, and laugh simultaneously. While the teens were respectful, they were also funny and ironic with the narration and music. We all absolutely love it and make them replay it twice. Gordie promises to distribute copies once the releases are all signed.

I heard that yesterday, someone told Peg that Mary Helena was complaining that she had not been asked to perform. Normally, Peg isn't the type to enable that kind of whining, but I guess she did go to Mary Helena to invite her participation. Seems Mary Helena sings *Ave Maria* for weddings at her church. I imagine Peg is holding her breath wondering what Mary Helena would choose for tonight. And now the time has come.

Peg gives Mary Helena an upbeat, but slightly careful, introduction and steps back. And doesn't Mary Helena sing a *Danny Boy* that could rival Susan Boyle? After a stunned silence and a long round of applause, people start shouting for an encore. And would you believe, she has one ready. She has changed the words of *Galway Bay* to Sligo Bay she tells us. Then she steps out into the audience singing:

> *If you ever go across the sea to Ireland,*
> *Then maybe at the closin' of your day*
> *You will sit and watch the moon rise over*
> *Sea Side*
> *And see the sun go down on Sligo Bay.*

It is clever, but the best of it is how she hams it up, like a lounge singer at a Holiday Inn. We are all dumbfounded. It is great *craic*, as the Irish would say.

The next group, Peg announces, has a tough act to follow. It's the Boys Band, the guys with their tin whistles, Gordie with his *bodhran*, and Timothy with a ukulele-like string instrument. Everyone shouts and razzes him about holding out all trip and never admitting he played. We learn later he borrowed the instrument from one of the innkeepers so he could join the Boys. Add that to the fact that Jackson has joined the whistlers and actually looks like he is having fun. Wow.

Peg and Rob do a funny skit about visiting a dolmen, in the style of George Burns and Gracie Allen. Ready for prime time or American Idol? Probably not, but they get points for stepping up. It is very funny to watch them.

I am inspired by the fact my husband and I are going to the Dingle Peninsula when the tour ends. I chose a song popularized by Mary Black about living on the Western Shore. The line, 'sang a song for Ireland, hearts and minds restore,' speaks to all of us, I think.

Dorrie and Gordie prepared some limericks for the group, clean ones, a little lame, but all the more fun because folks get to pan them:

Timothy, Gordie, and Dorrie
Were thinking of renting a lorrie
It wasn't too long
Till a bus came along
And that was the start of our story.

There once was a lad they called Finn
Whose name came up time and ag'in
Then the women came 'round,
And look what they found!
The emergence of the Divine Feminine.

"There are a few more written to be shared at a later hour and after another round or two at the bar. That is, if folks are so inclined," adds Gordie. Everyone groans, as if on cue.

Melanie goes next. She chooses an edgy new song by Irish-Nigerian Laura Izibor, *If Tonight Was My Last*, which she makes rock.

Lily is next with her beautiful harp music. When she finishes, Dorrie and Gordie give her a small Belleek bud vase as a thank you for her generosity of spirit. It has one lovely yellow lily in it.

Trish and Megan then sing along with a CD by Celtic Woman, the song *Soft Goodbye*, a real tear jerker.

And then there are the toasts; Peg has arranged them as pop-ups between the songs. This is such a wonderful group and folks have really connected. Unlike a roast that often gets mean, these toasts are full of gratitude and well wishes.

The group also has a gift for Dorrie and Gordie: Herself and Himself beer mugs. They raise them often as the night goes on.

And then, of course, comes a final rendition of *Wild Rover* and lots of clapping with the *"No, nay, never..."*

The last surprise is Kevin with a Frankie Valli type rendition of *Oh, What a Night*. Not exactly an Irish group, but Kevin has changed the words to the verse and encourages everyone to join in the chorus. And we do.

Oh, What a Night!"

OUR LAST DAY

TUROE STONE *SHANNON AIRPORT*

We travel through the magnificent West of Ireland, passing through the countryside which has been the background for so many beautiful movies, The Quiet Man and Far and Away among them.
We will stop at the Turoe Stone, a very different and even more mysterious standing stone in what is called La Tene style.
Our Celtic Journey will end back at its beginning: Shannon Airport.

TIMOTHY

Morning comes early at the end, does it not? While folks have a final yoga or toning session out on the beach, I get the coach ready. Pity the last day has come, for what a fine group of people they are. Gordie encourages people to eat a hearty breakfast and pick up their carry-away sandwiches for noonday tea. Final trips to the loo, bags stowed, and good-byes and thank you's all get said. To add a wee bit of festivity to the occasion, I change the sign in the window to say "Journey Home" at the front and "Safe Home" at the back, both with tiny little shamrocks and spirals from Angie's party decorations.

There is a deep silence as we travel along the causeway. The scenic beaches disappear and the lush vegetation changes itself into the narrow ribbon of road that leads inland and then south toward the airport. Ach, 'tis beautiful, even to the likes of me.

No mind-reader am I, but I can tell each person is reflecting on our time together. Now, whether they are thinking of the days of the trip, or what awaits them on their return home, or of their life's journey, 'tis no way of telling. Me own mind races with thoughts of times spent with Kate these last twelve days, starting with her coming up to me coach that first day. I also wonder how me daughter and son will take to the news that I have brought home a woman after being on the road less than a fortnight, a woman of great interest to me, a Yank, a woman I am right thinking I might marry. 'Tis overwhelming. Will the family not be shocked altogether? Talk about paths taking a turn...But, for now, I need to focus, you might say to just focus on the road ahead, not bad advice, now is it?

Dorrie and Gordie anticipated that some of this kind of mental reflection time would be needed. "Reentry," the lass calls it. Yet, with this group, people need no facilitating. I right figure the music of James Galway will be all they need.

As I look into the mirror at the faces of me new friends, I wonder which have already turned their minds to home. What will they take away with them? What has been stirred? Have they unleashed any of the sacred mysteries that Dorrie introduced so artfully? How has me country changed their story? How will they be different? What will they do differently? Particularly the teenagers? Just what would me own life have been if I had gone on a trip like this to America at their age? Or, even when I think about it, a trip like this to the sacred mysteries of me own land?

I know that for some, the questions have already been asked and answered. I see some ride along with a look of someone savoring the most delicious meal of their life. Others are still chewing.

Then, Lily comes up front to see Dorrie. I hear her ask "Will you help me?" While I cannot see them whilst drivin', I imagine those big green eyes of hers beseeching Dorrie. In that silky, whispery voice of hers, she continues, "Will you help me learn to stay grounded? To deal with all this stuff and deal with this heavy body? To be fully human?"

Dorrie nods gently. I do believe the lass knows better than to react with any intensity to a fey lass like this one. Stories unfold and mysteries change their form as we all strive to make the most of this life we are given, but this is truly something to witness. I wait for Dorrie's reply. Her words to Lily are, "I will be there when you decide to walk through the gate." I am not even sure I know how to take the meaning of that, but Lily grins from ear to ear and hugs Dorrie. They seem to know what it all means and 'tis that what matters.

Just then we approach me wee surprise for everyone. I have planned our route along Lough Gill and am now looking for the car park and WC stop which has a good a view of the Isle of Innisfree. As it comes into sight, I tell people to take a look out the window while I maneuver the coach to a stopping place. I stand with the mike and say, " 'tis a wee parting gift I wish to give you, one of Yeats' poems I have known by heart since I was a lad.

> *I will arise and go now, and go to Innisfree,*
> *And a small cabin build there, of clay and*
> *   wattles made:*
> *Nine bean-rows will I have there, a hive for the*
> *   honey-bee;*
> *And live alone in the bee-loud glade.*
>
> *And I shall have some peace there, for peace*
> *   comes dropping slow,*
> *Dropping from the veils of the morning to where*
> *   the cricket sings;*
> *There midnight's all a glimmer, and noon a*
> *   purple glow,*
> *And evening full of the linnet's wings.*

I will arise and go now, for always night and
   day
I hear lake water lapping with low sounds by
   the shore;
While I stand on the roadway, or on the
   pavements grey,
I hear it in the deep heart's core.

Lots of love and praise and thanks I get as people get off the coach for their photos. "Aye, Innisfree is not to be missed by any a traveler coming to the West of Ireland," I reply.

"Timothy, that was lovely," says me Kate. "Is that the only surprise for the day, or shall we also tell people about us? I would like folks to know, but going about it feels awkward."

I almost said why not wait to surprise them with an invitation to the wedding, but that was getting ahead of meself. Instead, I do say, "Let's trust that we will know the time when it comes."

Back on the coach, folks lapse into another bit of quiet. The coach has not been so quiet since that first day when a group of strangers started off on their journey together. That first day, there was a nervousness to the energy, whispers among those traveling together and shy overtures being made to those traveling alone. Now, this is entirely different. 'Tis a community silence, like at a church communion, whole and full.

So our final published stop is the Turoe Stone, which seems fitting. After so much discussion and exploration of our Celtic mysteries, this one is the biggest puzzle of all. All the questions asked a million times on the trip about the ancient mysteries get asked again here, but even more so. The stone is unique amongst all the stones of Ireland.

Dorrie gives some background as we ride toward the site. "The Turoe Stone is sometimes referred to as a phallic symbol, but it is more accurately an *omphalos*, or navel stone. Most cultures, most notably Delphi, Jerusalem, Mecca, and many European centers have similarly decorated conical stones like this. The Turoe, however, is one of the best examples because it is in such good shape and because of the quality of the decorated surface. The Celtic art style used on this stone and others in Europe is called *la tene*.

"It seems certain the stones are related. Yet how? Were ancient peoples connected in ways we fail to understand? Phoenician boats on the Celtic crosses at Clonmacnoise, stone circles similar to medicine wheels, labyrinths, similar myths and symbols throughout the world make us wonder.

"One answer is that they are archetypal. Another hypothesis is the power and energy channels between earth and sky were much stronger or better understood by ancient peoples. That the spirals, crosses, and the other symbols we have been seeing tell a greater story than we imagine. That the rites of honoring the four directions and the four elements of earth, connecting to the stars and acknowledging the energetic properties of crystalline rock and water sources had significance in ways we are just beginning to remember.

"Almost all cultures have *axis mundi* symbols. Rebecca already described to us the symbol of the tree stretching up into the sky with its trunk as the pole, which sends its roots down into the earth. With the *axis mundi*, there is an image of a spiral or vortex of energy coming down from the sky as it wraps around the pole and a second spiral coming up from the center of the earth and wrapping around the pole in the opposite direction. Picture an hour glass. According to one theory, the *omphalos* stone was designed to hold, focalize or transform that energy where the top and bottom spirals met.

"The navel, of course, is also at the center of the body. Think of the diagrams of the human body with arms and feet spread to create five points on a circle, like the points of a pentagram, the Vitruvian Man. It all fits with what we are learning about quantum science. Holograms demonstrate it best for me. I think, more and more we are seeing science align with the ancient wisdom: 'As above, so below' and 'At every level we are One' or even 'In God's image.' All those ideas are being given new meaning by scientific findings."

Getting to this place is proving to be a wee bit of a challenge. I tune Dorrie out so I can concentrate. This place is in the middle of nowhere, even by standards of the West countryside. I read once of the speculation on where the original location had been. It had been described as at a rath or fort at midpoint, right in the center of Ireland. How it became privately owned or how the present owners got it, I do not know. And why, in the name of all the Saints, it was way and beyond like this, I have even less of a clue.

We pull up to what looks like an old farmhouse, except for the antique Travelers wagon, in the side yard. It has a petting zoo and a sweets and lemonade stand that make me wonder if I have the wrong place. If the lass were not so bent on the place, I would be driving right on. But, here we are, and here 'tis the stone.

An interesting metalwork circle has been built around the pedestal. It has nothing to do with ancient mysteries though. It is there to keep the livestock from rubbing up against it and scratching it. 'Tis a wee bit anti-climatic in my mind, but some seem excited. Sandra exclaims how much it looks like the *omphalos* she and Jake saw at Delphi. She says she can feel the vibration of the stone. Rose agrees. Little by little, everyone gives a go at touching it. I draw Nathan's attention to Penny who has made a dowsing rod of some nearby twig. The wee rod points right down at the stone. It does make a man wonder.

Dorrie is beside herself, "How perfect. You know, this is the only site on our trip that I had not previously visited. But when I read about it, I knew we just had to come. And, now so much of the trip has come to center around opening to the Divine Feminine, for both the men and the women. It is especially significant to end with this ancient symbol, seen as masculine by some and seen as both masculine and feminine by others. We have seen and felt its energy first-hand. We can only imagine its original power. But, I can tell that it was powerful in a creative not authoritative way. Can't you? I had envisioned the trip's theme as the story of Celtic spirituality. I now see that the story of the reemergence of the Divine Feminine is just as important. I am seeing the two stories as the serpents wrapped around a wand of healing: the *caduceus*, with which the Earth could be healed.

"So let us take a moment to gather around the stone, placing a hand on it and forming one huge human Celtic knot as we do. While we are so joined,

> We ask Spirit to bless us, our work, and this planet we love so dearly. May all be healed. May all be well."

'Tis a lot to take in. The lass is deep into it all. But, after a bit I put on some instrumental music and turn me attention to logistics. The Inn had packed sandwiches and bottles of drink and biscuits and fruit for us. We had planned to eat at the location of the Stone, but I saw a nice wee spot for a picnic back a ways. I suggest to Dorrie and Gordie we go there since this place and its petting zoo seemed a bit contrived after all the places we have been. So instead, we drive back to the banks of a lively stream.

Everyone chats on about the mystery of it all. No answers are forthcoming but the questions create a powerful stir. We all wish we knew more about the Ancient Ones. All we know is that their ties to water, land, and sky shaped a culture far beyond what we twentieth-century people ever imagined. And Dorrie has gotten our juices going thinking how the twenty-first century could benefit from learning about their ancient wisdom.

Thinking back to an earlier conversation at Salmon Run Lodge, I cannot help but think of all this. So now, would it not be true that 'tis at the intersection of science and spirit where magic and mystery truly lie?

Nathan wants his mom's attention and gets the attention of most of the rest of us as well when he calls over to her, "Hey, Mom, did I tell you what the leprechaun told me this morning?"

"You mean you dreamt about leprechauns while the rest of us were at yoga?"

"Well, sort of. It was more like a visit from him. I think I was awake. He was all dressed up with a fancy waist coat and shiny new boots."

Rose perks up and we all are all ears. Leslie looks skeptical and a little nervous for her son and his tale, but she remains quiet and encourages him to continue with a nod of affirmation.

"He said his name was Padraic, not Patrick. Then he said when I got to know him better, I could call him Paddy. He asked if 'me mates' called me Nate, but I said no."

"Anyway, he wants me to make a new movie. He and his people are very disturbed about *Darby O'Gill*. He said it is outdated. He did not think that Mr. Disney's film was very flattering nor very believable. He said with all the media available today, we ought to be able to tell the story better. He said he would be my advisor whenever I want."

"Well, if your video production last night is any indication, he's found the right film maker," inserts Peter with a smile.

"And, what do you think, Nathan?" asks his mom, noncommittally.

"It kinda excites me, but the idea overwhelms me, too. I've been thinking about it a lot this morning. It is kind of awesome. Padraic says it's my moral imperative to cast him and his people in a better and truer light. I never heard that expression before, but I guess it means, like, I must do it. He was very firm about it."

"You can do it, Nathan," adds Megan. "I know you can."

"Well, I was thinking that if J.K. Rowling can write Harry Potter books when she doesn't even believe in magic, I might be okay doing a video story about leprechauns, particularly if Padraic helps."

" 'Tis a shame to be disturbing the likes of the next Stephen Spielberg and his crew, but we better be boardin' the coach," I interject. With everyone telling Nathan he can do it, offering help, or reminding him to show it to all of them when it's finished, we finally are ready to drive on.

"Let's talk more about this on the plane home," is Leslie's last comment as Nathan takes a seat next to Megan.

Leslie turns to Jake, "Any advice on just how to present this to his father? The poor guy. His wife comes home planning to quit her job and start being an environmental champion and his son comes home co-producing videos with the Little People." Jake shrugs and they both just laugh.

The Boys Band, as they are now affectionately called, plays a few tunes as we head south. The group joins in singing and the men try their best to keep up. Unbeknownst to the group, Gordie and I had scoped out a dolmen on the internet that we planned to have as our final stop. I have never been to the place, but it is only a wee bit off the roadway and only about thirty minutes from Shannon. When I am certain that we will have the time to stop, I give Herself the nod.

Dorrie takes the mike to say, "As we were leaving the Turoe Stone, someone asked me if it had anything to do with the concept *vesica piscis*. I am no expert here. If anyone knows more, please speak up. But I will do my best to answer. The term refers to the place in the middle where two or more intersecting circles overlap. The pattern has been used artistically through the ages. It is part of sacred geometry and present day mathematics, as well. Can you visualize it?

Rebecca speaks up, "I've seen it a lot in motifs and religious symbols when researching the Tree of Life."

Kevin adds, "We use it a lot in management these days to show how different variables need to come together to get quality service. You know, like how that meeting in the middle is where integration and creativity come together."

Jackson even enters the discussion, "My physics teacher used the example of the sweet spot on a tennis racket or golf ball which gives the perfect hit to demonstrate it in physics class."

"It also represents the first two cells coming together to create birth," adds Mary Helena.

"Great! Then you all can understand that in esoteric tradition it represents a place of new beginnings; a gate to the Other Kingdom, to higher potentiality or the fifth dimension.

When people talked yesterday of how quantum thinking might be one of the keys to twenty-first century challenges, we were talking about this esoteric belief of the ages meeting the science of tomorrow. I think much of people's impatience and anger with specialization today is an instinctive feel that scholarship has led us to be so narrowly focused in our thinking that one discipline argues with another about the right answers. The common sense of overlapping ideas and taking the best from each gets lost in all the posturing. When we use the image of overlapping circles, we see new possibility.

"Back to the ancient mysteries, we don't know for sure how attuned ancient people were to electromagnetic force or if those forces were stronger in that time period. But some of us believe they knew how to focus energy and that these ancient stones worked to focus the energies in some ways.

"For me, I see the *vesica piscis* as the place where my intention meets spirit and opens me to new potentialities. I think that is why the dolmen is so special. Here, I sense I am at a gateway. I can step over the threshold and into a new place within myself. "

"One of the thin places," I add.

Nathan jumps in, "Yeah, that day at the dolmen was so awesome. It is my favorite thing of the whole trip."

"Well, glad to hear that, my friend, because guess what? We have time for one final stop."

"You mean we are going back to Poulnabrone?"

"Not Poulnabrone, but another dolmen that is more on our route to the airport."

"Cool."

"Gives new meaning to the expression 'In one door and out the other,'" quips Rob.

Dorrie laughs and continues, "So, along those lines, I thought we would take a bit of time to do a closing ritual. The first part will be your own personal opportunity to focus your energies on your return home. The second part will be our last coming together in a circle of gratitude and healing.

"I invite you to walk through the portal bringing together your thoughts and energies from this trip with your thoughts and energies for your return home to daily life. You can shout them out to us all or keep them quietly within. You choose.

"I know you all have been thinking of heading home and of letting go of that which must be left behind as we traveled this morning. So as we approach this place, I would like you to think about three questions:

What will I take home with me?
What must I leave behind?
What will I do with all I have seen and heard and experienced?

"As with the questions I asked you at the beginning of the trip, you're not expected to be able to completely answer these at this time. But, for those of you who are interested, the questions will stay with you. Those that are meant to be answered will then be answered in perfect time."

"Timothy, might you give us some more reflective music until we get there?"

Me response is clear and bright, "Aye, lass, would I not do whatever your heart desired at this point in our travels?" Many amongst the group are tearful and sober at the thought of all these goodbyes. But, I know in me heart of hearts that I have me Kate and the happiness of that 'tis all I think or feel at the moment. I have us to the dolmen in no time.

Dorrie gives some more opening words about the process of leave taking. She then repeats the three questions and invites people to step out of the dolmen opening and back to their daily lives as they wish them to be.

Nathan is first again, as he had been at Poulnabrone. He is grinning ear to ear and shouts out, "Watch YouTube for Padraic and me!"

His ma follows with her own statement and almost as much enthusiasm as the lad, "*Erin Go Bragh* and to a beautiful blue-green planet earth."

John and Melanie walk through together beaming and saying, "Expect the announcement of Patrick Timothy Williams-Price in nine months."

Bless them; now is that not altogether too much? A bunch more go through in dribs and drabs, some saying a word or two, others being silent. I stand by me Kate. We have been discussing what words to say and decide to say not a word at all. We hear Rebecca and Angie say something about their new artistic enterprise as we give each other the nod to go next.

We step through the portal together hand-in-hand saying nary a word. That is all as we planned. But, to the surprise of us both, at the moment of stepping through we both turn to one another and mouth the words, "I love you." No one hears, but the meaning is there for all to see.

Don't I lose track of what the others are saying as Kate and I kiss and as people approach us to acknowledge our only semi-veiled news of togetherness? People have questions beyond what we have for answers, but we are happy saying that we will "see what happens."

Lily has been playing the whole time whilst folks take turns stepping through. Now, though, I realize Peter has taken up playing the tin whistle. All eyes turn to Lily who is about to take her turn. She gives an intense stare at Dorrie for a long moment and then she leaps through the gate with great zest. The full meaning of that, too, is left an unanswered question, at least in me mind.

Does it not seem that all of a sudden we all are sensing that only Gordie and Dorrie are left on the far side and neither has taken a turn? People act like they aren't watching. But, of course, everyone is. Finally, Gordie, after a long hesitation, puts his hand out to Dorrie. The lass takes it with tears in her eyes and a smile as wide as Galway Bay. Together they step through the fateful, wee gate.

No one moves. No rush of talk, congratulations or questions to the two of them as they join us. The message, at least to me, is too vague and I know not what to say. Everyone dithers a wee bit, and 'tis a good bit of time before the lass collects Herself to invite us into our final circle. Me dear Kate has the presence of mind to start us off with a song. At the very first, I wonder as to her choice, but I am just glad for something light. But then it seems that before she gets to all the colors of the wee song, others join in. People are singing and swaying and enjoying it altogether.

Red and yellow and pink and green,
Purple and orange and blue,
I can sing a rainbow,
Sing a rainbow,
Sing a rainbow, too!

Listen to your heart,
Listen to your heart,
And sing everything you feel,
I can sing a rainbow,
Sing a rainbow,
Sing a rainbow, too!

Aye. Listen to your heart.

Blessed be and t'anks to Brigid, Patrick, and all the saints for the rainbows in our lives.

NOTES ON SPIRITUAL TRANSFORMATION

As our characters illustrate, spiritual transformation takes many forms. It can be sought out, it can come through pain and loss, or it can be spontaneous, a touch of grace. Sometimes the change is radical, sometimes the shift is subtle.

On my own spiritual journey, I found the Celtic *thin places* described in this story to be deeply spiritual and transformative. I felt a mind, body, spirit connection here that I had never experienced before. I now can recreate such a connection through spiritual practice. Perhaps you have already found the catalysts and approaches that help you do transformative work. If not, perhaps this story and the differing ways each character accesses Spirit will inspire you.

Steps to Spiritual Transformation

Create open space in your life for Spirit to enter.

Release emotional dramas and ideas that no longer work for you.

Set your intention with care.

Look and listen to what the Universe is telling you.

Practice gratitude and affirmation.

Live your values.

Surrender your ego.

Tune in to the energies and flow of the Universe.

Establishing a Spiritual Practice

Spiritual practice is essential to any kind of spiritual deepening and is a wonderful anchor to any transformation that you may be seeking or experiencing. Spiritual practice centers you, connects mind/body/spirit, helps clear away negativity, quiets the mind, and invites Spirit and Grace into your life.

Spiritual practice is a habit worth pursuing. Like any habit, it requires an initial commitment. If you commit to a 15-30 minute spiritual practice session every day and maintain the schedule for 30 days, you will establish that practice as a new positive habit. While at first the process may seem time consuming, once established, you will find the time easily absorbed into your day.

There are a number of options to choose from or you can create your own process. Finding a fit and determining how long to stay with a particular practice is a matter of personal preference and discernment. Going deeper within, finding ease in maintaining a practice and opening yourself to new experiences are factors to consider in making your choice. Also, consider whether you prefer to choose a process or practice within your own faith tradition or to try something totally new.

Many people develop a morning practice or a routine time of day for their spiritual work. This, too, is a matter of preference. The important thing is that you quiet mind, body and heart; and that you do so regularly. Try out a number of options but then stick to one until you develop it as a discipline or practice. Once you have done so, you may vary or shorten the process of achieving the desired state.

In this story, you were exposed to a number of spiritual practices, including meditation, guided visualization, and rituals for creating sacred space. Morning practices of yoga, sound toning, giving thanks, walking in nature, journaling, and reading poetry were introduced.

Many forms of prayer, including prayers of petition, prayers of supplication, and liturgical prayers were also practiced within this story. Some were free form and spontaneous, while others were based on sacred or secular readings.

Various forms of meditation were also illustrated. Not everyone has the temperament for "sitting" or the emptying-of-the-mind meditation. Some are better suited to a mindful meditation where one actually concentrates the mind rather than tries to empty it. Some use a mantra, a phrase or word as in Transcendental Meditation. Slow, mindful walking is another option. The simplest form may be simply deep breathing, concentrating on the breath, in and out and the moment between. If you cannot do any of these, sit quietly with your cat or dog and listen to their breath and become mindful of your own breath for fifteen minutes a day.

As the book further illustrates alternative options such as movement, dance, singing bowls, drumming, singing, and chanting are also possibilities. The options are endless. Be creative and choose what works for you.

The important thing is to find something that feels right and provides you with a quieting of your mind and a relaxation of tension within. A few minutes a day, dedicated to centering and to the opening of your heart, can do wonders for your health and wellbeing. Time spent in deep meditation can widen and deepen your spiritual life.

If the information below is helpful, you may also want to see my Kindle single *Paths to Spiritual Transformation* for more information on the process of transformation for individuals and organizations.

BOOK AND RESOURCE NOTES

Book List

DAY ONE

Jackson is reading James Joyce *Ulysses*, later he also reads *Portrait of a Young Man* and Peg reads *The Dubliners*.

DAY TWO

Dorrie refers to *Life's Companion: Journal Writing as Spiritual Quest* by Christina Baldwin as her spiritual primer. For other recommendations see the author's Kindle single *Paths to Spiritual Transformation.*

Readers might also be interested in Neil Douglas-Klotz, who writes of sound embodying prayer in original Aramaic and Hebrew Scripture. Start with *Desert Wisdom: Sacred Middle Eastern Writings from the Goddess through the Sufis.*

Peg mentions theologian Matthew Fox's *One River, Many Wells.*

The Keeners by Maura D. Shaw is the novel mentioned about County Clare families during the Famine. *The Irish Dresser* by Cynthia Neale also portrays this horrible period of Irish history.

Dorrie's definition of mystery is taken from Jean Bolen's *Crossing to Avalon*, an insightful, richly and personal memoir of pilgrimage, mystery and the Grail legends.

See Tanis Helliwell's CD on *The Celtic Mysteries*, available through Amazon.

DAY THREE
Rob is reading *Anam Cara* by John O'Donohue and refers to *When God Was a Woman* by Merlin Stone. There are a number of other books on this topic. *A God Who Looks Like Me* among them.

Dan Brown writes about symbology in *The Da Vinci Code*, *Angels & Demons* and *The Lost Symbol*, mentioned here. All are fiction.

How the Irish Saved Civilization is by Thomas Cahill.

Peg refers to Rebecca Parker and Rita Nakashima Brock and their work when discussing early Christianity: *Proverbs of Ashes: Violence, Redemptive Suffering, and the Search for What Saves Us* and *Saving Paradise: How Christianity Traded Love of This World for Crucifixion and Empire.*

See *Celtic Wisdom: Seasonal Rituals and Festivals* by Vivianne Crowley for more on the circle of the Celtic Year.

DAY FOUR
Kate cites questions chronicled by Angela Arrien.

Trinity by Leon Uris is mentioned in the discussion of Northern Ireland and The Troubles. It appears again in Day Ten when the women visit Croagh Patrick.

DAY FIVE
Mary Helena is reading *Tara Road* and refers to other Maeve Binchy novels *Circle of Friends* and *Quentins.*

The men at the pub discuss David Korten's *The Great Turning: From Empire to Earth Community.*

Peg refers to *Angela's Ashes,* the bleak tale of an impoverished family in Limerick city, by Frank McCourt. He also wrote *'Tis.* She buys a copy of Joyce's *The Dubliners.*

There is a wonderful two volume historical fictional account of Dublin that gives an easy and enjoyable explanation of the English in Ireland, *The Dublin Saga* by Edward Rutherfurd.

DAY SIX
The Avalon series by Marion Zimmer Bradley is a brilliant retelling of Arthurian legend from a feminist perspective.

DAY SEVEN
The Star in My Heart by Joyce Rupp is the book Sandra found so helpful and to which she refers on a number of occasions.

Rebecca is influenced by Joan Borysenko's insightful *Fire in the Soul* and the novel *The Red Tent* by Anita Diamant, which looks at the story of the women of the *Old Testament* from a feminist perspective.

Shalom, Saalam, Peace by Allison Stokes offers a nice discussion of the commonalities among the desert religions of Judaism, Islam and Christianity and promotes interfaith work in general.

DAY EIGHT
Ley lines are discussed extensively in *Pi in the Sky: A Revelation of the Ancient Celtic Wisdom Tradition* by Michael Poynder.

The Triads of Ireland is from the 14th century.

The Power of Myth by Joseph Campbell becomes an inspiration to Megan.

The work of Marija Gimbutas, the celebrated but also controversial archeologist and author of *The Goddesses and Gods of Old Europe,* is the foundation of much of what the women refer to when talking about an early goddess culture.

Readers looking for great fiction about Celtic fantasy will enjoy Charles de Lint, especially *Into the Green* and *The Little Country.*

DAY NINE
Walking a Sacred Path by Lauren Artress and *Exploring the Labyrinth: A Guide for Healing and Spiritual Growth* by Melissa Gayle West are my favorite among many books about labyrinths.

The Heart Aroused: Poetry and the Preservation of the Soul in Corporate America is by David Whyte.

Many works by W. B. Yeats are cited over the course of the trip. Most of the quotations are from *Celtic Twilight.*

DAY TEN
Trinity by Leon Uris is the novel on Northern Ireland where Melanie recalls first hearing of Croagh Patrick.

Robert Bly wrote *Iron John* His work inspired the discussion among the men about the Divine Feminine.

See the books *Summer with the Leprechauns* and *Pilgrimage with the Leprechauns* by Tanis Helliwell for more on these uniquely Irish elementals or visit the International Institute for Transformation website, www.iitransform.com.

Other Resources

Sounds True has a wonderful selection of sound healing tapes, including those of Jonathan Goldman.

Celtic Wisdom Sticks: An Ogham Oracle by Caitlin Matthews and any of the books or cards by Matthews are terrific.

The Druid Animal Oracle: Working with the Sacred Animals of the Druid Tradition by Philip and Stephanie Carr-Gomm are also wonderful.

Sacred Circle Tarot, *The Green Man*, and *The Celtic Tree* are three favorites. Be careful, some of the Celtic sets focus more on kings and battles than spirituality. These three are very much aligned to the spirit of this book.

The song *Roses in Your Heart* is by Gabriella Kapfer, www.peace-trails.com. Her music is magical and truly transformational. The workshops mentioned are led by Terry Frank and Gabriella and often held at The Bridge Between the Worlds Conference Center in Virginia.

Look for local and regional groups for additional inspiration. Many Celtic festivals are held throughout the USA and Canada.

I spoke on Celtic spirituality at the multi-faith Mary Magdala Celebration in Sedona, Arizona in 2010. Visit www.marymagdalacelebrationsedona.com for current programs.

The Rochester New York Women of the Well group is one of many that offer public liturgical drama performances. www.womenofthewell.com.

Finally, for more details about the ancient sites visited in the book, see the author's Kindle Single *Visiting the Thin Places of Celtic Ireland* and visit her web site CelticSpiritbooks.com.

ACKNOWLEDGEMENTS

I want to thank my friends for their support and help. First, to Beth Van Winkle, Poppy Nelson, and Sylvia Strobel. who were there from the beginning, read the rockiest of drafts, and kept listening and lovingly giving me feedback.

Heather Proctor, Sally Crosiar and Jen Sutton then read a still rocky draft and offered insightful suggestions.

Nancy Reed was willing to create "Angie's" sketches that brought life to the structure of the book.

Judy Cadle gave so generously of her time and talent as more than just the book designer. She patiently untangled my formatting errors and joyfully brought the book to completion.

Barbara Van Meter of Lake to Lake Designs created a concrete rendering of my vision of Celtic Spirit for both the book cover and website design. Peter Blackwood of Peter Blackwood Studio provided the author's head shot. The folks at CreateSpace saw to the final touches in both the print and e-book additions.

I am so grateful for them all.

And with special thanks to Gabriella Kapfer for permission to use lines from her beautiful song "Roses in your Heart," *Songs of the Dove* CD, 2003, recorded in Scotland. www.peace-trails.com.

And, of course, to W.B Yeats for his amazing poetry of Celtic Spirit and all the writers, poets and song writers that so inspired me.

The Author, Jeanne Crane.

My first trip to Ireland was as a teenager. I immediately felt a deep connection to my Celtic roots. But, it was on a much later trip that I was introduced to the ancient sites, the dolmens, standing stones and beehive structures that so intrigue me. These places stirred me beyond any cathedral, temple or sacred site I had ever visited. While Unitarian Universalism provides my spiritual home, it is Celtic spirituality that has been at the heart of my spiritual transformation.

My own calling has been as life coach, organizational consultant, and facilitator of change. Helping individuals and organizations develop their potential and open to emergent challenges has been the thread running through all I do. See JeanneCrane.com for more on that work.

The inspiration to write this book came to me while in deep meditation at Glendalough. I sensed the need to tell a story of the universality of Spirit, the desperate need for us all to reconnect to Mother Earth, the Divine Feminine, and to commit ourselves to peace, love, and the will to live sustainably.

For me the power of the Celtic lands and the Celtic spirit have been a wonderful source of inspiration. I hope this book gives you a sample of that Spirit as you take this wee journey to visit these thin places of Ireland with me.

Celtic Blessings,
Jeanne Crane 2012